How to Sell Online

How to Sell Online

The experts' guide to making your business more successful and profitable online

Christer Holloman

PEARSON

Harlow, England • London • New York • Boston • San Francisco • Toronto • Sydney
Auckland • Singapore • Hong Kong • Tokyo • Seoul • Taipei • New Delhi
Cape Town • São Paulo • Mexico City • Madrid • Amsterdam • Munich • Paris • Milan

PEARSON EDUCATION LIMITED
Edinburgh Gate
Harlow CM20 2JE
United Kingdom
Tel: +44 (0)1279 623623
Web: **www.pearson.com/uk**

First edition published 2016 (print and electronic)

ISBN: 978-1-292-14840-3 (print)
978-1-292-14841-0 (PDF)
978-1-292-14842-7 (ePub)

British Library Cataloguing-in-Publication Data
A catalogue record for the print edition is available from the British Library

Library of Congress Cataloging-in-Publication Data
Names: Holloman, Christer, author.

Title: How to sell online : the experts' guide to making your business more successful and profitable online / Christer Holloman.
Description: 1 Edition. | New York : Pearson Education, 2016.
Identifiers: LCCN 2016032743 (print) | LCCN 2016034325 (ebook) | ISBN 9781292148403 (pbk.) | ISBN 9781292148410 (PDF) | ISBN 9781292148427 (ePub) | ISBN 9781292148427
Subjects: LCSH: Internet marketing. | Customer relations. | Success in business.
Classification: LCC HF5415.1265 .H65435 2016 (print) | LCC HF5415.1265 (ebook) | DDC 658.8/72--dc23
LC record available at https://lccn.loc.gov/2016032743

10 9 8 7 6 5 4 3 2 1
20 19 18 17 16

Cover design by Two Associates
Print edition typeset in 9.5/13pt ITC Giovanni Std by iEnergizer Aptara®, Ltd
Printed in Great Britain by Ashford Colour Press Ltd.

NOTE THAT ANY PAGE CROSS REFERENCES REFER TO THE PRINT EDITION

I dedicate this book to Anders Hallsten and Fredrik Borgquist and the whole team at Divido!

Contents

About the author

Source: Chris Mann (www.chrismannportraits.com)

His bestselling *Social Media MBA* series, published in multiple languages, has sold over 10,000 copies worldwide. The *Evening Standard* named him, 'One of London's Most Influential Individuals Within New Media' and he is frequently invited to write for *The Guardian* about new technology trends.

Holloman is also a popular keynote speaker because his message is always tailored to the client and the audience. In presentations, Holloman will share the most up-to-date data and showcase the best business use of new technologies by taking the delegates on a journey via outposts, such as Silicon Valley start-ups, tech buzzwords, emerging opportunities and more. All his talks are peppered with case studies and real-life examples to bring the topic to life and illustrate the ROI for businesses, with actionable takeaways throughout the presentation.

What makes Holloman unique as a writer and speaker is that he consults for businesses regularly, so he will not be providing theories, but instead tried and tested hands-on advice. Prior to setting up his own VC-backed consumer finance company Divido, he launched Expedia founder Rich Barton's £100 million start-up Glassdoor.com in Europe. Holloman was previously head of digital product development at *The Times* and *The Sunday Times*, responsible for award-winning apps and delivering new digital revenue streams.

Holloman holds an MBA from the University of Oxford and is a member of the National Union of Journalists.

For more information, please visit www.holloman.info or to discuss possible speaking engagements, email him directly at contact@holloman.info or Google speaking agencies that represent him.

Acknowledgements

We are grateful to the following for permission to reproduce copyright material:

Author photo on page ix © Chris Mann (www.chrismannportraits.com); figure on p xiii courtesy of eMarketer (www.eMarketer.com); figure on p xvi courtesy of Athlon, a design and innovation company; tables on pp 148 and 149 courtesy of Spot Studio (www.spotstudio.net).

Foreword

In this book I explore, with the help of the best people I come across in their respective fields, some of the most critical business areas for a growing online retailer (etailer) to get right, end-to-end. My main goal is not just to equip you with the latest thinking, but, more importantly, also to inspire you to take action to fuel the continued growth of your online business.

Each section begins with a general discussion and is then analysed and applied further with the help of:

- *Expert commentary* – learn from experienced industry leaders.
- *Case studies* – see how other retailers overcame specific challenges.
- *Deep dive* – sections exploring a given topic in more depth for the advanced reader.

Feel free to jump to the section that interests you the most, and skip the analysis and applications you do not think are relevant to your particular situation.

I will cover some aspects in more detail, and what I think has already been covered well and extensively elsewhere, I will discuss on a more high level, e.g. marketing. Think of this as an opportunity for you to identify gaps in your own knowledge or strategy, to see where you might want to compliment this book with further reading to complete your own 'business toolkit'. You will also notice that some themes are reoccurring throughout the book, e.g. omni-channel, this is just to highlight it from different angles and emphasise its relative importance.

Looking ahead,

The UK is already the world's leading ecom economy according to eMarketer's latest forecasts, when it comes to retail ecommerce's share of total retail sales, increasing from 14.5 per cent in 2015 to 19.3 per cent in 2019

UK ecommerce sales are expected to top £70 billion in 2017, helped by a strengthening economy and impressive growth in smartphone-based buying. The UK is already the world's leading ecom economy according to eMarketer's latest forecasts, when it comes to retail ecommerce's share of total retail sales, increasing from 14.5 per cent in 2015 to 19.3 per cent in 2019. The only way we can stay on the top is by constantly reevaluating our current approach, testing new things, to make sure we are on the top of our game.

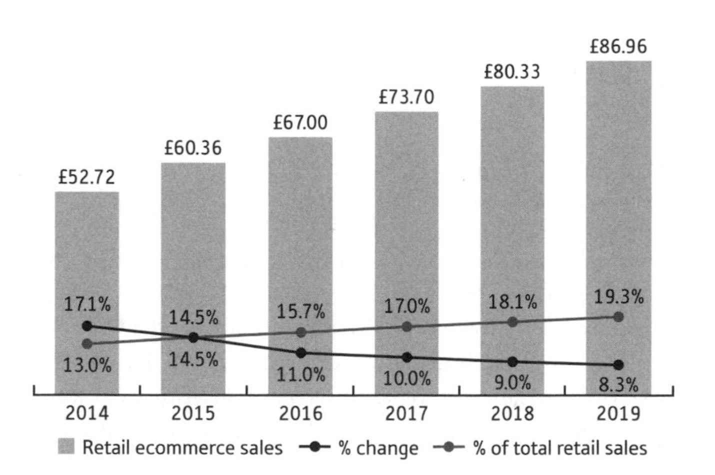

Retail ecommerce sales, 2014–19
Source: eMarketer, September 2015, www.eMarketer.com

Henri Seroux is the Senior Vice President, EMEA, at Manhattan Associates, supply chain commerce solutions provider (www.manh.co.uk) that recently conducted market research on behalf of its clients. When it comes to choosing between online or instore shopping, most consumers are not prepared to rule out one or the other. Almost half say it depends on what they are buying – with only 21 per cent saying they prefer to shop online. However, given the increase in competitive prices, convenience and enhanced personalisation (such as product recommendations and wish lists), it does make retailers wonder, what do customers really want from a shopping experience?

Online vs offline

Henri explains that on the back of the success of digital personalisation, retailers are recognising both the rise in customer expectation and the differentiation that personal service can offer. But what does that experience look like into the future? From individually created recipe ideas and ingredients lists in supermarkets to intuitive, customer-inspired fashion recommendations, retailers have the chance to transform customer engagement.

Over the past decade, the internet and smartphone revolution have started to change the rules of shopping and presented retailers with the challenge of their lives as they strive to stay ahead of the digital curve. Whilst retail companies have focused much attention on honing their online offering, a recent survey of 2,000 UK consumers highlights that shoppers are still increasingly frustrated with both the online and instore experience of many retailers.

Most consumers who shop instore do so for one simple, self-evident reason: the opportunity to see, touch and try products. The second most popular choice for shopping instore is usually 'immediacy of purchase', which was chosen by 54 per cent of consumers in recent research. This demonstrates how consumers want instant gratification from their shopping experiences, making it even harder for online-only retailers to keep up.

51 per cent of shoppers research products online and then purchase instore

Omni-channel

However, it is also clear that shoppers are embracing multi-channel shopping. According to a survey by Google and Ipsos OTX research, 51 per cent of shoppers research products online and then purchase instore, whilst 32 per cent visit the store, research online then finally return to the store to purchase.

This is being fuelled by the rise of smart devices, but it is also an opportunity for retailers to empower store associates and capitalise on the opportunity instore as well as online. How? By store associates connecting online and offline experiences to increase sales on both channels.

To match the online experience, a store associate needs access to a customer's complete online and offline transaction history. By knowing who the customer is, how they shop and with real-time access to inventory availability across all stores, fulfilment centres and suppliers, store staff can, effectively, sell any item located anywhere in the network, and provide an experience that matches that of the website.

Within this omni-channel model, the role of the store assistant is becoming critical. The fact that mobile-toting consumers have more information than the assistants has become widely recognised – with 71 per cent of consumers claiming that this is the case.

Of course, if the online channel was a smooth experience, then the customer simply collects the item, likes it and goes away happy, it is all good. When a problem arises – if the customer does not like this product and wants to swap it for another, for example – the whole situation gets far more complicated and a retailer's lack of end-to-end omni-channel support becomes patently clear.

Today, for example, just a handful of retailers can offer a single swipe option in this situation, requiring, instead, customers to embark upon a complex mix of cancelled and new transactions. Not so good.

In order to increase sales online, retailers must ensure that they have a frictionless experience on all their channels. And that means buying online, collecting instore, swapping that purchase for a product of different value or spending vouchers to buy something a little more expensive – all in one transaction. It also means an experience that includes pertinent recommendations – a pair of shoes to go with the dress bought last week or a cashmere throw to balance the cushions being collected from store. Today, just a few – some of the world's most innovative retailers – have the tools, technologies and processes in place, which enable their sales assistants to deliver that quality of experience.

Ranzie Anthony is the founder and executive creative director of Athlon, a design and technology agency that employs 60 people, and he sums up the multi-layered nature of the omni-channel experience like this:

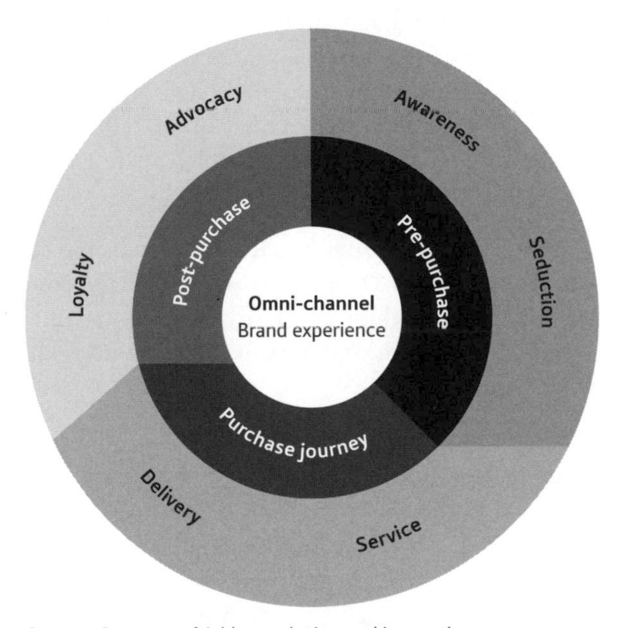

Source: Courtesy of Athlon, a design and innovation company.

What consumers really want

The research from Manhattan Associates showed that across both online and instore shopping, price is the number one attraction for two-thirds (67 per cent) of shoppers. No surprises there, but what is next on the list? Fast delivery, at 51 per cent, and flexible returns at 42 per cent, take the second and third spots.

The message is clear: if you are not competing on price, you are competing on speed of deliveries and your returns policy.

In addition to this, a quarter (26 per cent) of respondents stated a consistent experience across all retail channels as important, underlining the need to provide consistent information, personalisation and fulfilment options to online customers and instore customers alike.

And it does not stop there. Personalisation is a huge driver for many consumers, with 49 per cent saying they would interact more with store associates if the shopping experience were tailored; showing that a personalised, relevant and timely experience is absolutely key.

However, a one-size-fits-all approach will not work here; the model, therefore, must be customer-led. Retailers should be using information about a customer's shopping habits – including products browsed but not bought – as well as a single view of available stock across the business, to deliver a far more personal and truly engaging shopping experience. And with 45 per cent of Millennials shopping both instore and online, retailers need to be prepared, and equip themselves with the technology to offer the same personalised experience across every channel.

Customer expectations have changed radically over the past decade and the online experience has become a powerful, engaging and increasingly personal event. That personalised, relevant and timely experience should also be delivered across all channels in order to provide the best possible customer service. The tide is turning and retailers urgently need to reconsider the quality, relevance and personalisation of the overall experience.

Customer expectations have always outpaced retailers' ability to meet them

Mark Woodhams is the senior vice-president and managing director for EMEA at NetSuite, a global ecommerce infrastructure provider, and he suggests that, 'Customer expectations have always outpaced retailers' ability to meet them. It's the nature of the industry.'

To compound their challenges, the surge in promotional discounting means retailers are virtually in constant sale mode. In particular, retailers are struggling to produce profits on Black Friday and Cyber Monday, the busiest sale days of the year. In 2015, the average percentage of sales of marked down goods has eroded retail's contribution to the UK economic output by more than £20.3 billion, according to research from Planet Retail in March 2016.

So, therefore, the main themes we will explore throughout this book are:

1) *Embracing omni-channel* Today's savvy omni-channel shoppers are connected at every step of their ideal shopping experience from start to finish; they know exactly where to find things on your website, which retailer offers the best click & collect service, and which will let them return without a receipt.

   It is time to connect the dots with technology and information that allows retailers to provide a great, if not superb, service. Consumers now do their research before even entering the store, which means they know what they want. So, when they come into the store, do not leave them hanging around whilst your staff check the stock room or ask another member of the team. Empower your staff with the technology to make the purchase there and then, the same as they would online.

   Shopping is not just a hobby, it is a science and retailers must start connecting the offline and online customer journeys in order to make the grade. Consumers are going to become only more and more connected, so retailers who want to sell more online must not forget the importance of the store, especially when it comes to the upsell opportunity. Store assistants are key to this and they must have the knowledge, skill-set and desire to offer the best possible experience. How about going one step further still and providing technologies that allow store assistants to match up online and instore data in order to get to know a customer's preferences, with real-time access to inventory availability across the whole store network. Or take the ultimate leap of faith and follow in the footsteps of retailers like

Apple or Dixons, where the store experience is very similar to that of the website and the store associate plays an interactive and fundamental part in the buying process from start to finish.

These retailers are great examples because they did not only invest in the staff and technologies, they provided them with everything they needed to ensure the customer not only feels looked after, but also leaves the store with everything they wanted and more. This team approach will be one that continues to pay off for the retailers that embrace it, way into the future.

2) *Increased customer centricity* Consumers are stating openly that they crave a personal experience. Therefore, it is time to not only understand the individual, but also the segments they fit into and their different requirements. For example, Millennials appear to be the generation of personalisation, with 56 per cent of them saying they would interact more with a brand if the experience was tailored, compared to 46 per cent of over 55s.

   Retailers must embrace this and build those personal relationships you find at local butchers and bakers. This change in mindset will allow retailers to take advantage of technological innovation and engineer a cultural shift that will help to deliver a personalised experience across every channel.

   However, this model will, of course, need to vary from retailer to retailer. Not all supermarkets, for example, can ensure a personalised service online as well as every sales assistant offering that same personal shopping experience instore – not only would that interfere with essential jobs, such as restocking shelves, but many will not have the skills or desire to deliver such services. However, within a luxury environment, where the majority of customers are likely to want a more personal service, the experience can be more personal and tailored to the needs of the individual.

   It is also important to remember that today's consumer wants a frictionless experience. And that may mean buying online, collecting instore, swapping that purchase for a product of different value or spending vouchers to buy something a little more expensive – all in one transaction. It also means an experience that includes pertinent recommendations – a pair of shoes to go with the dress bought last week or a cashmere throw to balance the cushions being collected from store. Today, just a few – some of the world's most innovative retailers – have the tools, technologies and processes in place that enable them to deliver that quality of experience. You could be one of them.

3) *Conquer the final impression* More than half of consumers stated fast delivery as a key component when deciding what is most important to them during a shopping experience. So, what should you be doing to address this?

   With 20 per cent of consumers saying they prefer to shop online, long gone are the days where shipping in five to seven business days was acceptable. Delivery expectations have changed; consumers are now expecting action on an order within minutes of when it is received and, subsequently, they think processing should be complete within a couple of hours. It is time to assess your fulfilment performance and see where it can be improved. Consumers want the instant gratification they can receive instore to be matched online, which means retailers must make every effort to get their products to their consumers as quickly as possible at the lowest cost.

   The simple way to achieve this is to work the whole network harder by moving fulfilment responsibility away from just the distribution centre and bringing it to the high street, where stores can be empowered to pick and pack orders, process returns and see where everything is in the supply chain.

   And today's forward-thinking retailer needs to not just overcome these challenges but also create a foundation to build on success for the future. With more and more online retailers jostling for space on the high street, the old 'it'll get there when it gets there' mentality will not cut it any more.

   Creating a single stock pool with real-time availability across the business network gives retailers with physical stores a unique opportunity to create outstanding customer experiences, across the entire gamut of bricks and clicks, moving from a siloed, expensive supply chain to a unified omni-channel business where profits are protected.

   And do not forget it is not just about delivery. What if the consumer does not like the item or it does not fit? Do not underestimate the importance of a flexible returns policy, with 43 per cent of consumers saying this is most important to them during the shopping experience. Some consumers even said they would buy more online if they could return to store; showing all aspects of the journey must be considered.

Lessons for you

1. Consumers do not necessarily see online as channel. You are a brand, they expect consistency and an exceptional, personalised service no matter where they purchase.
2. Consumers want their products quickly; they do not like to be left waiting. Make the whole network work harder so that when a customer buys something online they receive it as soon as possible.
3. Make the whole experience personal. Consumers want to feel like they are the only customer you have and crave a tailored experience created directly for them and their needs.

Christer Holloman

London, September 2016

P.S.

For a digest of the latest advice straight to your inbox, sign up to the free mailing list on www.sell-online.co today!

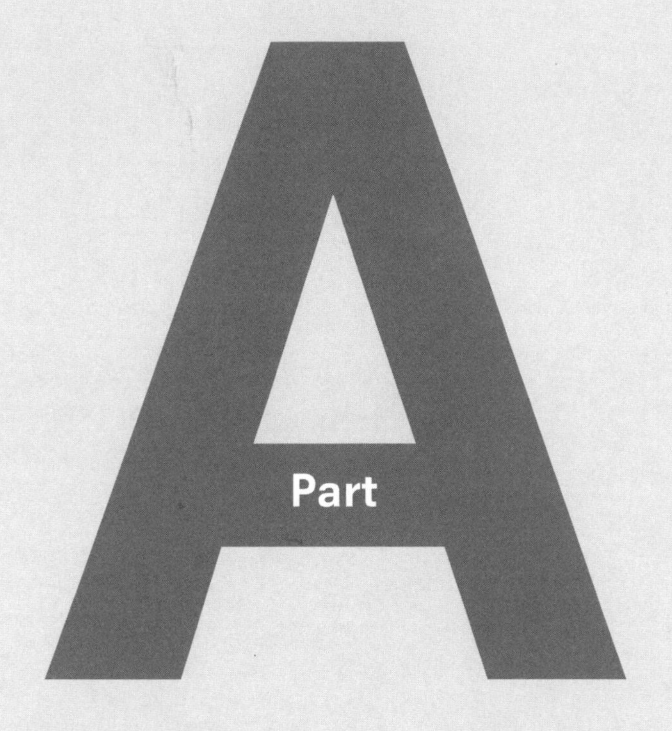

Retail truths

1. Some things never change

Even though this book is, indeed, about online retailing, it is worth pausing and reflecting on some of the truths from the offline world that still hold true as we move online with our customers. At the end of the day, the fundamentals have not changed; the customer experiences a need, shops to satisfy the need and then consumes or uses the product purchased (I need a hat, I buy a hat, I wear it). Think of this chapter as a checklist before proceeding.

The advice

Truth 1: Look drop-dead gorgeous

Window dressing, or visual merchandising, is one of the most important tools in terms of communicating with your customers. What you display in your windows gives you not only an idea of what is sold inside, but it also allows customers to get a good understanding of brand values. As well as showcasing the products that they want to push, the store also takes the opportunity to show where they sit in the market – is it all about luxury or does it reflect a more typical domestic scenario? Is the company product-led, as Lakeland's window displays, which include low-key collections of time-saving cook and bakeware, suggest? Or, does the company rely on lifestyle values, as with window displays in the House of Fraser? Whilst the brand sells everything from furniture to face cream, the message of buying a little bit of glamour usually spills forth from its window displays.

Window dressing serves not only to attract customers to one particular store, but also to pull them away from other retailers who may be in direct competition. Critically, when it comes to a little bit of retail therapy, the objective is to spend some money rather than to have a particular item in mind. This means that window dressing is crucial when it comes to pulling customers in through the doors so that they can make impulse purchases.

In some chain stores and in larger department stores, the job title has evolved from 'window dresser' to 'visual merchandise manager', with each display being strategically created and measured in terms of subsequent sales.

With the bigger retailer, there is a move towards emotionalisation. This is the concept of drawing the customer in via the window display whilst continuing the narrative throughout the store, across many departments. There are also occasions when a retailer takes the story of the window display on to social media, through the use of hash tags. Retail TouchPoints Social Commerce Survey highlights the fact that, whilst 79 per cent and 77 per cent of retailers promote their social presence via email and their website respectively, 24 per cent utilise the POS and 22 per cent do it through instore digital signage.

Truth 2: Offer a life-changing solution

One of the great secrets of selling is learning where your 'in' point is in terms of your customer and working out how to leverage that, in other words, what do they need and how can you fulfil their needs?

It is not a one size fits all, and a good sales person will know exactly when to change tact and morph their message to suit their prospect's need. After all, there is a huge difference in selling a tin of paint that will be used to lighten up a dark room and a paint that is being bought to make a statement to anyone who sees the finished result. Both customers are looking for the same thing, but need different outcomes and are at different stages of the same DIY journey.

It is the same with clothing. Some buy luxury-clothing brands because they connect with the brand values of timeless chic and sharp tailoring, whilst the very next customer could be buying the very same item so that their friends can see they are financially buoyant. A great sales person will be able to identify each customer need and adjust their techniques accordingly. Not only will this result in a great opportunity for sale, but it will also be more likely that the customer leaves feeling positive, regardless of whether they purchased or not.

As well as making customers feel valued, demonstrating how your product can meet their needs is a critical element of the sales pipeline. Bringing a product's benefits to life is an important way of reaching out to the customer via the product.

> *A kettle boils water. A kettle with a high wattage boils water in 60 seconds. A kettle with a glass jug and a blue light within brings a little bit of life to a reasonably boring appliance.*
>
> *A hairdryer dries hair. An ionising hairdryer will remove flyaway frizz whilst another model will operate with less noise than others.*

Picking apart the features of any products and transforming them into benefits is one of the cornerstones of retail. To work out the benefits for any given customer, you must first identify their needs and see your product in terms of the solution it will offer them. On a large scale, this is taken care of by market research.

To understand the leverage that your benefits have, the question to ask is 'so what?' Stand in your customer's shoes and query every benefit. Then make sure your answer fulfils their need and you swiftly move along the sales pipeline to the resolution stage, where you seal the deal.

Truth 3: Honesty is the best policy

Customers are not the wide-eyed and bewildered targets of decades gone by. Today's customers are savvy enough to know when you are being honest with them. They also understand how it feels when they shop online and the only voice that they can hear is their own internal decision-making process. With the click & collect concept estimated to be utilised by 76 per cent of the shopping public in 2017, consumers are also leveraging the ability to shop from home whilst preferring to take advantage still of the instore customer service.

Over-egging your sales position can have the double impact effect of not only making customers leave empty-handed, but also ensuring that they will not make a return visit or give you another opportunity to freshly impress them.

It is ok to not know all the answers that your customer needs, but you do need to access an information source quickly and add the response to your own knowledge bank. In digital terms, this is a lot like a constantly evolving FAQ section and responding to reviews to show that you are engaged.

Whilst the universal retail truth of honesty still holds true, today's retailer is up against a huge digital social space that can be hard to undo. Before the internet age, people may have made their excuses and left the store, mentioning their negative experience to a friend or two in the days following. Today, shoppers can leave the store, stop for a coffee and share their negative experience across the many friends and family members they connect with, across multiple social media accounts. Not only will their post circumnavigate the world in seconds, but there is a strong likelihood that it could impact connections who live locally and who may even be shopping in the same high street.

Truth 4: Go all out when it comes to consumer rights

A returned item is not always a lost cause. Carefully handled, a return can, instead, be the start of a long enduring customer relationship. To have a good returns policy or guarantee is a highly valued aspect of any brand for customers. Primarily, a returns policy is in place to protect the consumer from sub-standard goods, but, conversely, a store's returns policy can, instead, give the customer the confidence to take a risk and purchase something they might otherwise not, because of the ease of bringing it back, particularly for online retailers. In a virtual retail environment, a returns policy may help to give customers that extra bit of confidence they need to make the purchase. It is estimated that 8–9 per cent of goods are returned on average, but this will, of course, vary by product type.

Making it simple for customers to access and understand a returns policy is an important step towards transparency. Display it throughout the store and ensure there are not a string of caveats attached. Reducing the fine print does not equate to stripping back the terms of the return. Let your customers know that you are happy for them to take time to think about their purchase outside of the sales environment and still have the ability to return something they later decide is not for them.

It is perfectly reasonable to try to minimise the chance of a return. A good brand will allow and encourage customers to interact with products before they bring them home. Installing comfortable and spacious changing rooms with a controlled climate will allow your customers to try things on in comfort and without turning into hot sweaty messes who will more likely feel worse about their appearance than better. In terms of technology, walking the customer through the features and benefits of the product is a great start – even if it means rocking out the store to let them hear the crystal clear sound from speakers or a television.

Truth 5: It is the little things

Maximising your transaction by increasing the value of the basket by using add-ons, upsells or cross-sell is an important retail methodology that means that you get the most from your instore customers.

These methods of leveraging your opportunity are not an attempt to undo all your good and honest work in securing the trust of your customer. Instead, it is about showing customers how you can add to the excellent value they already enjoy with you.

There are many cross-sells that feel much more like basic common sense.

How do things pair up? Make sure that you know your stock well enough to be able to suggest a tie that will complement a shirt. Customers may well begin to seek you out as a knowledgeable sales consultant that they can trust and from whom they know they can buy with confidence. It is a great technique that will help you add to customer satisfaction, whether it be finding the perfect pair of matching earrings or making sure that they have a king-size duvet to match the size of their new mattress. Just make sure to keep the cross-sells logical.

If there are complementary items and common pairings, then make sure that you are already displaying them clearly instore. Many customers do not believe that they have good taste in terms of pairings, so suggest an outfit or combination that knocks their socks off and display prominently. This stands as true for home furnishings as it does for haute couture and should be displayed prominently on the sales floor. Value points are important and your cross-sell should be less than a certain percentage of the first sale. A guide figure is around 25 per cent, but tailoring in situ is equally important.

Add-ons are another way of upping the transaction value. Rainproof spray for a pair of new shoes will ensure that the shoes stay looking fresher for longer and so give the product a longer lifespan. Whilst it does cost to buy the rainproof spray, its application actually will increase the value of the shoe purchase by months or years, therefore making them better value. Empowering your customer to say yes to extra cream and marshmallows on their hot chocolate can also add to a feeling of wellbeing and self-reward.

Lessons for you

Retail has undergone a massive evolution from its early days. From the opulent days of the very first department stores through the pile 'em high and sell 'em cheap days, to the chain-store takeover of the independent high streets, one element has never changed – smart retailers understand that people return in order to feel like they did last time they bought from you.

Recommended actions

- *Short term/quick win*

  Add click & collect as a new delivery option.
- *Medium*

  Redesign your website to give it an up-to-date look.
- *Long term*

  Embrace omni-channel, make sure your customers can view and buy from you via their mobiles, too.

1.1 Expert commentary: from bricks to clicks

I met up with Professor Kim Cassidy, Dr Sheilagh Resnick, Dr Julie Lewis and Nelson Blackley, academics in the National Retail Research Knowledge Exchange Centre (NRRKEC) at

Nottingham Business School (Nottingham Trent University) to discuss the transition from bricks to clicks.

We will look at how some UK and US retailers have successfully followed a *clicks to bricks* strategy and we will go on to identify and highlight three basic principles that appear to underpin the effective development of this channel strategy and so offer insights for independent retailers pondering the *bricks to clicks* or *clicks to bricks* dilemma.

Bricks to clicks or clicks to bricks; the principles of successful retailing remain the same

The question for retailers is no longer whether to operate an omni-channel strategy, but how to implement it most effectively. Just a few years ago, in the face of the continuing and unstoppable rise of online retailing, developing a bricks and mortar presence might have been considered a high-risk strategy. However, as consumers now shop both online and offline, retailers have to be there, too. The goal for retailers is to fully integrate offline and online sales channels and so create a seamless 'holistic' customer experience.

The strategic response to this omni-channel challenge has been mixed. Some retailers have made few strategic adjustments, retained only a physical estate and, consequently, struggled to survive. Others ('pureplay' retailers), benefiting from a strong brand or niche product or service positioning, have chosen to maintain an online presence only with varying success. A third group, the majority, who have, historically, prospered through their physical estate, have reduced or maintained their store offer whilst simultaneously striving to develop an integrated online offer, i.e. followed a *bricks to clicks* strategy. A fourth group, and the focus of this white paper, are those who have adopted a *clicks to bricks* strategy – retailers who have a heritage in catalogue and/or online retail, but have now actively also developed a physical store presence.

As Zhang et al. (2010) point out, clicks to bricks in itself is not a 'new' strategy: Sears, for example, became a multi-channel retailer in 1925 when it opened its first store to complement its catalogue channel which was launched in 1886 (p. 168).[1] However, it does appear to be a strategy being embraced by more and more retailers. In addition, a recent study of these *clicks to bricks* retailers suggests that not only are they performing particularly well in an increasingly competitive retail environment, but they appear to be doing so because this strategy allows them to focus on some basic principles of successful retailing that can be implemented by any retailer, irrespective of size.

> *First, they have an in-depth and personal understanding of the changing demands and behaviour of their consumers.*

Extensive consumer databases, accessible through the catalogue operations, have given clicks to bricks operators a head start and ensured that decisions are customer-focused and market-driven. Powerful datasets and integrated data processing systems enable them to sense and rapidly respond to changes in consumer behaviour and expectations.

This is illustrated by *Screwfix*, part of the Kingfisher Group, and the UK's largest direct and online supplier of trade tools, accessories and hardware products to tradesmen, handymen and serious DIY enthusiasts all over the UK.[2] Screwfix started life in 1979 as a niche retailer called the Woodscrew Supply Company, selling screws to small tradespeople via a one-page catalogue.[3] In 1992, the retailer launched its first catalogue under the name of Screwfix Direct, selling a wider range of hardware products, though still aimed at small tradespeople. Acquired by Kingfisher in 1999, Screwfix now operates over 450 stores across the UK and makes a significant contribution to the group, with total sales increasing 26.3 per cent to £1.05 billion for the year ending 31 January 2016 with like-for-like sales jumping 15.3 per cent versus Kingfisher Group in the UK and Ireland total sales

---

[1]Zhang, Z., Farris, P.W., Irvin, J.W., Kushwaha, T., Steenburgh, T.J., and Weitz, B.A. (2010) 'Crafting integrated multi-channel retailing strategies', *Journal of Interactive Marketing, 24*, pp.168–180.

[2]www.screwfix.com.

[3]www.screwfix.com/jsp/help/pressoffice.jsp.

increase of 5.6 per cent and like-for-like 4.5 per cent.[4,5] This history has given Screwfix 37 years of customer data focusing on a relatively small segment of the market (i.e. small trade customers). They have been able to draw on this information to make effective, responsive marketing decisions. In addition, the company has adopted a holistic rather than channel-centric approach to data integration from the outset, generating and combining insights from all customer touchpoints. In 2011, the retailer rolled out its innovative Fusion Platform, a large-scale initiative developed to transform the company's multi-channel ordering process.[6] Fusion enables store staff, at the point of purchase, to view a customer's purchase history across all channels, automatically generating product recommendations for staff to use to upsell and cross-sell products to customers.

Made.com is another example of a clicks to bricks operator who has focused on integrating customer data across all channels.[7] The etailer (online retailer) was launched in 2010 and claims to offer unique design-led furniture at affordable prices. The company has opened three UK showrooms in addition to a pop-up showroom in Brighton and is seeking more 'unusual locations' to expand its European network.[8] The company has joined forces with retail analytics company CloudTags to pilot the connected showroom in Brighton which uses tablets and beacon technology to capture the preferences of its shoppers.[9] Using instore tablets to showcase Made's full online offer, CloudTags' technology gathers data on shoppers based on items they have looked at online, but did not buy. The pop-up store also houses an interactive wall featuring images from the retailer's social media platform, Made X Unboxed. Shoppers can tap on the images to reveal product

---

[4]www.screwfix.com/jsp/help/pressoffice.jsp.

[5]www.retail-week.com/sectors/home-and-diy/kingfisher-full-year-profits-slide-but-bq-and-screwfix-sales-up/7006011.article?blocktitle=Top-story&contentID=17831.

[6]www.lets-do-diy.com/News/2011/03/Benefits-for-trade-recognised-as-Screwfix-celebrates-latest-win.aspx.

[7]www.made.com.

[8]www.retail-week.com/sectors/home-and-diy/madecom-launches-amsterdam-showroom-as-it-ramps-up-european-expansion/7004211.article.

[9]www.cloudtags.com.

information. CloudTags combines beacon technology with data on products that shoppers have interacted with instore, allowing Made to send personalised marketing communications to individual customers based on the products that caught their eye in the showroom.

Clicks to bricks retailers clearly realise from consumer feedback that digital innovations have to be an integral part of the retail offer whether online or in a physical space. For this reason, many are maximising the potential of novel digital uses instore, taking advantage of the latest high-tech applications to interact with customers and gather data. Arguably, this is not simply about being able to access and use new technological innovations but being in tune with changes in customer behaviour. Consumers are using more and more technology in their daily lives and expect retailers to mirror this activity when shaping consumption experiences.

However, the use of technology needs to be underpinned by customer insight, highlighting that an understanding of customer behaviour remains, and always has been, a principle of successful retailing.

> *Second, clicks to bricks retailers appear to have a strong brand identity and positioning within the market and a clear view of the role stores play within their channel 'mix'.*

They have recognised that a physical presence offers the consumer different benefits and can be used strategically to reinforce a consistent brand image. The first most obvious benefit is that stores can be used to 'showroom' products and give customers the opportunity to touch goods and assess the quality themselves prior to purchase. This is clearly more important for some product areas than others. *Ocado*, for example, is reportedly considering a move into bricks and mortar with the etailer eyeing a showroom for its health and beauty business.[10] According to chief financial officer Duncan Tatton-Brown, 'We don't expect to add a physical presence in grocery but in health and beauty we would think of having a showroom to help the supply chain

---

[10]www.retail-week.com/sectors/grocery/ocado-mulls-over-opening-its-first-bricks-and-mortar-showroom/7003004.article.

to showcase their products.' Similarly, *Sofa.com*, established in 2005 as a bespoke furniture design service, has recognised how important it is for customers to be able to touch and feel fabric swatches and now has showrooms in Chelsea, Edinburgh and Bath for those reluctant to buy before they try.[11] Stores have the potential to engage all of the customer's five senses and so demonstrate how the brand looks, sounds, smells, feels and even tastes. This is not possible (at least at present) in the online world, which can appeal only to the visual and, sometimes, auditory senses. Sensory engagement has become even more important to retailers, given the empirical link to increased customer spending and dwell time.

The second related benefit is the opportunity to facilitate the 'experiential' or the 'theatrical' with a store setting. Many clicks to bricks operators are using the store presence to enable consumers to experience products in situ using innovative theatrical design principles to create realistic, interesting or dramatic settings. Stores are being developed as 'destinations' rather than simply places to see and collect product. The US clicks to bricks preppy 'eyewear' retailer *Warby Parker*, based in New York, illustrates this trend.[12] With its unique 'try five pairs of glasses for a week and keep the pair you like' service, the company has moved from being exclusively online to include physical stores in 2013. Since then, the company has expanded its bricks and mortar presence and now has almost 30 stores across major US cities.[13] Warby Parker's retail stores have been designed to capture a sense of theatre and fun and include pneumatic tubes that shoot glasses from the stocking area to the sales floor. This fun environment aligns closely to the company's mission, which stems from a belief that, 'Buying glasses should be easy and fun. It should leave you happy and good-looking, with money in your pocket.'[14] The use of theatrical installations to generate instore interest and excitement is certainly not new. Harry Selfridge was considered to be a pioneer of retail theatre and in 1909, after

[11]www.sofa.com.

[12]www.warbyparker.com.

[13]www.warbyparker.com/retail.

[14]www.warbyparker.com/history.

the first cross-Channel flight, Louis Blériot's monoplane was put on display at Selfridges, in order to attract 'new customers to Selfridges and thus generate both immediate and long-term sales'. What does appear to be new is the amount of thought being given to the strategic role of such installations within the retail promotional mix and the nature of the new customers that the retailer might attract. Armed with consumer data obtained from multiple contact points, retailers are in a much stronger position to evaluate the effectiveness of such initiatives, establish whether interest is generated amongst new or existing customers and the contribution it might play in reinforcing the company image and positioning.

Another example is furniture etailer *Loaf*, established in 2008.[15] It is one of the fastest growing companies in the UK and has recently ventured into bricks and mortar, opening an 8,000 square foot store in Battersea called Loaf Shack. As well as beds and sofas, the company also sells gifts and accessories, including organic candles, tableware and cashmere blankets. As the name implies, the interior design focuses on helping consumers to relax and chill out with products showcased in realistic settings. The store features a Little Loafers corner for younger visitors as well as a traditional-style ice cream parlour. There are plans to develop a further 10 Loaf Shack stores across the southeast of England by 2018. According to Charlie Marshall, who founded Loaf under the original name of The Sleep Room in 2008, the focus is on, 'getting the brand magic absolutely spot on. Our move to bricks and clicks is all about reaffirming our core values and giving customers a fantastic shopping experience.'[16]

The key here is that clicks to bricks retailers are using the physical space strategically to complement rather than compete with their online operations. They are acutely conscious of the potential dangers of cannibalising sales from existing online operations and carefully consider what role stores might play in reinforcing a

[15]loaf.com.

[16]www.retail-week.com/stores/store-gallery-loaf-moves-into-bricks-and-mortar-with-loaf-shack-launch/5079639.article.

clear brand message. This approach has always been regarded as part of good retail practice, i.e. making sure that all elements of the retail mix are working consistently to reinforce the message. John Lewis, for example, goes to great lengths to ensure that its sales staff reinforce its quality positioning through their interactions with customers on the shop floor whilst, at the same time, spending £7 million pounds on developing a high quality Christmas TV advertising campaign.

Third, and finally, our clicks to bricks retailers appear to have an entrepreneurial culture or leader.

This enables them to respond quickly and flexibly to change in the retail environment.

One of the best examples is Jason Bannister, founder of *Oak Furniture Land*.[17] This is a business which began life as an eBay retailer in 2003, opened a website in 2006 and now operates a physical estate of 68 stores.

In April 2015, the company owner, Jason Bannister, was shortlisted in the London and South region of the Ernst & Young Entrepreneur of the Year Award.[18] The development of the business demonstrates clearly Jason's personal skills and expertise as an entrepreneur as well as an opportunistic approach to store development which capitalised on changes in the retail environment. Jason originally set up a business to sell a container of Mexican pine furniture he had bought for £10,000 from a wholesaler, instead of using the money to build an extension on his house.[19]

He realised that furniture sales represented a growing market opportunity and was aware of leasing deals available in the retail property space. He took a financial risk investing in a shed from which to operate his business. The gamble paid off because Oak Furniture Land became eBay's largest retailer within three years.

---

[17] www.oakfurnitureland.co.uk.

[18] http://swindon-business.net/index.php/2015/04/27/swindon-bosses-join-battle-for-britains-top-entrepreneur-award/.

[19] www.retail-week.com/technology/innovation/analysis-retails-new-entrepreneurs-three-businesses-taking-the-industry-by-storm/5063849.article.

By 2006, and with a turnover of £2.7million, it was time for Oak Furniture Land to move again. A 100,000 square foot aircraft hangar in Kemble, Gloucestershire, became the etailer's home. Again, timing played its part as the economic downturn enabled Oak Furniture Land to get space at a cut-down rate. Bannister noticed there were 13,000 square feet of empty offices at the entrance to the airfield and he asked the landlord if they could trial these as a showroom and experiment with the first store.

The showroom at Kemble turned over £5 million in its first year, proving that customers wanted to see and feel the furniture first hand. Bannister realised that having a shop was growing the overall business and not, in fact, cannibalising online sales and so, from that recognition, came the short step to opening their first bespoke showroom in Cheltenham in 2010.

Whilst other large retailers have been reassessing the size of their store networks to reflect growing online sales, Oak Furniture Land bucked the trend by embarking on an aggressive store opening programme in 2010, opening 56 new stores over the next four years, adding close to 700,000 square feet of sales floor area.[20]

Screwfix is a company also known for having an entrepreneurial, fast-paced and dynamic culture. According to the Screwfix.com website, 'The Screwfix Head Office in Yeovil is a dynamic, diverse and exciting place to work.'[21] As a member of staff in the marketing department observes, 'screwfix is unlike any other business I have worked for; the fast pace and innovative outlook makes it a very refreshing environment.'[22]

Missguided is another etailer with plans to open standalone UK stores to enhance brand awareness and to complement existing online operations.[23] Established in 2009 by Manchester-based

---

[20]www.alixpartners.com/en/Publications/AllArticles/tabid/635/articleType/ArticleView/articleId/1600/The-AlixPartners-Growth-Retailer-Report-2015.aspx#sthash.mHUWwb62.dpbs.

[21]www.screwfixcareers.com/business-areas/head-office/.

[22]www.screwfix.com.

[23]www.missguided.co.uk.

entrepreneur Nitin Passi, the trendy own brand women's wear etailer has embraced digital marketing and invested heavily in search engine optimisation (SEO) and pay-per-click services. The etailer has experienced seven years of rapid growth, with its founder attributing success to speed, reactivity, agility, value for consumers, a strong social media presence and a little luck in terms of timing.

To conclude, whether a retailer is bricks to clicks or clicks to bricks, the principles of successful retailing remain the same. To succeed, retailers need to understand customer behaviour across all channels, create and maintain a strong brand identity and a clear view of the role stores play in the channel mix and establish an entrepreneurial culture. As Simon Burke, director of the Co-operative Group, comments, 'One important way of doing this is to be courageous about getting involved in new things that are happening in our space. Another is to make changes along with, or better still just ahead of, our customers. So, if you look around your business and see that everything is carrying on just as it used to, with the same people doing the same things, and your retail offer has been doing business the same way for generations, this is not a cause for quiet satisfaction. You should be worried.'[24]

1.2 Becoming omni-channel

Retail has come a long way since the birth of ecommerce in the 1990s, as have consumer expectations. Brands are now expected to give customers access to 'infinite aisles' that extend well beyond the four walls of the store. Shoppers expect an equally seamless experience whether they buy a product in person, pay for it online and collect it instore, or order it directly to their homes. In all these cases, the end result must be that they receive their purchase when and where they want it.

[24]http://www.retail-week.com/analysis/opinion/comment-embracing-change-is-central-to-retail-success/5072658.article.

I met up with Mike Webster, senior vice-president and general manager, Oracle Retail and Oracle Hospitality, to discuss the move to omni-channel retailing. Webster is responsible for strategy, enablement, development, sales, service and support. Oracle provides retailers with business applications and server and storage solutions that are used by 20 of the largest retailers worldwide. For more information about Oracle, visit: www.oracle.com/industries/retail/index.html.

Key takeaway

It has been well established that ours is the age of customer-centricity, arguably more so in retail than in any other sector. What sets this industry apart is that shoppers' habits change extremely fast, and retail merchants need to keep evolving even faster to stay ahead of the market.

There are many factors involved in getting it right, but three elements in particular are crucial to success when it comes to delivering 'commerce anywhere'. These are:

1. *A single view of customers*

   Customer data is widely viewed as one of a retailer's most valuable assets. Being able to collate, analyse and then execute against customer data is an essential component of a successful sales approach. This information allows brands to deliver an individualised experience to every shopper that visits their website and, if used effectively, the insight retailers extract from this information improves the chance that a shopper's visit ends with a purchase.

2. *A single view of stock*

   Retailers require the confidence to deliver on their customers' expectations regarding availability, but they also need to know where their stock has come from, where it is in the supply chain at all times, and how it can be optimised to deliver the greatest margin.

   Oracle research from 2014 found that 46 per cent of consumers are more likely to be loyal to a retailer that provides accurate information on the availability of goods, with 30 per cent of shoppers saying they would spend more, if that were the case. In fact, more than half (58 per cent) said the availability of a product was more important than its price.

3. *A single view of transactions*

   Delivering a consistent purchasing experience across all channels requires that all transactions are treated equally. Customers are bound to get frustrated when they are told they cannot return something instore that they bought online, when a sales assistant is unable to look up their online transactions, or when a retailer's pricing is different in a store from on its website.

The insight

Modern retail is about customers, not channels

Whilst it may seem counter-intuitive to start a chapter that is supposedly about omni-channel retail by suggesting retailers stop using the term 'omni-channel', it is worth reconsidering the vocabulary around this trend. Customers today do not think of the shopping experience in terms of channels or interactions; they consider their experience with a brand as a whole.

The term 'commerce anywhere' is, therefore, the more accurate way to describe a fully-formed omni-channel approach. Put simply, it is not about the number of platforms retailers use to service customers but, rather, about ensuring they can cater to shoppers' changing expectations at all times and on all devices in a seamless way. It is hardly surprising, then, that Oracle's research found that nearly 60 per cent of consumers want retailers to deliver a converged commerce experience.

▶

In the words of Roberto Merlini, group marketing & ecommerce director, Prénatal: 'Retailers have to decide if they want to serve customers the old way and disappear or the way their customers want to be served – everywhere and anywhere.'

Retailers accept that shoppers have more choice and flexibility than ever in how they make purchases and understand that they need to adapt to this reality. However, many brands still cannot deliver a consistent experience across online, mobile and instore that brings all these platforms together harmoniously.

1. Culture

Innovations in technology, from new mobile services to cloud-based inventory systems, certainly have a vital role to play in building the future of retail, but getting the technology right is only one element of a larger evolution. Retailers must also embrace cultural change within their organisation if they are to break down the barriers that stand in the way of delivering 'commerce anywhere'.

Ensuring a seamless flow of information internally is essential to delivering a seamless retail experience to shoppers. There is a distinction to be made between just selling across any and every channel and delivering an experience that is joined-up and consistent across all platforms. The latter is what retailers must aspire to.

Achieving this often requires a rethink of business processes, with a particular focus on working more quickly. Speed is critical to success and brands must promote a culture across their organisation that encourages faster decision making.

This requires them to abandon their notions of hierarchy, which includes putting an end to internal competition between online and offline sales. The time has come to move past a culture that puts instore on a pedestal as the company cash-cow, and onto one built around ensuring consumers get what they want, wherever and whenever they want it.

We're moving away from the culture of the highest paid person is the only one making the call. We're making decisions based on quantitative and qualitative customer data

Leading UK retailer Shop Direct has seen first-hand how implementing cultural change can help retailers get more out of modern retail technologies. Speaking at an event in Amsterdam, Shop Direct's head of ecommerce, Paul Hornby, said: 'We're moving away from the culture of the highest paid person as the only one making the call. We're making decisions based on quantitative and qualitative customer data.' The approach, alongside a new approach to mobile and click & collect orders, has been successful: Shop Direct saw its profits surge to a record high in 2015.

Retailers must also reexamine the physical store and rethink its purpose as part of a 'commerce anywhere' ecosystem. There is no doubt the store has, traditionally, been the place where retailers made the most money, but today they must also consider its role as a service centre, as a collection point, as a showroom and as a place where customers simply want to hang out.

In light of this shift, retailers should not penalise themselves when customers shop online rather than in their shops. Instead, they should find ways to enhance the instore experience to drive even more online sales. At the same time, they must focus on finding ways to make online purchases, product deliveries, after-sales service and returns equally convenient, regardless of which channel their customers use.

2. Convenience

True 'commerce anywhere' also requires a new approach to customer service.

Shoppers have grown used to getting what they want, when they want it. The takeaway for retailers is that the more nimble and technologically savvy consumers become, the more selective they can afford to be when choosing from whom to buy.

▶

People today expect zero friction, whether they buy an item online and collect it instore, purchase it instore and opt for home delivery, or use a voucher code instore that was issued online. In this environment, retailers must deliver a consistent experience that does not fall apart when the lines between online, mobile and instore are crossed in the course of a purchase.

From the pricing of goods to the availability of inventory to returns, every component of the retail experience must be developed with convenience in mind. Even a single barrier can prove insurmountable for time-stretched consumers in a world where the competition is only a click away.

To that end, it is worth reiterating, yet again, that the physical store is far from dead. If a customer wants to try on an item of clothing or test a television's picture quality for themselves before committing to payment, they will do so. In fact, they often prefer to. Oracle's research found that 62 per cent of consumers still prefer to visit a store as part of their shopping experience.[25]

What retailers must realise is that serving customers instore is no longer just about making a sale right away, although that will remain the initial reflex, but rather to give consumers every reason to buy an item, either in the moment or later in time, if they prefer to order it online.

This is the key to building customer loyalty, in addition to higher sales. Oracle's research found that knowing the right product will be at the right place at the right time is the most important element of the shopping experience for 31 per cent of shoppers.[26] Tellingly, more than 50 per cent of consumers would be more loyal to a retailer that gets this right.

John Lewis, one of the UK's most respected and enduring department stores, has been taking advantage of new technologies to improve its customer experience across all channels. A strong focus on its ecommerce site has helped John Lewis to drive online growth and complement its instore offering. David

[25] Retail Without Limits, Oracle Retail 2015.

[26] Retail Without Limits, Oracle Retail 2015.

Hunn, director of IT delivery at John Lewis, explains the motivation behind this approach: 'Our ongoing customer commitment includes adopting new technology to enable us to better serve customer needs and meet their expectations for convenience, choice and experience.'

Part of John Lewis's success has also come down to the improvements it has made to its search engine optimisation (SEO) approach using Oracle Commerce. By providing fast and responsive search and navigation tools on its website, John Lewis has reduced cases of customer searches yielding no results by 30 per cent. The company's SEO growth has contributed to a boost in sales from £1 billion to £1.7 billion in just three years.

3. Confidence

A seamless experience for customers demands an equally seamless retail operation; from the assortment and shipment of goods, to inventory management, to a convenient purchasing journey. Just as crucially, these individual retail operations must also be joined up in a seamless way.

Achieving a single view of their operations gives retailers the confidence to plan more proactively, in addition to giving them more confidence in the strength of their relationships with customers.

With transparency across all their processes 'behind the scenes', companies can make better informed decisions when it comes to pricing, range, assortment, fulfilment and growth, which, in turn, means they can deliver on shoppers' expectations and foster higher levels of loyalty on the front lines. Seventy per cent of shoppers say being provided with real-time information on the availability of a product adds significant value to their interaction with a retailer.[27]

▶

[27] Retail Without Limits, Oracle Retail 2015.

For brands, delivering on the expectations they set for consumers also requires confidence in their merchandising system supply chain and that no surprises will disrupt the on-time delivery of customers' orders. Modern supply chain technologies offer retailers total transparency in their relationships with trading partners, as well as into the procurement and provenance of their inventory from the source. Complementing these, today's merchandising systems allow brands to easily marry supply and demand by reconciling their sales and financial data, purchase orders, item availability and suppliers.

Visibility into these processes puts businesses in the best possible position to ensure the accurate and on-time delivery of the thousands or, in some cases, millions of orders that their online customers place. This is paramount to the 'commerce anywhere' generation for whom the guarantee that a product will be delivered to a certain address by a certain date is not taken lightly, and who will be quick to express their discontent if a retailer cannot fulfil their promise.

A reliable, transparent operation is particularly important for online merchants eyeing international growth. With each new market it sells to, a retailer adds a new layer of complexity to its merchandising and supply chain processes and, having a single, consolidated view of these operations becomes the only way to manage them effectively.

Recommended actions

In short, keeping pace with changing consumer demands will require retailers to continue becoming better at listening, both to shoppers – who are no longer shy when it comes to expressing their needs – and to signals within their data that can help them spot and act on potential issues before they result in a poor customer experience.

Deckers Brands, the parent company behind UGG, is one retail brand leading the way in this regard. In the words of its president,

Dave Powers: 'Customers seek out the UGG brand online, on their mobile devices and in stores. By creating a single, accurate view of their engagement with us, we can better align our service, marketing and merchandising with their needs.'

What this all means, fundamentally, is that there is no finish line. The retail market has never been more competitive, and retailers must make a long-term commitment to continue innovating and becoming more agile if they are to differentiate themselves from the competition in the face of an increasingly discerning public.

1.3 Expert commentary: John Lewis moves to mobile

John Lewis is the UK's largest department store business and a leading omni-channel retailer, serving over 11 million customers every year. Sienne Veit, director, online product at John Lewis, works with teams across ecommerce, stores, marketing, customer service and IT to achieve customer, commercial and strategic growth targets through product development and harnessing new technologies. Veit was previously head of mobile and research and development at Marks & Spencer and head of mobile at Morrisons. For more information, visit: www.johnlewispartnership.co.uk.

I met up with Veit to talk about how the mobile device is used by their customers.

Optimising mobile for shopping success

'Our customers are increasingly using their mobile devices to shop with us. In the past year we have seen mobile traffic grow 60 per cent whilst desktop has taken a step back.' Veit explains that mobile has become the default device on which inspiration and search happen in the moment, in the spaces in our busy lives. It is increasingly becoming the shop window for consumers and also the glue between John Lewis' channels. It is the one device that is used for shopping everywhere: on the bus, at work during breaks, at home on the sofa and in bed late at night, but also, in shops.

To optimise this trend, John Lewis has made several changes to its mobile offering over the past 18 months. It has both a mobile-enabled website and also native smartphone and tablet applications for both Android and Apple devices. You need mobile web, as many journeys still start in a browser with search, or use media as a jumping off point to shopping. But you also need apps, so customers can use the native mobile device capability, such as the camera, as a scanner to check prices, fingerprints and touch ID to log in and make payments, as well as push notifications and location features to provide relevant information, reminders and prompts.

'We constantly track and measure data about how our customers shop and have learnt that many shopping journeys start in our shops and are then completed at home online or vice versa. This is even more so for higher value, considered purchases, like furniture, TVs and large appliances,' she explains.

Veit says that the business recognised that it needed to ensure that customers could use their mobiles to assist the purchase journey in a shop and cross the boundary between shops and home. So, all their shops now have free WiFi, which is easy to log on to. This means their customers can use the John Lewis app in shops to help them choose the right product by scanning product barcodes to find more images, product information, product reviews, pricing, offers and online stock availability (which is especially useful when there are colour and size variants not available in shops).

In 2015–16, John Lewis also updated its wish list capability to make it easier for customers to create wish lists and add items to them so that, if the journey starts at home or in a shop, the customer always has the products they are considering with them.

The company has also created a digital version of its loyalty card in the app so that customers never forget to scan their card to receive the benefits that it brings: points that lead to rewards and vouchers and also Kitchen Drawer, a first-of-its-kind feature that saves all of a customer's online and instore receipts in one place and makes it easier to keep them for returns or reference purposes.

'We researched how customers use their cards in our shops and made sure that the app version was really easy to use: you simply shake the phone to activate the card (making it easy to scan at a till point) and the card works offline (if the store WiFi or 4G signal isn't available at the time). Our most recent iPhone release has enabled the myJL card, barcode scanner and product search to appear from the app icon on the phone using force touch on iPhone 6S for faster availability in a shop.'

How do you know if you are doing the right thing on mobile?

Veit's team are constantly tracking and closely watching how customers shop. They track app store reviews (which is a good measure of customer happiness with a new feature) and take all negative feedback or requests for change from the app store reviews and feed these back into development.

They keep the customer front of mind and bring them into the design process early and often. If what they create is not right for customers, it will not be commercially successful.

Shopping is not just something that happens online. John Lewis recognises that the shops are a key part of the customer's shopping journey and that for some journeys they are essential. The company designed its online and app experiences with shops in mind (sometimes putting the development team in the shop for a week). Veit says that if they just focused on 'online shopping', they would ignore a key part of how their customers shop.

As a final recommendation, Veit says that you have to foster a culture of experimentation and innovation. She makes sure teams are given the freedom to pursue new ideas and trial them and to improve upon or quickly abandon them, if they do not work as planned.

1.4 Expert commentary: mobile shopping opportunity

I met up with Kevin Jenkins, MD for VISA UK & Ireland. For more information, visit: www.visaeurope.com.

Jenkins explained that consumer behaviour is different when shopping on mobile. McKinsey last year reported on evidence from South Korea (the world's most developed ecommerce market), showing smartphone shoppers are more impulsive in their purchases than those who shop on their laptops.[28]

First, these mobile customers tend to go straight to a retailer's website or app (if they have one), rather than using a search engine as their route. This is particularly valuable for a small retailer, who may lack the resources to constantly manage its search engine rankings, as it presents an opportunity to build greater brand recognition and direct loyalty with your customers; music to the ears of any small retailer on the high street.

Second, shoppers are blurring the lines between online and instore. Research that Visa conducted in 2015 confirmed that shopping trends, 'web-rooming' and 'show-rooming', are here to stay. Over 74 per cent of consumers web-room, i.e. research items online, then go to purchase instore; whilst 40 per cent show-room, i.e. visit a store to examine a product before buying it online.

Much of this happens on mobile, which, in turn, generates a very different kind of shopping experience. If you are selling goods both online and offline, then thinking about the mobile browsing experience and how it matches what is seen instore is going to matter.

Third, the payment experience can be different. Shopping on mobile often hits a barrier at the point of payment; no matter how smooth the browsing process before it, entering card details on a touchscreen can feel cumbersome. That is why we are seeing the growth of mobile payments and digital wallet services that remove the need to enter payment details every time you shop. It works on a traditional laptop set-up, but really comes into its own in the mobile environment, because it addresses the payment barrier.

---

[28]http://www.mckinsey.com/industries/retail/ourinsights/learning-from-south-koreas-mobileretailing-boom.

Finally, Visa's research shows 68 per cent of consumers cite fraud and security as a reason for reservations towards mobile shopping and, clearly, there is some historic baggage concerning security. But, in reality, this need not be a concern. The authentication systems for mobile or laptop purchases are identical, whilst mobile technology is actually becoming even safer, with the rise of fingerprint-authorised payments (known as biometrics).

To be successful, online retailers need to avoid the temptation to treat all online avenues the same

A decade ago, smartphones did not exist. Today, half the world's adult population owns one and shopping via mobile is booming. To be successful, online retailers need to avoid the temptation to treat all online avenues the same. Mobile is different and successful retailers will consider the unique opportunities mobile shopping presents and how these can be addressed.

Successful retailers are ensuring that a well-developed and differentiated mobile offering complements their other channels. By doing this, they can offer a seamless retail experience to their consumers: online, on mobile and instore. Consumers may not make a conscious distinction between retail environments any more, but ensuring you cater to their needs, whilst joining up the experience across platforms, is the key to success.

In conclusion, Kevin says that consumers will continue to expect secure shopping experiences that suit their preferences, habits and the latest changing technology. As always, the most successful retailers will do all they can to meet their customers' requirements, whilst keeping transactions secure and convenient, no matter where, or on which device, they are made.

1.5 Case study: Graze.com

Omni-channel is not just about offline retailers going online, but, as we have seen in the case of Made.com, more and more native online retailers are expanding into the real world. Another example is Graze.com. This is a case study about how Graze leveraged its online retailing experience and business model to compete with traditional fast-moving consumer goods (FMCG) companies in stores.

As part of its rapid growth ambitions, online snack subscription brand Graze recognised the scale of the business opportunity presented by omni-channel operations. With the synergies available from the existing online business resources, and by enabling the brand to extend its reach to new customers and snacking occasions, it was a significant and cost-effective commercial opportunity to drive profit and strengthen brand awareness and loyalty. Unlike other start-up food brands, the success of its online business created a strong launch platform. Graze had strong brand awareness already and had been proactively approached by flagship grocery and high-street retailers to establish a retail proposition, reflecting a shifting regulatory focus on healthy snacking.

This case study looks at how Graze defined and launched its retail proposition, including:

- preferred form factor;
- recipes;
- brand positioning;
- packaging;
- internal launch;
- trade marketing, PR and CRM.

Key findings

- As an omni-channel brand, existing marketing spend now drives multiple channels.
- Graze can now support online and offline customer journeys, which is driving profit – in the first three months over 1 million customers tried Graze offline.
- It has been a cost-effective expansion for the brand, and it could invest ahead. Graze was able to utilise existing online business resources; namely marketing, new product development, operations, facilities, supply chain and technology.

Interviewee

Anthony Fletcher started at Graze in November 2009 as head of marketing, sales and innovation, becoming its third employee after the founders. He then became CMO in July 2011, MD in November 2011 and, finally, CEO in December 2012. Prior to joining Graze, Fletcher was innovation manager at Innocent Drinks.

About Graze

Launched from a bedroom on the same day Lehman Brothers collapsed in 2008, graze.com was the brainchild of seven friends, including the co-founders of film rental company LoveFilm. Graze was devised to provide office workers with healthy, convenient and exciting alternatives to vending machine snacks, by sending a selection of personalised, portion-controlled snacks by mail.

Graze designs, manufactures and brands its own snacks and its mission is to reinvent healthier snacking with pioneering technology. Food is one of the largest consumer markets in the world, yet is underpenetrated by technology. Adopting a direct-to-consumer subscription model, the consumer signs up to graze and receives four different snacks in a recyclable box as often as they choose. Consumers (called grazers) select the kinds of snacks they would like to eat, from a range of over 120, and can rate the snacks afterwards. Graze sells in both the UK and US markets and competes with traditional FMCG snacks.

The company has grown from 7 founders in 2006 to 500 employees in 2016. Graze has a proven track record for growth, with revenues up 29 per cent to £68 million in the year ended February 2015.

Its online sales strategy

As the business has grown, Graze has, typically, launched one large initiative every year – expanding into a new snacking segment or occasion, such as broth boxes or sharing bags. In 2013, Graze launched into the USA, having established an office in Manhattan and a manufacturing site in Colony. The company was delivering to all 50 states within two weeks and achieved a

US sales run rate of $35 million per annum in the first year. Rapid profitability was also achieved, with US operations EBITDA positive in month 13. In 2014, Graze committed a further £45 million to be invested over the following three years, including $3 million to open a factory in New Jersey to fulfil US demand. Graze's ambitious online strategy has always been driven by the vision to be the number one healthy snacking brand in the world.

The Case

The problem

With the growth of healthy snacking in the UK, Graze recognised a gap in the market for wholesome on-the-go impulse options, which would also deliver on excitement and taste. It is estimated that 98 per cent of UK adults snack, with 68 per cent snacking at least once every day. But there was also considerable commercial demand for healthier options.

Big retailers and manufacturers alike were under pressure by the UK Government's 'Responsibility Deal' to reduce salt and sugar in foods and promote healthier alternatives to high sugar and high fat products. As a result, space instore traditionally designated to confectionary – particularly 'guilt lanes' at tills – needed to promote fresh or healthier alternatives. These areas represent the highest rate of sale space in stores and retailers looking to boost profitability and expand their on-the-go healthy single-serve snack offerings approached Graze directly to develop a range.

Benchmarks for small- to medium-sized snacking brands that have entered the UK retail healthier snacking category were strong, so it offered a significant commercial opportunity. Going omni-channel would also drive profit and the synergies available to Graze from being able to utilise the online business resources – marketing, new product development, operations – gave it confidence of driving strong EBITDA quicky.

Fletcher, CEO of graze.com, commented: 'There was no doubt in our minds that an omni-channel presence would strengthen the Graze brand. Trust, reach and familiarity are, traditionally, a problem for online brands, so combining our direct-to-consumer online business with a retail offering would raise awareness and build brand trust and loyalty. A clear advantage of omni-channel operations is being able to cross-sell both ways – to drive consumers to and from the online subscription business and offlline retail business using promotion codes and awareness emails.'

The background

Unlike most start-up food brands, being a well-established online business meant that there were a number of significant factors that gave Graze a strong launch platform into retail.

First, Graze had strong awareness and scale already. Graze was the second largest manufacturer of dried fruit, nuts and seeds in Europe by value, and the number one snacking brand in these products in the UK by value. Graze's annual marketing spend put it in the same league as household names, such as Lindor and Jacobs, and above big brands Pringles, Doritos and Kettle Chips. Its main competitors in the healthier snacking space were spending far less and the result of this was that its brand awareness statistics were high. Graze was cited as the number one 'healthy snacking brand' in the UK amongst females, ahead of significant players, such as Ryvita, Special K and GoAhead and, when asked to describe Graze, the top words used by non-customers were: modern, unique, imaginative, innovative and credible.

Second, a Graze retail proposition was in demand. Unusually, Graze had been proactively approached by some 'beacon' brands and accounts to establish partnerships – such as a major cinema chain, national airline and major grocery and high-street retailers Sainsbury's and Boots.

Third, Graze could utilise the power and minds of an existing organisation, critically in communications, new product development, supply chain, data and technology systems. It had the ability to test products online before introducing instore and

▶

was able to self-finance. Graze's online business is profitable in both the UK and US markets and was, hence, able to fund the FMCG launch and invest ahead.

The solution

To implement the omni-channel expansion, a UK retail director was appointed in December 2014 and, by July 2015, Graze launched an impulse 'on-the-go' range of 12 stock keeping units (SKUs) nationally in three strategic accounts. With the advantage of having a deeply vertically integrated business model with manufacturing, in-house creative and product team, the retail launch was delivered by a tight and flexible team led by the new retail director and marketing manager with the support of an existing product developer, insight manager, project manager, designer and finance manager.

The resulting proposition was 12 sleeved punnets, but Graze went through a careful process to define this retail proposition. With the online subscription business generating 15,000 customer ratings an hour, and with 7 years of product ratings under its belt, Graze had a good idea of what the UK public liked to snack on.

Originally, it considered the idea of launching a narrower range with only one type of product, i.e. six low-calorie recipes. However, Graze was aware that consumers enjoy a wide variety of snacks, from sweet to savoury, and felt it was important to reflect that same variety to retail.

A two-month trial of nine test SKUs in Boots, the UK's leading chemist, from February to April 2015, was critical in honing the proposition and gathering insight on offline customers. With zero marketing or promotional support, Graze delivered the highest rate of sale across the store's total snack business; with the range representing five out of the top ten revenue selling SKUs for the period it was trialling. In addition, the Boots loyalty Advantage Card data revealed that, during the trial period, almost 50 per cent of purchases were made by consumers who had not actually bought from the Boots snacking category in the last five months at all, indicating that the new Graze offering was set to drive significant category value. After the trial, Graze decided that launching 12 SKUs would allow it to launch 3 snacks under 4 different umbrella varieties (pillars) to ensure there was a healthier snack for everyone. In this way, each of the 12 SKUs would have a nutritionist-approved badge, such as 'less than 100 calories', 'high in fibre' or '8 g of protein' – to appeal to the different needs of consumers, and so there would be a reason to feel good about eating each portion-controlled product.

In terms of the preferred form for this range, alternative options were assessed, based on the following criteria: differentiation to its competitors, value perception versus the competition, how well it fits with the existing Graze brand, consumer understanding of packaging/concept, cost/capital expenditure, complexity to implement, and launch date achievable. Eventually, Graze opted for a punnet (as per its online products) and cardboard sleeve (with window). This had some key attributes – first and foremost, as a differentiated format in the category, which was seen as a major brand asset. It enabled visibility of the ingredients and product, whilst also leaving space for brand messaging and communications. By following the same punnet format as for the online product, there was no new manufacturing equipment required or CAPEX concerns and Graze already had the capability to deliver the right volumes. The packaging would also be sustainable, which was important for the Graze ethos.

In terms of the retail snacks in the range, 11 out of the 12 snacks launched were the same or similar products to online. This meant there were synergies with existing supplier relationships and ingredient bases. However, creative product names were tweaked to make sure they were immediately recognisable to a time-poor retail customer.

The run-up to the retail launch prompted the broader Graze brand team to agree on and define the global brand positioning 'good just got exciting'; a message that Graze would roll out across geographies on all communications, including

▶

its packaging, website, social media platforms, PR, advertising and inserts. Similarly, when designing packaging for retail, Graze soon realised it had some core brand assets it was keen to incorporate into the packaging material and creative design. Going omni-channel forced Graze as a business to establish and align on key brand assets, including its recognisable brown logo, brown, textured Kraftpak and clear, plastic punnet. The design team believed they were missing colour identity with the Graze brand so, in July 2015, launched the Graze brand colour 'electric moss' to provide consistency across different channels.

To drum up internal excitement, engagement and support for the launch, Graze branded all three office locations and handed out goody bags during launch week. It also launched an internal social media competition to kick-start a wider Instagram campaign.

Retailer support was key to landing a successful launch. Each of the launch partners – Sainsbury's, Boots and WH Smith Travel – enabled the use of on-fixture point of sale, which included 'new' posters, 'new' barkers and branded display units. Additional support secured included car park advertisements, A-frame posters and secondary-site display units. Ian Rankin, senior confectionary buyer, Impulse, WH Smith Travel, comments: 'No other product launch in snacking and confectionary over the last three years has driven the same level of excitement and opportunity for store managers to get behind.'

Also integral to launch was a solid PR launch plan. Along with appointed consumer and corporate PR agencies, four key tactics were employed. There was an announcement to the trade media to reveal the Graze retail range to industry publications one week before launch, followed by a media house tour at two key publishing houses – inviting journalists from the UK's biggest household titles to come and meet key members of the team, learn about the Graze story and try the new 'on-the-go' range. Graze also conducted an Instagram influencer campaign with eight well-known foodie bloggers, with each of the influencers paid to post three images of the Graze retail products during launch. Their PR agencies met their established press contacts to seed the retail story to them in advance.

Finally, Graze made use of its 7 million strong existing customer database. Emails to the Graze database at each of the retailer launch dates enabled communications and key messages to be delivered to 7 million engaged or previously engaged Graze consumers for free.

Results

Graze used a number of different measures to monitor success, of which the most valuable was free electronic point of sale (EPOS) data available from key accounts. Graze used both its own, and category data, where it was available – allowing it to compare base rate of sale both in value and volume, against its competitors. Graze purchased category data from its biggest account, Sainsbury's – measuring all healthier snacking brands in the retailer. This would indicate the average number of units sold of each punnet per store per week – an important measure because that is how a retailer buyer naturally compares products and makes ranging decisions.

Second, loyalty card data from Sainsbury's Nectar Card and Boots Advantage Card revealed an additional layer of detail that flat EPOS would not, and put performance into perspective versus the competition. Graze's retail director Emma Heal comments: 'As we were seeing similar performance in both Sainsbury's supermarkets (a grocer) and Boots (a high street retailer), we could make a safe assumption that this was being replicated in other key accounts across the country. We could see that we were attracting new consumers into the snacking categories of Sainsbury's and Boots – meaning we are driving incremental sales, not just stealing market share from our competitors.' Loyalty card data also allowed Graze to assess the number of repeat customers in a week versus those trialling it – revealing a strong repurchase rate against its competitors. It could also calculate the average number of units bought per week per customer off promotion, which informs its promotion strategy.

▶

Another benchmark that Graze used was in retailer take-up, assessing the percentage of total retailer estate. For instance, Graze launched into 850 Sainsbury's stores in June and, by September, was listed in all 1,100 stores – reaching 100 per cent distribution.

Retail also ran its own internal P&L, detailing profitability at three stages – gross, contribution and EBITDA. Results were assessed through weekly reporting by the retail director until a commercial team was in place three months after the launch, later supported by a commercial finance head recruited within six months of launch.

Critical success factors

There were a number of critical success factors for Graze. This included spicing up its packaging so that it could hold its own on supermarket shelves, whilst still ensuring that it strongly reflected the Graze brand that online customers were familiar with – keeping the trade mark Kraftpak box look and feel by importing a Kraft sleeve. Balancing profit with an accessible price for consumers was also vital to a successful proposition.

Fletcher adds: 'With over 150 products available online, for Graze, omni-channel success meant being brutal with the range – identifying which products cut the mustard for retail. Ultimately, you have got to test, learn and be agile. And be prepared to learn that people shop differently online and offline, and that your approach might need to fluctuate accordingly.'

Lessons learned

Looking back on the omni-channel expansion, Emma Heal, Graze's retail director comments, 'Graze has always been a trailblazer and, from being one of the first mail-based providers of snacks to becoming one of the first omni-channel FMCG retailers, the number of direct analogues in the market they have been able to learn from or look to is limited. But something we've learnt for ourselves is that we should have launched into retail sooner. Having spent seven years building a strong online business, going from clicks to bricks took a long time. We'd also be bolder with our launch assumptions. Within two days, we were out of stock on shelves in Central London, and it was lucky our dynamic supply team could react quickly to meet such significant demand – we had to treble our forecast. The beauty of going omni-channel from online is typified in Graze's agility and ability to innovate quickly. Within five months, we'd replaced two SKUs with stronger recipes.

'Ultimately, you've got to be bold and go where your customers want you to – even if that means a significant change in your business model.'

Recommended actions

- Create synergies with the existing online business – capitalise on CRM and customer databases, to cross-sell against different channels with promotion codes and awareness emails.
- Align core brand assets and brand positioning to create consistency of identity across all different geographies and channels.
- Test and hone products online before introducing into store – use existing data and feedback to determine the make-up of the range.

1.6 Deep dive: omni-communications

Can retailer-consumer communications increases sales, retention and customer satisfaction across the board for online retailers? According to mGage, global mobile engagement provider (for more information, visit: www.mgage.com), this is certainly the case and it has never been truer than now.

Modern audiences are the most fragmented in history. Gone are the days of single points and methods of contact. Consumers have an ever increasing amount of access to content delivered in a plethora of forms, from the written word to images, audio to video and many more. Not only is there a multitude of content available, potential customers can also access this information through a huge and growing list of channels, be it social media, TV, radio, snapchat, email, etc. The points of contact are countless.

How does a brand reach this new and fragmented audience?

In short, the only way to achieve any form of lasting connection with this new type of consumer is to become omni-channel. Retailers the world over are breaking down the data from customer communications and are coming to the same conclusions. The customers that engage with retailers across multiple channels are much more valuable to the brand as a whole.

Still not convinced that your business needs to adopt such an approach?

Research into omni-channel engagement for retail shows that:

- businesses that successfully employ a consistent cross-channel marketing strategy enjoy a 14.6 per cent year-over-year increase in annual revenue and a 13 per cent annual improvement in customer retention rates;
- omni-channel customers have a 30 per cent higher lifetime value than those who shop using only one channel;
- a poll of 7,000 people across 7 countries revealed that 64 per cent of customers expect to receive real-time customer support, regardless of the channel, and 75 per cent of customers will return to companies they deem to have good service;
- seventy-one per cent of instore shoppers who use smartphones for online research say their device has become more important than their instore experience;
- omni-channel campaigns are highly measurable, so you can find out which channels are the most efficient for reaching your customers and optimising your communications campaigns. Every dollar spent in tracking the output of your channels returns $13.

By definition, omni-channel is inclusive, it involves conversation between the retailer and the customer wherever, whenever, however the customer feels comfortable.

In recent years, the retail giant Macy's has conducted huge amounts of research into the benefits of switching to omni-channel marketing. It found that shoppers who use a number of communication channels are eight times more valuable than those using a single channel.

Similarly, MasterCard claims that customers who shop both online and offline spend 250 per cent more on average. Can this be ignored?

To put it simply, businesses that employ an omni-channel engagement policy have better customer relationships, higher lifetime value and generate more revenue, year on year!

How can other retailers leverage the power of omni-channel communications?

The next stage is to work out the best channels to target for your business; becoming truly omni-channel takes time and should be taken in steps.

Mobile is vital for reenforcing communications. For consumers, text messaging is the preferred channel of communications – 20 billion SMS messages are sent daily; to put that in perspective, that is 40 times more messages than the 500 million tweets sent out daily. Messages are short, non-intrusive and even the least tech-savvy amongst us feel comfortable with them.

Today, there are more connected mobile phones than there are people:

- The current global population is 7,289,122,584.
- The number of mobile phones is 7,352,011,604.

The shift to mobile has been huge and the importance these phones play in people's lives can be shown by the need to replace and protect new technology over the norms of times gone by – it is 26 hours before someone reports a lost wallet. In comparison, it takes only 68 minutes for someone to report a lost mobile phone.

Recently, the shift to personal messaging for enterprise has grown and is predicted to boom this year. It is thought that, by 2017, customers will be talking with brands through

WhatsApp, SMS, Facebook Messenger and many other platforms. This transition is happening already and customers have barely noticed, for one reason in particular: it is already second nature. Customers are completely comfortable with messaging because it is already intuitive for almost all demographics.

Thanks to growth in all these channels, the average person checks their phone 221 times per day and time spent on mobile phones increased by 117 per cent in 2015 compared with 2014.

Who, then, should retailers target?

Now that the importance of mobile has been covered, selecting the demographic with the most growth is key.

Born between 1980 and 2000, Millennials are the first generation to grow up with mobile phones, the internet and computers. They are tech-savvy, educated and have serious purchasing power. Millennials want information at their fingertips, instant gratification and want to be able to self-serve – mobile phones make all of this possible.

Millennials already make up 28 per cent of the global population and, according to Deloitte, will fill a staggering 75 per cent of the UK workforce by 2025.

As retailers, there are some extra bits of information to take into account. Seventy-four per cent of Millennials browse the internet on their mobile devices whilst they watch TV, meaning that they are accidentally using multiple channels at the same time.

Furthermore, when outright shopping, 84 per cent of them are using mobile devices whilst instore for comparing prices, checking availability and styles, and so on.

In terms of uptake on new technology, mobile payments have been widely available only in recent years but, for Millennials, it is already booming: 73 per cent of them are onboard.

How do we reach Millennials?

When someone thinks mobile, they might instantly think, we need an app for that . . . You do not. It can help when done properly but, of the apps downloaded, the majority of them get opened only once. There is, however, one app that is number one amongst all demographics, users do not have to change notification settings or locations settings with it, it never gets deleted and does not even need the internet to function. It is SMS.

SMS is the ideal channel to further engage shoppers:

- Ninety-eight per cent of all SMSs are opened within five seconds.
- Forty-five per cent of SMS campaigns are successful compared with 6 per cent of email campaigns .
- Engagement from an SMS is eight times higher than email.

How best to harness SMS for retail

Two huge developments for retail, in particular, when it comes to mobile engagement, have been click & collect and basket abandonment retargeting.

Click & collect as a whole is on the rise and smartphones provide almost infinite access to stores from sofas and offices across the country. Fast food establishments, like Hummus Bros, are already using mobile to enable customers to preorder and pay before they arrive at the shop, negating the need to queue and, therefore, having more time to enjoy their lunch.

Click & collect does not only mean shorter lunch queues; we are seeing more and more pickup locations near major transport hubs, allowing items to be ready and waiting as customers get off the train. Whether they are picking up a coffee from Starbucks or a new computer mouse from Argos, customers are increasingly using click & collect to streamline their lives.

Click & collect is a great example of how mobile can help to bridge online and offline – a great online user experience allows for seamless integration from online purchase to offline collection.

According to Deloitte, home delivery services are struggling to meet demand and we will see a 20 per cent increase in click & collect uptake over the next 12 months.

The most effective ways to remarket to 'basket-abandoning consumers'

- Do not let the opportunity go cold. The best conversion rates from remarketing are achieved by reaching out to a customer within an hour of cart abandonment.
- Use a service lead message. Customers respond extremely positively to remarketing activity based on providing a service to help them overcome problems they experienced on a website. Customers respond well when the retailers understand the reasons why they abandoned in the first place.
- Vary the remarketing channel according to the value. High-value basket items with the highest margins of profit should be valuable enough to justify using outbound phone calls to remarket to a customer with an abandoned cart. Lower value baskets can be targeted with both email and SMS-based remarketing activity.

Remarketing to online basket abandonments becomes an even more attractive solution when you discover that abandoners spend 55 per cent more when successfully remarketed to.

As previously mentioned, customers are comfortable with messaging; something that has not been pointed out is how the language used affects customers.

An SMS can be informal, friendly and to the point. Using these short and concise messages, retail companies can speak the language of the customers they are targeting, the Millennials. Currently, brands can use a base of increasingly intelligent CRM systems to create a sense of conversation with the customer, but there is more to follow.

Tech giants the world over are looking at an increasing number of ways to incorporate their sales within messaging. Conversational commerce is a recently coined phrase that encompasses this. For example, Uber is testing Facebook Messenger integration in North America; consumers planning to meet up can discuss where to meet and when, in a chat thread, and then order their respective vehicles from within the same thread, without opening the Uber app.

All this leads to mobile 2.0, the shift in approach for mobile that has arrived and that nobody spotted until very recently.

With the launch of the first iPhone and most smartphones since, we had mobile 1.0 – the constant drive to replicate the web on a mobile screen.

Mobile 2.0 finally recognises that mobile is now bigger than the desktop web and marketers are taking this on board by grasping messaging as the future, not just an addition to the past.

Recommended actions

There are various ways in which companies, large and small, can adopt to an omni-channel approach. There is, however, a strong argument that says, when ready, the first recommended step will be mobile, whether this is to gain new users or improve relationships with current users or both.

2. Getting technology to work for you

Picking the right platform for your retail business is just the first step in making the most of technology to get ahead of the competition. Having the ability to integrate quickly with a wide variety of third-party services and tools is critically important to maintaining a competitive advantage and to ensuring that you are always at the cutting edge of what is possible online. No web business has a shortage of raw data, but intelligently managing and extracting useful information from that data is the skill necessary to get ahead of the game in terms of marketing automation, operational efficiencies and profit driving insights.

I met with George Graham, CEO, and Alex Crawley, CTO, at Wolf & Badger (W&B) to understand how they grew sales by over 200 per cent year-on-year by making use of technology. Here the team explain how they implemented tools to manage processes and automate marketing in order to grow successfully. For more information on this innovative multi-channel retail platform please visit www.wolfandbadger.com

Key takeaway

- The company developed its own technology, but retailers moving online should assess the relative benefits of a fully hosted platform, a self-hosted platform, building your own technology, or selling via a marketplace.
- Regardless of platform choice, connecting the right third-party tools can increase sales, reduce operational burden and improve

▶

profitability. The successful implementation of tools led to 213 per cent year-on-year increase in online revenue for the company in Q1 2016 alone.

- Easy integrations can deliver quick wins, even seemingly boring ones. Accepting PayPal led to an immediate boost in sales, with 35 per cent of customers utilising this payment method. Similarly, introduction of fraud tools reduced fraudulent transactions by 80 per cent, producing a material impact on the bottom line.
- Marketing tools can be easy to integrate and deliver incredible results, particularly those making good use of product feeds. The introduction of triggered emails increased repeat purchase rate by 60 per cent, for example, and tech-driven marketing tools now drive 39 per cent of online sales.

The insight

Wolf & Badger was established in 2010 as a boutique in Notting Hill, focused on selling a curated edit of the best independent fashion brands from around the UK. Following initial expansion offline, including the opening of a flagship store on Dover Street in Mayfair, the business pivoted online in 2013 and, following a merger in 2015 with Boticca.com, has now become a leading European retailer for independent brands. The company now carries 13,000 individual items from over 700 fashion, jewellery and homeware brands from across Europe and has started to expand into the USA and other markets.

In its first year of launch, the wolfandbadger.com website jostled for success with the two award-winning London stores for which the brand is best known and the website would bring in just a small fraction of sales. During this time, web sales would reflect no more than 10 per cent of monthly sales. Jumping ahead by just three years to 2016 and, whilst the stores remain integral to the business, the website now represents 84 per cent of overall sales. The transition from boutique to successful online player demonstrates the enormous potential to grow a successful online business whilst maintaining a strong offline presence.

Choosing the right platform to meet your needs

There is certainly no one-size-fits-all solution when it comes to choosing the right platform on which to build your ecommerce business and, rather than seeking to provide an exhaustive list of available options, the following is intended simply as recommended considerations for when deciding on which route to pursue. Generally speaking, the more flexibility and customisability you need over specific processes, the more expensive and technically difficult your online operation will become, so think about how much you really need to do before you get started.

Considerations

- How much control do you need over things like order processing and reporting?
- Are you willing to let your platform dictate some operational business processes?
- Do you have the resources to manage technical development yourself?

Platforms overview

The following is an outline of available platform options, roughly in order of technical complexity, flexibility and long-term cost, from lowest to highest.

Marketplace: brands who are focused on production rather than retail may find it most beneficial to simply sell via a marketplace. If you have a product range that you think may be accepted, then selling on a curated marketplace could be the fastest and most cost effective way to launch your online presence, bootstrapping your online credibility by partnering with an established online brand and benefiting from extensive technical infrastructure and marketing expertise. Alternatively, selling on an open marketplace, such as Etsy, Amazon or eBay, is a quick and easy option for many brands.

Fully managed platform: these are, typically, the quickest and cheapest options for getting a fully featured site off the ground, but are also likely to offer you the least flexibility for customisation. A good thing to look at when deciding if one of these is going to suit your needs is to look at whether there is a healthy ecosystem of third-party apps or plugins. Good examples of these platforms include Shopify and Squarespace, both of which provide intuitive interfaces that even non-technical users can use to build an attractive and functional site.

Self-hosted framework: probably the most well-known and widely used platform is Magento, a proven framework written in PHP that provides core ecommerce functionality out of the box, a healthy ecosystem of third-party integrations and a large community of developer familiarity and support. Frameworks such as this can offer a good balance between speed to launch and common functionality, and an ability to customise processes as your requirements evolve over time. It is recommended to be cautious of less well-known frameworks that have been developed in-house by an agency or that are not community supported, as building on these can lead to becoming dependent on that agency for support. A good way to assess this is to check that the source code for the framework is freely available on a repository site, such as Github or Bitbucket, and that it has regular and recent community contributions.

Custom build: larger ecommerce businesses or those with bespoke needs may consider building their own framework from scratch. This route gives absolute freedom to create the unique features that you may want or need for your business as you are bound, ultimately, only by your own creativity and the capabilities of your development team. This is the route the company took due to the complex requirements of its multi-channel business and, in the long run, it has been a decision that allowed the team to build out an extensive feature set of custom integrations and working processes that have driven exponential growth in recent years and allowed the business to scale technical operations efficiently to keep pace with that growth.

Recommended actions

- Take care not to become dependent on proprietary or poorly supported technology.

- Make sure you own your source code and are not tied in to using a specific agency for any further changes.
- Ensure that your platform provides a fully-featured CMS that allows your non-technical team to easily make changes to things like content, stock levels, inventory and pricing.
- It is an easier and more natural progression to migrate to a more advanced platform than a less advanced one, if necessary, at a later date, so the recommendation is to err on the side of ease and speed to launch if you are unsure which platform is best for you.

Although picking the right platform is important and should be evaluated thoroughly, it is just the first in a series of design and development decisions that must be made when building and growing an ecommerce business. It is also important to consider how to connect your new online systems with any legacy offline systems.

What to do with your existing offline systems

Regardless of the current state and complexity of your offline systems, an important step towards becoming a scaleable online business is to ensure that you have a centralised database containing your most important data, including customer records, inventory information and stock levels. Having a single overview of customer behaviour and inventory management across your various sales channels will be critical to your ability to make informed decisions and manage your operations as you grow.

Be aware that the technical difficulty and risks associated with this process increase quickly as your disconnected systems and data grow so, although this task can seem daunting, it is strongly recommended that it be undertaken as early as possible whilst transitioning to an online-focused business.

When integrating its online and offline channels in 2014, Wolf & Badger initially took a conservative approach to migrating its disparate, legacy data to a centralised system. The team spent a disproportionate amount of time attempting to salvage records that, in retrospect, contained little value, before reassessing and taking a more ruthless approach to discarding messy and outdated records.

Assessing and implementing third-party tools

Regardless of your choice of platform, there are countless tools and third-party services that can be leveraged to punch above your weight with limited resources. If using a hosted platform, many tools can be simply plugged in with no need for any technical expertise, whilst, in other cases, an implementation from a developer may be required. If self-hosted or using a custom-built site, it may be useful to make use of a tag-manager so that non-technical teams can easily and quickly introduce new tracking features that will help their department.

Whilst this retailer has evaluated and implemented many tools that it finds the most useful, there may be numerous others that are being used by ecommerce businesses in your sector. An easy win to get some ideas is to use Ghostery, a browser plugin that can be used to quickly examine which tools have been integrated on other sites you may be interested in. Similar tools, such as Siftery and Builtwith.com, exist that provide a more thorough breakdown of which frameworks, services and tools are being used by other businesses relevant to you.

The tools touched on here reflect just a handful of those available that can reduce operational burden and improve efficiencies across various departments within an ecommerce organisation:

Marketing department

For newsletters, updates or marketing emails, an initial integration that you will want to consider is with an email service provider (ESP). Although you can use your ESP as a stand-alone tool, an integration allows for a single customer record and much greater visibility and control. In this case, Wolf & Badger (W&B) integrated directly into Mailchimp, which, although reasonably expensive in comparison to competitors, is very easy to use and integrate with other tools. W&B has over 450,000 active user emails on its database and, with a proper integration in place, the marketing department is able to make full use of the ESP functionality to get the most from this valuable marketing channel.

Many ecommerce platforms will often have their own basic email tools built in for transactional emails but, if you are developing your own site or want more power and functionality from your existing solution, you may also wish to use a dedicated transactional email provider. The team at Wolf & Badger opted for Mandrill to give visibility over sending volume, open and click rates, run split testing of content and much more. Do not underestimate the power of your transactional emails as a selling tool – customers are far more engaged when opening order confirmation emails or sign-up emails, for example, than they would be with a regular newsletter, and it is also possible to set up 'lifecycle' emails, such as abandoned bag, abandoned browse or repeat-purchase encouragement emails, if correctly tied together with customer analytics data. W&B uses Ometria for this and the marketing team now sees triggered emails generating eight times open-rate when compared to newsletters.

Customer support department

As a small business, it might be easiest to simply interact with customers and answer queries via a personal email account, but any established ecommerce business will tell you that this does not scale well. For the sake of your customer support department, it is worthwhile investing in a subscription to a good help desk tool in order to keep all customer communication in one place. The team at W&B trialled numerous providers before settling on Groove for this. Variable pricing by user met the needs of the expanding customer service team; and for those just starting out, many tools are even free for single users. By implementing templated response macros, sharing support tickets between the team and, most importantly, integrating with customer records, the support team was able to cut average first response times by 50 per cent.

Order processing department

Tools can help with even the dullest processes. For example, there is now an abundance of third-party options for processing payments on your site that often will be far superior to those that come as standard with hosted solutions. In recent years, a proliferation of new payment providers such as Stripe have enabled a much simpler integration without the need for separate merchant accounts, which is a big time-saver for start-ups. W&B utilises a payment gateway that facilitates multiple currencies and card types to encourage and boost cross-border transactions and, thanks to this, it now sells regularly to over 80 countries. The team also integrated with PayPal, which has proven to be a very popular payment method, representing 35 per cent of all online transactions on the site during 2015.

Numerous other tools have been integrated into the site in recent years and some of the most important, and yet least talked about, of these are around customer security and fraud mitigation that further reduce operational burden for the order processing department and allow for efficient scaling of processes. For example, certain payment gateways include fraud-detection tools, but many of these lack the power and functionality of a specialist tool, such as Sift Science. Since implementing this tool, the fraud rates dropped from 0.5 per cent of attempted transactions to fewer than 0.1 per cent.

Understanding your data and what to do with it

With third-party tools in place to ease operations, focus can be moved to growing sales on your ecommerce site, but first a step should be taken to collect, maintain and understand data across your site. Again, tools and technology are key and having the ability to easily navigate, compare, and visualise your key metrics is fundamental to being able to understand and drive your online business.

With an explosion in the availability and rate of production of data, however, it can be hard to know what are the important things to measure, and easy to get over-ambitious in your ability to process that information in a meaningful way. Finding the right analytics tools for your business is, of course, subjective, but the day-to-day usefulness of any tool will hinge on how easy it is to gather a few of your most important metrics into one place, and be able to assess their health and movements with a quick glance.

If you do not already have any analytics in place, then start with Google Analytics. This is the industry standard analytics tool that is installed on almost every website, not just ecommerce, and it provides a powerful set of features for tracking and measuring relevant data points. A number of departments use Google Analytics in formulating marketing, merchandising and other decisions as well as for a starting point in investigating what else to measure, before choosing a more specialised tool. Google Analytics is also an excellent resource to cross check the accuracy of other services.

Beyond the quantitative data, it is important not to underestimate the importance of qualitative data, too. Understanding how your customers interact with the site and getting feedback on their experience is essential to understanding your strengths and weaknesses and identifying what you can do to improve. For this, make use of carefully worded surveys or feedback forms and, if you have a real-world presence, then speak to your customers in person.

Getting more technical, dedicated tools, such as Hotjar, exist to view heat maps of where users are clicking on your pages, create funnels to identify where users are dropping off in the user journey through your site and even create recordings of actual users browsing your site. With the latter, it is easy to lose hours just watching recordings, being amazed at how real users are using the site in ways far different from how you intended. By looking at all of this data, the team at W&B are able to identify weaknesses, evaluate new features and continuously improve the customer experience.

Collecting customer reviews, using a tool such as Feefo, from those who have recently completed purchases can also be a great way of gaining invaluable feedback, as you continue to grow and develop your site. Seeing positive reviews can encourage new users to purchase and, in addition to building consumer confidence, the addition of independent customer reviews has the added benefit of being able to push star ratings to your Google Adwords listings. This is something that Google has stated can increase the click-through rate by an average of 17 per cent and the marketing team at W&B have found this to be even higher. This is just one of many ways that you can use technology to drive marketing.

Using technology for marketing

Using tools is not just useful for implementing new features and improving efficiencies across departments, it can also help directly in driving an increase in sales through boosting conversion rate on your own site, delivering additional sales by selling via other sites and through marketing automation to drive new customers and increasing lifetime value.

By putting integrations and data at the core of business strategy, an ecommerce retailer is well positioned to use technology as the primary driver of marketing strategy and generate a significant increase in sales. Whilst traditional marketing efforts such as PR are still central to the approach adopted by W&B, using technology in this way to drive marketing efforts has been central to the rapid growth experienced in the last year and is a strategy that can be replicated by ecommerce retailers in any sector.

Product feeds

The first step in marketing automation should be to produce a high-quality XML product feed using the widely accepted Google specification. As usual, there are tools that can help with this, although W&B manages the process internally in order to ensure that all data fields are included and the feed is regularly updated.

This product feed will be the core of your marketing efforts and can be used for multiple purposes. It will prove invaluable in facilitating sales via third-party marketplaces, listing on shopping comparison sites, powering social shopping feeds, showcasing on Google Shopping, providing content to affiliate marketing channels and much more. With 13,000 individual products from over 700 independent brands, getting the stock data in shape was particularly important to W&B, but, for any retailer, it is worth taking the time to put in a little upfront work to ensure your data is robust.

The team work continuously to improve product listings, not only for conversion rate optimisation onsite, but also to enrich the data feed to drive more traffic and of a higher quality. The difference in sales between those products with detailed and well-written product descriptions, sizing information, material content and multiple photos per product has been found by the team to increase sales by as much as 55 per cent when compared to a lower-quality product listing. By putting the maintenance and improvement of data as a core competency of its merchandising team, the business has been able to drive a significant portion of its sales through channels utilising its product feed.

Marketing automation

Stock data in a standardised product feed is just one half of the equation, and not the only type of data on which a savvy ecommerce manager should be focused. Maintaining good customer data is also central to the marketing strategy and also should be for any site focused on customer acquisition or retention.

With both customer data and inventory data available in the correct format, an ecommerce retailer can make efficient use of new marketing channels and take a real data-driven approach to ecommerce marketing, often in an automated way. For example, W&B chose Ometria to help manage customer marketing across different stages of their lifecycle. This tool is used to trigger automated email campaigns using product data relevant to the right audience at the right time; this led to an increase in repeat purchase rate by 60 per cent and overall online revenue by 4 per cent in the first few months following implementation.

This is just one example, utilising an ever-expanding suite of marketing tools all driven using this customer and inventory data to deliver a strong return on investment across various channels, not just email. Technology-driven marketing tools now drive 39 per cent of W&B's online sales and have even been shown to increase offline sales, too. Making good use of data and third-party tools should become central to the marketing efforts of any ecommerce business.

Recommended actions

- *Short term/quick win*

  Selling via a marketplace can be a quick way to get up and running online. Going to an open marketplace, such as Amazon or

▶

eBay, may work for some, whilst, for others who meet the selection criteria, it may be beneficial to consider a curated marketplace, such as W&B, who will do much of the hard work around customer acquisition, support and fulfilment.

Unless selling via a marketplace, integrating with third-party tools should be central to your business; do not be afraid to experiment quickly with new services, and be willing to drop them if they are not working for you.

Take a look at what others in your industry are doing with third-party tools. A quick tip is to use simple browser plugins, such as Ghostery or Builtwith, to see what tools are in use on any other site on the web.

- *Medium*

  Creating an automated product feed will allow you to boost your online presence and marketing ability by pushing content through to other sites, including online shopping search engines, such as Google Shopping or using affiliate marketing programs, such as Rakuten Linkshare.

- *Long term*

  Carefully assess what platform is right for your business. There are some great ready-built hosted platforms available to small businesses, such as Shopify, which make integrating with third-party tools very straightforward, although they may lack flexibility and scalability and you will still need to put in a lot of work to build a successful online channel.

2.1 Deep dive: importance of speed

Simple common sense suggests that the longer a consumer has to wait for a web page to load, the more likely they are to abandon that page and look elsewhere. However, there are also case studies dating back to 2008 to support the claim.[1] Big retailers, such as Walmart, have shared case studies showing a correlation

[1] https://wpostats.com/tags/2008/.

between load time and conversion.[2] More recently, in 2015, Etam increased its conversion rate by 20 per cent after cutting 0.7 seconds from the average load time for its online store.[3]

Yet, despite the fact that the importance of a fast-loading website is no secret, many of the UK's top retailers fail to implement even the most basic best practice.

Why is this? And does it open the way for smaller, more agile organisations to steal a march on their larger competitors?

I reached out to Alex Painter to discuss this further. Painter is a consultant at NCC Group. They are a FTSE 250 cyber security and risk mitigation business with 1,800 employees and more than 15,000 clients worldwide. For more information, visit: www.nccgroup.trust/uk.

Why speed matters

The idea that a website's performance can affect the revenue it generates is not new. Some of the case studies making the connection date back to 2008. Jakob Nielsen was also writing about the importance of computer response times in the context of usability way back in 1993.[4] Nielsen referenced earlier work that put response times into three broad categories:

- 0.1 second – user feels that the system is reacting instantaneously.
- 1.0 second is a noticeable delay; above this, a user's flow of thought is interrupted.
- 10 seconds – the user's attention is lost.

These timing points still inform website performance goals today. For example, in 2014 a team at *The Guardian* set (and met) a goal of delivering core content in under 1 second.[5]

---

[2]www.slideshare.net/devonauerswald/walmart-pagespeedslide.

[3]http://blog.quanta-computing.com/etam-earns-20-of-conversion-by-optimising-its-online-store/.

[4]Nielsen, J. (1993) *Usability Engineering*. Boston: Academic Press.

[5]Hamann, P. (2014) *Breaking News at 1000ms*: https://speakerdeck.com/patrickhamann/breaking-news-at-1000ms-front-trends-2014.

A website's performance is not just important from a user experience perspective. It also has an impact on search engine optimisation (SEO). Google has used page speed as a ranking factor since 2010 and has factored landing page load time into its quality score for pay-per-click (PPC) advertising since 2008.[6, 7]

Many organisations see a knock-on effect on cost as well. Faster websites will use less bandwidth and need less storage, which can mean less investment in infrastructure.

However, despite a burgeoning web performance industry and a growing list of case studies pointing to a link between a website's performance and the money it makes, many websites, especially in the retail sector, are still failing to get the basics right.

Three of the biggest barriers to a fast website

1. Increasing page sizes

As a general rule, bigger web pages (in terms of cumulative file size) take longer to load than small ones, and page sizes are growing. According to the HTTP Archive, average page size increased by 14 per cent between March 2015 and March 2016.[8] The main cause of bloated web pages is imagery, with images making up 63 per cent of the content on an average web page on 1 March 2016 (again, according to the HTTP Archive).

So, why are we building bigger, image-heavy websites?

Part of the explanation is likely to lie in recent design trends, which have favoured large hero images, whole-page background images, carousels and infinite scrolling pages. The growing popularity of responsive design (where web pages reflow to fit different sized displays) has also played a part: some implementations of responsive design involve sending unnecessarily large images to mobile devices with small screens.

---

[6]https://webmasters.googleblog.com/2010/04/using-site-speed-in-web-search-ranking.html.

[7]http://adwords.blogspot.co.uk/2008/06/landing-page-load-time-now-affects.html.

[8]http://httparchive.org/interesting.php.

Perhaps the assumption has been that steadily increasing broadband speeds mean that size no longer matters – that it is possible to deliver ever-larger web pages without any negative consequences. However, the rise in mobile browsing means that the infrastructure we rely on to deliver web pages is, in some ways, actually getting slower, not faster. What is more, bandwidth is not the only bottleneck. Latency is (broadly) the time it takes a packet of data to travel from a web server to an end user's device. It is important because it is usually much higher on mobile networks, and it means that including large numbers of files on a web page can have a serious negative impact on performance for mobile users.

2. Third-party content

Another trend that is holding back page load times is the rise of third-party content. This is due, in part, to a growing appetite for more complex functionality. Increasingly, web pages are feature-rich user interfaces rather than simply a means to deliver static information. As a result, designers and developers rely on the vast array of pre-packaged, one-size-fits-all libraries that have grown up as a result. Why build your own solution if someone else has already done it for you? The problem is that the greatest strength of these solutions is also their greatest weakness. Developers do not need to 'look under the hood' to find out how they work. This means that they can end up embedding a lot of redundant content in a website.

Then there are third-party services offering such things as A/B testing, remarketing, advertising and analytics. These normally are delivered by small pieces of code embedded on a web page (tags) and they can deliver immense value, particularly to retailers and publishers. Unfortunately, website owners are all too often unaware of the toll they can take on their site's performance.

In the past few years, tag management solutions have sought to mitigate this impact. Tag managers can help to make sure that third-party content is loaded in a way that is least likely to slow the web page down. That does not mean that tag management solutions are risk-free and one drawback is that they almost make adding third-party content too easy. The effect has been that, largely, they have taken such services out of IT departments and placed them firmly in the hands of marketing, where the effect on performance is less likely to be understood, measured and controlled.

3. Company culture

Perhaps the biggest barrier to performance is not technical but cultural.

In some ways, the larger the organisation, the easier it should be to reap the rewards of a faster website. The process of auditing a website's performance and identifying opportunities for improvement is, essentially, a fixed cost. It takes the same amount of time and effort, regardless of the size of the organisation (unless there are multiple websites). And, if the end result is a 1 per cent increase in conversions, this is worth a lot more to the likes of Amazon or Walmart than it is to the average SME.

However, whilst many retail giants could benefit from investing in improving their website's performance, the fact remains that relatively few of them actually do it.

One reason for this is the sheer number of people with a stake in the design, structure and content of the typical website. Building and maintaining a fast website means considering performance at every stage. The importance of performance needs to be understood not just by the designers and developers, but also by the people specifying requirements, approving designs and carrying out day-to-day updates.

This presents a considerable challenge, especially for larger organisations with teams that may be distributed over multiple locations. For example, product images might be uploaded by the marketing team, using a content management system (CMS) and working in a different office from their colleagues in IT. They are less likely to appreciate the impact of uploading a large, unoptimised product photo than if they were working in the same room as those responsible for making sure the website meets its performance targets.

Driving change in such organisations takes leadership, vision and time. It involves managing different teams and individuals with all kinds of different priorities, and that gets harder as organisations get larger. Only in a very few cases does website performance find its way into the boardroom, and it still does not have quite the same level of visibility as related disciplines, such as SEO.

All this should mean that SMEs are well placed to steal a march on their larger competitors. Smaller, more agile teams should be better able to work together to make sure the website's performance is adequately considered as it is designed, built and maintained.

How do you know if your website is as fast as it should be?

Measuring a website's speed is not as straightforward as it might sound. How fast a page loads at any given time depends on a range of factors and everyone's experience will be slightly different. Bandwidth, latency, device, browser and even the time of day can have an impact. Part of the challenge, then, is deciding on the conditions in which to test.

Then there is the issue of what to measure. Do you wait until everything on the page has finished loading? Recently, the trend has been to try to measure performance in a more sophisticated way by looking at what is likely to have the biggest impact on the user experience. For example, Pat Meenan at Google developed a metric known as Speed Index, which looks at the rate at which a page becomes visually complete above the fold.[9]

Ultimately, the way you measure performance should be determined by what you are trying to achieve, and the tools of the trade fall into five broad categories:

1. **Synthetic monitoring**

   Synthetic monitoring regularly checks a website's load times and availability under carefully controlled conditions. It does not necessarily replicate a typical end-user experience, and the times it records may or may not be representative. However,

---

[9]https://sites.google.com/a/webpagetest.org/docs/using-webpagetest/metrics/speed-index.

synthetic monitoring excels in benchmarking and tracking changes in performance over time, and it can be invaluable in helping organisations identify and understand slowdowns, as well as other errors, such as missing objects on a page.

2. **Real user monitoring (RUM)**

   RUM aims to measure a website's performance from the point of view of everyone who visits it. This makes it less good for benchmarking – for example, a website might look as though it has suddenly become much slower simply because it is getting more visits from people with a slow internet connection. However, it does give organisations useful insight into how their website is working for customers in different regions or on different devices. RUM also tends to benefit organisations with very large volumes of web traffic because more data makes it easier to identify patterns and trends.

3. **Application performance management (APM)**

   APM tools typically look at a website's performance 'from the inside', and often they are used by web operations teams to debug back-end performance issues, such as slow database queries, rather than measure performance from the end user's perspective.

4. **Load testing**

   Load testing examines how a website responds to different levels and patterns of traffic by subjecting it to increased load in a controlled environment and measuring the impact on performance. It is particularly important for organisations whose websites are about to enter uncharted territory – for example, a retailer that is about to launch its first TV ad campaign.

5. **Real-browser performance testing and analysis tools**

   Finally, there are a number of tools that offer performance testing from real browsers under controlled conditions. These can be very versatile. At one level, they can be used to create dashboards, giving an overview of performance, both over time and in relation to the competition. But they also offer a lot of detail, giving analysts insight into how every object on the page loads, with reports to help them understand performance from the visitor's point of view and pinpoint the bottlenecks.

Many organisations use a combination of tools to understand how their website is performing, what they need to do to improve it and how performance relates to key metrics, such as conversion.

Simple steps to optimise performance include:

1. **Set goals and communicate them effectively**

   Web performance key performance indicators (KPIs) do not need to be complex, and a simple goal such as 'The home page should be visually complete above the fold within 1.5 seconds at a download speed of 5Mbps' is better than none at all. Precisely where KPIs should lie depends on a range of factors, but a good starting point is to benchmark the website against the competition.

   Everyone involved in the website also needs to know what they are aiming for. This does not just mean the people building and maintaining the site – it also means anyone specifying requirements. For example, do branding guidelines require the use of certain custom fonts? If so, how might this delay the point at which text on the website is displayed? And will the business value of custom fonts outweigh the negative impact of that delay?

2. **Test – and report – regularly**

   The only way for an organisation to know if it is meeting its KPIs – and how any updates will affect performance – is to test. Ideally, tests should be carried out in carefully controlled conditions, so that results are not affected by external factors.

3. **Focus on the big things**

   The factors that have the biggest impact on performance are often the simplest ones. For example, most site owners could make big gains just by auditing and optimising the images on their website. Others could benefit from activating compression for text files.

4. **Change one thing at a time**

   It is important to know whether and to what extent changes designed to improve performance are working, and this means taking a scientific approach to optimisation. This is important because some techniques for making web pages faster come at a cost. Some could even make the website slower in some circumstances. Following a pattern of 'test, change and retest' will help to ensure that every improvement has the desired effect.

5. **Remember why you are doing it**

   Website performance optimisation is not a goal in itself. From a business perspective, it means delivering important content to potential customers as quickly as possible, so that they are more likely to make a purchase. In this sense, it is just one of a whole range of factors that affect buying decisions. It just happens to be one that is too often overlooked.

In summary

Speed matters: faster ecommerce websites tend to deliver better results. It is, therefore, important to understand how a website's performance correlates with key metrics, avoid common mistakes and ensure that performance is addressed at every stage of the website's lifecycle.

- A retailer's revenue and costs are both affected by how fast its website loads and/or displays.
- Recent trends have led to image-heavy websites with large volumes of third-party content, which, in turn, have led to slower load times.
- Improving the performance of an ecommerce website is as much an organisational and cultural challenge as a technical one – larger organisations could find this challenge harder to overcome than smaller ones.
- There are a number of different ways to measure a website's speed – how quickly a web page displays is at least as important as how long it takes to finish loading.
- It is possible to make big performance gains by focusing on a few, simple things, but it is important to be methodical: test, improve and retest.

2.2 Case study: Watchfinder

By definition, new technologies and tools emerge all the time and it can sometimes feel overwhelming to know where to start.

In this case, we get to follow the evolution of strategic technology projects, answering the question, what is the best way to adopt your technology over time?

This case study will focus on how Watchfinder used technology to push the business forward.

We will look at four of the key stages in the development of Watchfinder's IT solutions that have raised the company from one level to the next, explaining the reasoning, practicalities and processes that went into creating them. The case study will cover:

- the catalogue editor, the foundation of the Watchfinder IT solution;
- backoffice, the stock and order management system;
- the Cloud, online hosting with instant flexibility;
- machine learning, the future of Watchfinder.

Key findings

- Watchfinder's growth to £55.5 milion turnover has been made possible thanks to the evolving IT capabilities.
- The introduction of ecommerce following the implementation of 3D secure targeted business focus.
- Machine learning will drive the optimisation of the company going forwards.

Interviewee

Jonathan Gill has spent over 10 years developing the company's hardware and software systems. His interest in coding started in his teens, inspiring him to cut his teeth at software development agency Illuminaries and launch a 20-plus year career in software development. Gill joined Watchfinder on a consultancy basis in 2003, making the move permanent two years later.

About Watchfinder

Since 2002, Watchfinder has developed from a homegrown business to a multi-million-pound business shipping to multiple countries.

Watchfinder is one of the world's largest pre-owned premium watch retailers, founded in 2002 as a purely online business by two friends and watch enthusiasts, Stuart Hennell and Lloyd Amsdon. The company stocks over 3,000 watches at an average unit price of £4,000, with a turnover of over 13,000 units and £55.5 million annually. There are over 50 brands available, including Rolex, Omega and Breitling.

Watchfinder diversified into traditional bricks-and-mortar retail solutions in 2012, with the opening of its first boutique in The Royal Exchange in London. It has since opened 3 more boutiques, 2 private showrooms, and a manufacturer-certified service centre, staffing over 110 employees nationwide. This unusual approach has been led by the strong development of an IT-based infrastructure, building a core business online that has then naturally flourished into a fully rounded commercial entity.

Its online sales strategy

The approach to Watchfinder's online retail strategy is to have a strong paid and organic search presence, to reach users that know what they want but are not aware of Watchfinder. This is achieved by feeding the top of the funnel with programmatic real-time buying of display targeted to strong audiences. This complements offline marketing strategies.

The path to purchasing a £4,000+ watch is around 30 to 90 days, so the process is, mainly, about nurturing the customer through the consideration stages to conversion. By offering the opportunity to win a pre-owned Rolex, visitors are encouraged to sign up to the Watchfinder newsletter. They will then receive emails with new arrivals and offers; this targeted approach gives the company high open rates and click-throughs.

As customers move further down the conversion path, and they start spending a significant amount of time onsite browsing certain brands, they will receive targeted remarketing messages via display. These messages are designed to tread that fine line between 'top of mind' and 'ad fatigue'.

From here it is about delivering the premium level of customer service that someone spending £4,000+ on a watch expects. Regular emails put new customers back into the consideration phase, where they are presented with more watches that they could part exchange for.

Much of this strategy has evolved over the last couple of years as the tools that facilitate remarketing become more widespread and through Watchfinder's long-term relationship with paid search and display agency Periscopix.

The key challenges over the next 12 months are to make use of these new features within its mature market in the UK, whilst rolling out, testing and developing the current UK strategy within the global market.

The Case

The evolution

There have been several key moments in Watchfinder's history that have moved the company up a level in terms of its business efficiency and operation as digital entity.

2003: the development of the catalogue editor

At Watchfinder's genesis, the business was little more than a website run from home. An enquiry form was its core, with the transaction completed via a follow-up telephone call. Watchfinder held only a small amount of stock at this stage, sourcing from a national network of retailers for the right product and the best price for its clients, but, with the customer base growing, it was obvious that a solid IT infrastructure was going to be needed.

The early days of the online transaction presented a multitude of issues: customers were wary of purchasing big ticket items online; banks were also wary, offering no protection to businesses that used online card transaction systems; and, although off-the-shelf cart systems existed, none would work with the Watchfinder model.

Because Watchfinder stock covers both contemporary and historic models, there is no one catalogue structure for each brand. Watch manufacturers revamp their lineups every so

▶

often, which would be fine if the only stock catered for was new. However, in the case of Watchfinder, all historical model data needed to be accounted for. This flexibility did not exist in off-the-shelf catalogue solutions, so the IT team was introduced, at this stage, to build a catalogue editor that could cope with all these variables, developing what would become the foundation for the Watchfinder back-end system still in use today.

The system in place required ground-up redevelopment for customers to choose the model they required from a list of drop-down menus, submitting an enquiry and then waiting to hear whether or not said watch was available. Naturally, this line of filtration channelled customers towards general enquiry telephone calls, preferring to speak to a person about their preferences rather than picking from lists.

The new catalogue editor used brand, series and model as its variables, neatly allowing any model of any age to fall under the correct brand without requiring a catalogue restructure. The accumulation of historical sales data began at this point; watch brands are very protective of RRP lists, and this accumulation of data over time has since proven to be a very valuable and useful resource. The catalogue data was pushed through to the front end, allowing customers to browse an index of watches rather than selecting with the previous drop-down system.

Although, at this stage, the business was still enquiry led, the change sparked an immediate variance in the enquiries themselves: customers were sending enquiries about specific models rather than the general ones of before. This laid the groundwork for the next stage of development, which was the development of the back office system.

2006: the BackOffice system

The wider introduction of 3D secure online payment, which removed the burden from the retailer in the case of credit card fraud, opened up a new avenue for direct online transactions. For Watchfinder, this was the opportunity to move from the enquiry-based system to an ecommerce-based system and also coincided with the development of a new back office system.

At the company's beginnings, spreadsheets had been used to keep track of stock, orders and finance, but, as the company grew, employing more people and acquiring more stock, a consolidated, trackable solution was becoming a priority. This back-end management would need to tie in the catalogue editor with an order management and stock control system to make sure nothing went amiss. With such low-volume, high-value sale items involved, nothing could be left to chance.

Once again, an off-the-shelf solution could not cut it. The need to integrate with the catalogue editor, plus the specifics required for the stock and order data, required heavy modification of existing software – and still would not achieve the ideal solution. A need to constantly update and develop the software was a must, in order to keep the business flexible, and relying on third-party developer support would not give the company the response times needed.

BackOffice introduced the ability to keep a record of every single watch within a singular database. Using individual stock numbers for every watch, BackOffice allowed not only brand, model and series data to be attributed to a specific stock reference, but also order data, customer data, servicing data and more. With everything so tightly integrated within the one custom package, every last piece of information was able to be recorded. With this protective system in place, the ecommerce online transactional part of the site could be introduced.

The benefits of this development were twofold: the strict data management and control gave a strong base to build the company securely and also positioned the company for the introduction of 3D secure and online transactions. A third-party solution was used for the implementation of the front-end search system: Solr. The company was keen to use ready-built systems where possible to avoid unnecessary work, allowing them to focus on the custom software the company needed to progress.

As the company expanded and opened additional locations, a new solution was needed to manage the location ID of stock

►

items travelling from department to department, location to location. The custom-built nature of BackOffice allowed for the integration of a new stock tracking and management system to keep each stock item under strict control throughout all stages of its journey through Watchfinder. Travelling from the purchasing department in one building to the service centre in another, then on to any one of the boutiques, the risk of loss demanded a secure and precise tracking system.

By this point, around 2012, a new software developer was hired, tasked to research and develop a hardware solution to allow watches to be scanned from location to location, and the initial direction was towards radio frequency identification (RFID). Testing proved that RFID, although it could be used with batches of watches, yielded only a 92 per cent hit rate – not enough for a business where a single loss was unacceptable.

Barcode scanners were finally decided on and implemented in 2013, working with BackOffice to move data IDs from place to place. It was also designed to automatically calculate maximum insurance combinations, generate stock manifests and push ownership to other departments or to a neutral 'transit' status, if between buildings. If BackOffice had been provided by a third-party developer, integrating additions like these would have proven a lot more difficult.

2011: the Cloud

As Watchfinder grew, so did its marketing spend, and placements in print and on television were expected to bring in spikes of traffic to the website. An advertising placement on Channel 5's *The Classic Car Show* in 2015, as an example, saw spikes of over 350 per cent – this could have resulted in a downed website was it not for the fact the website had been moved to cloud-based servers.

Before moving to the Cloud, Watchfinder was run from Rackspace servers, as was the norm. Additional space required the purchase of additional server space, at a cost of tens of thousands of pounds. Preparing for a spike in traffic meant significant outlay versus letting the website go down under heavy traffic load. From late 2008, Amazon was marketing a new kind of flexible, rentable server space that could be purchased over small periods for a fractional outlay.

With the Watchfinder website hosted on the Cloud, the firm had the flexibility to expand server space indefinitely in the space of just half an hour. When *The Classic Car Show* broadcast its first episode in 2015, the company simply upped the Cloud space to easily compensate before the episode, and brought it back down again the next day. It cost less than £50.

The future

Machine learning

The development of BackOffice and the catalogue editor from an early stage in Watchfinder's development has accumulated a huge amount of data over the years.

The company is now able to use machine learning pattern recognition to pull logical conclusions from the data. The team will pose questions to data scientists, who will use machine learning to answer those questions, to see if there are efficiencies or behaviours that can be understood more fully to improve the business performance. Perhaps there are patterns in behaviour in upgrading a watch, or patterns in journey to committing, or even patterns in how much customers are willing to spend, based on time. Fine-tuning the operation of the website, based on the answers to these questions, will continue to push the company ever forward.

And the machine learning does not stop there: in-house, the development team are working on a recommendation engine that uses self-learning preference patterns to determine algorithms for concepts like auto purchase pricing, time- and stock-sensitive pricing and servicing job optimisation. Auto purchase pricing is currently on trial, with overall positive results. The ability to push the idea further and create a system that can

▶

keep prices at the perfect point so stock flow and cash flow remain smooth, or to optimise the flow of stock through the service centre based on time to completion or stock requirements, has the potential to maximise the efficiency of the business enormously.

Results

Rome was not built in one day, and your website and IT infrastructure will not be, either. By tackling key projects systematically, it is possible to prepare the company for the future whilst still providing for customers today.

Recommended actions

- Put the business first, focusing attention on ideas that will drive efficiency and performance.
- Research technology before investing – make sure there is not a more appropriate in-house solution.
- Conversely, swallow your pride and know when the time is right to go third party.

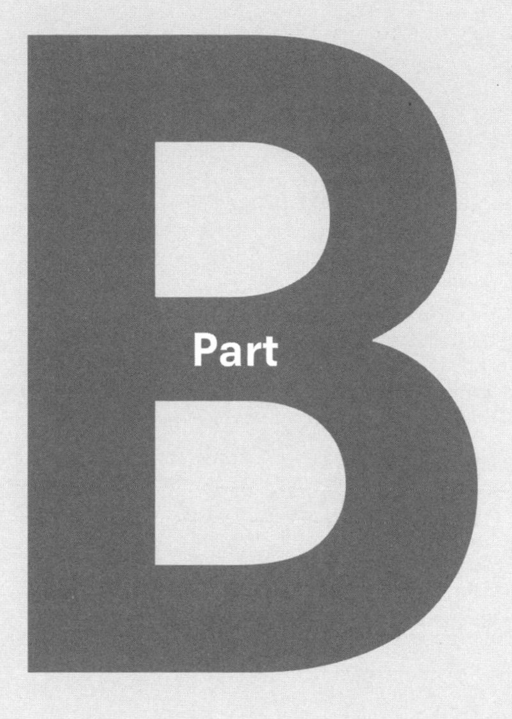

Part B

Attracting more customers

3. Understanding your demographics

Consumers are more free than ever to construct lifestyles and mindsets of their own choosing, regardless of their age, gender, location and more. To thrive in this environment, brands and businesses need to embrace new strategies.

I met with David Mattin, the global head of trends and insights at TrendWatching and author of *Trend-Driven Innovation*, published by Wiley. TrendWatching is an innovation advisory firm with over 1,200 clients and a global network of 3,000+ trend spotters helping them to stay on top of the latest around the world. For more information, visit: http://trendwatching.com/.

Key takeaway

Demographic segmentation of customers is no longer an effective way to predict customer behaviours and mindsets. Instead, we are entering an age of post-demographic consumerism.

- It is no longer possible to predict customer behaviour and mindsets effectively by demographic segmentation according to age, gender, location, income bracket, and so on.
- Instead, thanks in part to the global brain and the erosion of traditional social norms, consumers are more free than ever to construct lifestyles and mindsets of their own choosing.
- As a result, new ways of consuming, and new products, services and campaigns, can now spread rapidly and unpredictably across the old demographic customer segments.

The insight

Consumer behaviour can seem increasingly unpredictable. In a recent poll, 67 per cent of men say they would be willing to change jobs to better balance family life, against 57 per cent of women.[1] Asked to plot themselves on a sexuality scale, 49 per cent of British 18–24-year-olds choose something other than 100 per cent heterosexual.[2] A full 74 per cent of Chinese consumers are likely to consider whether a product is fair trade, sustainable or helps a charity, a higher proportion than in New Zealand.[3]

These data points give glimpses of one of the most important recent shifts in consumerism, and one which will require a fundamental overhaul of the demographic-focused approach that companies have turned to in order to understand and predict consumer behaviour for decades.

In short, we're entering a world of post-demographic consumerism, in which consumption patterns are much less defined or predictable by traditional demographic segments, such as age, gender, location, income, family status and more

Mattin believes this trend will have a fundamental impact on those in online retail who previously have relied on demographic frameworks to segment and target consumers. But it will also have a far-reaching implication for senior executives in *all* consumer-facing businesses: namely, that little, if anything, will remain the preserve of a single demographic for long.

A strategic landscape where *any* product, service or business model that solves a pressing need, or satisfies a fundamental desire, will rapidly spread beyond its initial demographic is a

[1]EY & Harris Interactive, April 2015.
[2]YouGov, August 2015.
[3]MasterCard, April 2015.

very different one from what most B2C professionals are used to, and many still assume exists.

What is driving this trend?

This new era is driven by the convergence of many of the mega-trends that have shaped the economy and society over the past decades: globalisation, urbanisation, mass affluence and expanding consumer markets, widespread adoption of digital technologies and increasing socio-cultural diversity. For consumers, these mega-trends manifest themselves across four increasingly post-demographic dimensions:

1. **The global brain**

   Consumers of all demographics and in all markets increasingly buy and use products and services from the same mega-brands: Apple, Facebook, Amazon (the technology sector is especially universal), IKEA, McDonald's, Uniqlo, Nike, and more. Alongside these global mega-brands, the global reach of information has also created a convergence in tastes and outlook among consumers, from 16 to 60 and from Boston to Beijing. BBC Radio 1's head of music recently observed, 'If you look at the list of the 1,000 favourite artists for 60-year-olds and the 1,000 favourite artists for 13-year-olds, there is a 40 per cent overlap.' It is arresting to note that pop music, once one of the most reliable indicators of generational boundaries, is now becoming increasingly cross-generational.

2. **The erosion of social norms**

   Perhaps not always politically, and certainly not uniformly, societies around the world have become more socially liberal as many conventions – from family structures to gender roles – have collapsed. Cities, with their greater social freedoms and exposure to alternative lifestyle choices are a key factor here: 87 per cent of BRIC feel that living in a city has expanded their

▶

worldview, whilst 85 per cent like the freedom of city life.[4] The choice and freedom found in cities gives individuals more opportunities to construct their own identities outside of the traditions of their specific demographic.

3. **Choice explosion**

   Individuals are now able to personalise – and express themselves through – their consumption to a greater degree than ever before. This is being driven at a macro level with the global expansion of the consumer class and the explosion of product choice in mature markets, but also on an individual level where digital experimentation allows for greater experience at lower cost, and by online social networks (enthusiastically used by *all* demographics), which allow people to identify with brands, products and services, even if, perhaps, they cannot or do not purchase them.

4. **New forms of consumer status**

   The pursuit of status is one of the key drivers of all customer behaviour in affluent societies. Traditionally, status has been about wealth display: the sports car, designer handbag or expensive jewellery. But today we are *so* affluent that even these status markers are losing their power. Instead, consumer status in affluent societies is starting to orbit around a more diverse set of issues: taste and sensibility, ethics, creativity, and more. That has made it harder to predict how affluent consumers – who typically are older – will behave, think and spend.

What does all this mean?

So, powerful forces are driving the emergence of post-demographic consumerism. What does this mean for customer behaviour and for the brands trying to serve those customers?

When it comes to customer behaviour, the top line implication is clear. That is, it is no longer possible to reliably

[4]JWT Intelligence, 'Meet the BRIC Millennials', September 2013.

predict how customers will act, think and spend by looking at their demographic profile: that is the age, gender, location, income bracket, and so on. Of course, no one ever claimed that the demographic model was perfect when it came to predicting customer behaviour. But today, its predictive power has been significantly weakened by the forces discussed above and the emergence of post-demographic consumerism.

These changes were powerfully summed up by the vice-president of product innovation at Netflix, Todd Yellin, when discussing how Netflix predicts what its users will want to watch. Yellin said: 'Everyone thought, "if you find out their age and gender data, that's fantastic", and what we learned was that it was almost useless. It's not who they are in a superficial sense, like gender, age, even geography. It's not even what they tell you. It's what they do.'

It is hard to imagine a more powerful and straightforward acknowledgement of post-demographic consumerism.

As for the consumer arena and the brands moving in it, the key implication of this trend is the way that new products, services and campaigns will spread much faster across demographic boundaries.

Yes, younger, affluent consumers are still (usually) the earliest adopters of new products and services. They are more open, more experimental and have fewer commitments. But *any and all* revolutionary – or simply just compelling – innovations will be more rapidly adopted by, and/or reshape the expectations of, *any and all* demographics. Society is now too fluid, ideas now too available, the market now too efficient, the risk and cost of trying new things now too low (led by the digital world, but increasingly the case for physical products, too) for this not to be the case.

Indeed, we see this again and again when looking at the adoption of novel and supposedly niche consumption habits. Another example (to add to the ones opening this article):

►

a 2014 study showed that whilst 48 per cent of those who had used collaborative consumption platforms (such as Airbnb, Zipcar and Kickstarter) were aged 18–34, 33 per cent were aged 35–54 and fully 19 per cent were aged over 55.[5]

How should brands respond?

How should consumer-facing brands respond to the rise of post-demographic consumerism? Mattin and TrendWatching see four main opportunities and responses from successful post-demographic brands:

1. **New normal**

   Embrace and celebrate new racial, social, cultural and sexual norms.

2. **Heritage heresy**

   Be prepared to re-examine or even overturn your brand heritage.

3. **Cross-demographic fertilisation**

   Look to seemingly foreign demographics for inspiration.

4. **Taste-led targeting**

   Use data to target the 'segment of one'.

Below we explore each in a bit more detail.

1. New normal

Embrace the new normal. To thrive in a post-demographic world, celebrate and cater to the new and diverse range of lifestyles and attitudes that it is creating. In January 2016, for example, the men's deodorant brand Axe unveiled its latest TV ad for the US market. The 'Find Your Magic' clip shows a variety of men – from a dancer wearing heels and women's apparel to a political protestor running from the police and one man in

---

[5]Crowd Companies, 'Sharing is the New Buying: How to Win in the Collaborative Economy', March 2014, www.slideshare.net/jeremiah_owyang/sharingnewbuying.

a wheelchair dancing with his girlfriend. The brand states, 'No must-have, must-be, fashion norms or body standards. The most attractive man you can be is yourself. So find what makes you, you.' Meanwhile, UK brewery Brew Dog launched the No Label beer in November 2015. Billed as the world's first 'non-binary, postgender beer', No Label is made with Jester hops, which naturally change sex during growth. The 4.6 per cent ABV beer is available to buy online and all profits go to Queerest of the Queer: a London lesbian, gay, bisexual and transgender organisation.

2. Heritage heresy

Be heretical towards your brand heritage. In a world where customers are no longer behaving as expected, neither should brands. Instead, brands will have to be prepared to reimagine or even overturn years, or even decades, of brand history and tradition that may be acting to hold them away from customers that might otherwise engage. Luxury female yogawear brand Lululemon – with a brand tradition that orbits around women and health – made a heretical turn in the third quarter of 2015: they partnered with Vancouver's Stanley Park Brewing to produce Curiosity Lager. Eighty thousand cans of the 4.6 per cent ABV lager were made, available to buy in liquor stores across British Columbia and Alberta. Can we discern in that a post-demographic move to engage with new kinds of customers – the same thinking that prompted Lululemon to open its first store specifically for *men* in New York City recently? The Savoy Hotel in London showed a similar kind of heretical thinking when it overturned decades of brand heritage around luxury to open a takeaway food counter, called Melba, in April 2015. The move showed an awareness of the new, post-demographic fluidity around who is a 'luxury' consumer.

3. Cross-demographic fertilisation

This should be encouraged. With consumer preferences being ever more universal, the opportunities to transfer innovations

▶

from an initial demographic to another have never been greater. Health and wellness is one vertical where these strategies have been especially successful. Ex-wrestler Diamond Dallas Page created DDP Yoga after finding that practising yoga helped him recover from injury. Targeting men who might be sceptical of conventional yoga programmes' spiritual elements, the variant incorporates additional muscle strengthening elements. Similarly, Crossfit Kids, a variant of the high-intensity workout phenomenon of recent years, can now be found in over 1,800 gyms and 1,000 schools worldwide.

4. Taste-led targeting

Target a segment of one. Consumers are spinning off more data than ever about their personal behaviours, preferences and past purchases. That means it is now possible to replace broad brushstroke demographic targeting with a targeting that is truly individualised. Meanwhile, the digital space lends itself to personalisation, making it possible to tailor your offering so that no two individuals experience them the same way. In August 2015, Spotify introduced Discover Weekly, a custom-made mixtape that is unique to each user and delivered each week. The playlists take Spotify users' previous song selections and use them to find tracks that have been played by other users with overlapping taste. Meanwhile, to celebrate the anniversary of its Milan–São Paulo route in May 2015, TAM Airlines created free personalised on-board magazines, *Ownboard*, for each passenger. The airline introduced a Facebook Connect request during the online purchase process in order to access information about passengers' friends, likes, places and photographs. The information was used to generate customised content for each passenger; their name and photograph were on the front cover of the magazines placed in their seats.

Recommendations

It is now a brave new post-demographic world, where consumer tastes and behaviours can no longer be understood by traditional demographic approaches. Successful products, services and brands will transcend their initial demographics almost instantaneously. As a result, executives who continue to attempt to navigate using demographic maps with their borders defined by age, gender, location and income will be ill-prepared for the speed, scale and direction of change. By contrast, those that encourage their organisations to look at winning innovations in often seemingly dissimilar, or even opposite, demographics and can incorporate what they learn into their strategies (no matter which demographic segment they target), will succeed.

- Overturn old brand traditions and do something (a new product, service or campaign) that runs *counter* to those traditions. In a world in which consumers are not behaving as expected, brands can win new customers if they also embrace the unexpected.
- To position yourself as a post-demographic brand and win new customers, celebrate and cater to new and non-traditional lifestyles.
  - Use data to personalise your offering around the individual customer; that is, the 'segment of one'.

Recommended actions

- *Short term/quick win*

Survey your customers, who they are, where else they shop, what makes them come to you, what improvements they would like to see, etc.

- *Medium*

Roll out a loyalty scheme to reward returning customers and to build a relationship.

- *Long term*

Use cookies and third-party plugins to start to personalise the customers' experience of your website.

3.1 Expert commentary: mapping the customer journey

I sat down with Neil Joyce, MD EMEA, at the ecommerce agency Signal to understand how anyone can map their customer journeys.

As marketing channels and customer devices have proliferated, understanding what makes a customer click 'buy' is no simple task. The journey is circuitous, meaning that marketers need to understand and optimise every relevant touchpoint.

One solution is customer journey mapping – a visual representation of all the points where customers interact with brands on their path to purchase. Every step on the map is a chance for a brand to show customers that they know their interests and preferences and is an opportunity to activate marketing at the right time, when the customer is in market. This will help make customer engagements more relevant and marketing spend more effective.

Here is a five-step process for customer journey analysis.

1. **Scope**

   Determine which part of the customer journey to examine. Will the map start with one channel, such as the web, or is the organisation ready to review every engagement point, such as mobile apps and retail stores? Defining the scope will determine the appropriate project owner and necessary resources.

2. **Hypothesis**

   Gather the organisation's customer journey stakeholders (marketers, website managers, social media teams, etc.) to review all customer segments and develop a hypothesis of what each segment's journey looks like. This might not be an accurate representation yet, but will be a basis for determining the data collection and analysis that needs to be done to understand the customer journey.

3. **Data collection**

   Quantitative data should come from the customer engagement touchpoints outlined in the scope. This data might live in separate locations and might not share uniform formatting, though solutions exist to help solve these challenges. As data is collected, offline and online identifiers should be linked to build persistent customer profiles that will be constantly available, even as the journey evolves. Qualitative survey data will also fill in the parts of the journey that lie outside of the organisation's visibility, such as research on an independent review site or at a competitor's store.

4. **Mapping/analysis**

   After data has been collected, analyse and reconstruct the mapped customer journeys created earlier. Be prepared for the data to directly contradict conventional wisdom. Perhaps it will show that customers who have made recent purchases are targeted with an average of five ads post-purchase. Or, perhaps a customer segment that's been targeted with desktop ads is engaging with the brand primarily through the mobile app. Uncovering these data-driven insights is the most valuable aspect of customer journey analysis. Keep an open mind and trust the data.

5. **Optimisation/evaluation**

   Once customer journey insights are uncovered, determine how to improve marketing efforts, such as:

   - Optimise efforts across channels. If a customer segment is only engaging through the mobile app, consider sending them mobile messages to increase the chances of engagement.
   - Plan retargeting and suppression campaigns, so consumers are not receiving irrelevant ads – and advertising pounds are not being wasted.

Persistent profiles are crucial for continued optimisation. The customer journey is fluid, but, over time, persistent profiles that survive even when cookies expire or are deleted will be enriched by each engagement, so customers can be reached consistently across channels and devices.

Mapping the customer journey is invaluable. Optimising the steps along the path to purchase provides the best customer experience possible and increases marketing ROI.

3.2 Case study: Thomas Cook

Thomas Cook Airlines wanted an affiliate marketing campaign that would not only drive sales but support specific business goals. Using data analysis to understand its affiliate network, the company was able to create a unique and intelligent affiliate programme.

The key to achieving this was understanding where the value lay within its existing campaign. By understanding which affiliates were best suited to driving the results that fitted with Thomas Cook Airline's wider goals, it saw a significant impact on the company's bottom line.

Key findings

- The targeted approach allowed Thomas Cook Airlines to increase its market share.
- It increased the cost efficiency of the campaign.
- It allowed Thomas Cook Airlines to identify and build relationships with its most valuable affiliates.

Interviewee

Helen Atkinson is the group marketing manager at Thomas Cook Airlines Group. She has over seven years' experience within digital marketing. She works with affiliate, meta search and display partners and also currently is involved with some key social media projects.

About Thomas Cook

Thomas Cook is one of the most recognisable names in travel and Thomas Cook Airlines is one of the biggest leisure airlines in the UK. With a fleet of 31 planes, they fly from over 20 airports across the UK, carrying 6.7 million passengers to over 60 destinations. They have over 2,500 employees across 10 UK bases, with head offices based at Manchester Airport. For more information, visit: www.thomascook.com.

Its online retail strategy

Thomas Cook Airlines operates across all key online marketing channels in order to drive customers to its website to purchase their flights. Whilst customers can also book instore, the company knows that today's traveller wants to be able to book and amend flights online and it has worked to make this process as easy as possible.

Its online infrastructure allows it to create bespoke campaigns for its customers and offer them their desired flights at the time that they wish to book. The company also twin this with geo-targeted offline campaigns, which are especially beneficial when, for example, launching a new route, such as Manchester to Boston and LA.

As customer service is Thomas Cook Airlines' focus area, it also uses its online marketing to highlight the benefits of this service, from investment in making journeys more comfortable to providing quality food, prepared by well-known chefs.

In terms of its affiliate marketing strategy, given that it already has a strong digital presence, one question then formed the basis of its strategic vision: 'How do we make ourselves excellent?' As it has a dominant affiliate channel, it knew that the key to achieving its goal of performance marketing excellence lay with the numerous affiliates the company worked with.

Identifying each affiliate's individual strengths and unlocking their potential to meet business goals would, ultimately, result in a more profitable relationship for both the company and its partners. In particular, the company looked to take an innovative approach within the performance marketing channel to mitigate revenue losses due to unsold seats.

The Case

The problem

Affiliate marketing is an important channel, driving huge volumes of online sales for Thomas Cook Airlines. There are thousands of affiliates from voucher sites to bloggers and identifying which ones are going to drive results for your businesses is essential.

In its purest sense, affiliate marketing drives sales. However, there is more to a business than simply selling. For Thomas Cook Airlines, it needed a targeted campaign to sell seats on very particular underperforming flights to mitigate revenue losses due to unsold seats.

It was more than a case of sell, sell, sell; the company needed an intelligent campaign that would sell the seats that would have the most positive impact on its business.

The background

Planning an intelligent affiliate marketing campaign relies on data and a deeper understanding of those affiliates who are a real asset to your company.

From a sales perspective, Thomas Cook Airlines had three objectives that a targeted affiliate marketing campaign would help to overcome:

- Minimise the average cost per sale (CPS).
- Increase the number of long-haul bookings.
- Increase the profitability of distressed routes.

To achieve this, the company needed to look beyond simply which affiliates were driving a high volume of last clicks and, instead, understand the role the entire affiliate network had in assisting sales.

Every affiliate adds value in a different way and at a different stage of the customer journey, depending on the nature of their site and the interests of their audience. From a strategy perspective, understanding this value would allow them to make the most of our existing affiliates and use them in the right way to drive the right type of bookings. It is important to appreciate that each affiliate the business works with is an asset to the business and understanding that they contribute in different ways is essential in allowing the company make the most of what they offer.

Beyond understanding its affiliate network, Thomas Cook needed to set out a clear vision of what it wanted to achieve from a sales perspective. Every plane that flies with unsold seats translates into a loss of potential revenue. As particular routes are affected more than others by this, campaigns with affiliates to promote distressed, particularly long-haul flights, would enable them to minimise some of this loss.

The company was also not aware of any competitor utilising the affiliate channel in this way, which meant that they could get ahead of the game by approaching this challenge in a unique way. They knew that affiliates are always looking for innovative ways to grow and test new ways of working with merchants, so the company felt this was a strategy that would encourage affiliates to work with the company.

The solution

With a clear plan of what the campaign needed to achieve, the activity was split into three categories:

1. **Looking at the value beyond simply revenue**

   Based on the aims of the campaign, the strengths of different affiliates were assigned differing levels of value. For example, as long-haul bookings were a particular target, those affiliates driving this type of booking were deemed of greater value.

   Thomas Cook also felt it was important to understand the role everyone in the network played in assisting sales. Often, affiliates are able to significantly influence a purchase several stages before the final click and this insight allows the company to value those affiliates that are having an impact higher up the purchase funnel.

   Affiliate sites each have a different focus and, as such, will drive different demographic sales. Understanding the type of sale each affiliate is able to drive allowed the company to reward those sites able to deliver high passenger numbers per booking.

▶

In doing so, Thomas Cook Airlines saw which sites had proven to be its greatest assets and allowed it to nurture the relationships with its most valuable affiliates.

2. **Understanding what each affiliate can do for you**

   Using data analysis to understand the strengths and, indeed, weaknesses of your network is the key to building a campaign that is streamlined and effective.

   Thomas Cook Airlines worked with its affiliate network to analyse past campaign data. All bookings made in 2014 had their path to conversion analysed, looking beyond the final sale and, instead, at the last six clicks before sale completion. This helped to identify each affiliate's contribution and actual cost per sale.

   By analysing everything, from routes, passenger numbers, booking classes and booking dates, the company was able to see which flights each affiliate would excel in promoting. This knowledge also allowed the company to personalise the commission to encourage bookings on high-margin flights as well as struggling routes.

3. **Putting this knowledge to use**

   The data analysis gave the company insight that could allow it to create an intelligent and efficient affiliate campaign and the final stage was putting this information to use. Powered by data, the company worked with its affiliate network to allow its partners to play to their strengths, creating a highly effective programme.

   By the nature of an affiliate campaign, each partner is one of many. However, using data to understand what each affiliate could offer, enabled the company to create a personalised campaign. Affiliates were granted higher commissions on particular routes, dates and booking classes, increasing sales of higher-margin products for Thomas Cook Airlines.

Results

As with the entire campaign, data was key in determining its success. A combination of detailed data analysis, affiliate mapping and fine-tuning of the programme saw Thomas Cook Airlines increase its long-haul share by 19 per cent. Not only this, but, by deploying an intelligent campaign, it was able to keep the average cost per sale below 2 per cent of revenue and reduced cost-per-click costs by 73 per cent. Most importantly, the impact of the campaign was felt where it was needed most and Thomas Cook Airlines sold thousands of seats on its distressed and underperforming routes.

The campaign allowed the company to step out of the shadow of the larger parent company and demonstrate itself as a competitive programme for affiliates to work with.

Critical success factors

The programme revamp and the insights it generated were an important part of Thomas Cook Airlines' long-term goal to distinguish itself as a separate entity from the wider Thomas Cook brand.

Lessons learned

The company had a clear vision of what it wanted to achieve from a sales perspective. Its approach to its affiliate campaign has been successful in achieving its business goals and maximising online sales. The company's advice would be that the key to achieving success with the affiliate channel is creating strong relationships with the right affiliate partners and working with their individual strengths.

Its advice to others looking to drives sales through the affiliate channel would be:

- It is not just about a high volume of last-click bookings. Look beyond this to understand the role of the entire affiliate network in assisting sales.
- Do your homework to find the right partners to fit your business strategy: every affiliate adds value in a different way

▶

and at a different stage of the customer journey, depending on the nature of their site and the interests of their audience.

- From a strategy perspective, understanding this value will enable you to make the most of your affiliates and use them in the right way to drive the right type of conversions to support your business growth.

Recommendations

- Data is the key to an affiliate campaign that supports business goals.
- Each affiliate has a different strength; understanding this allows you to play to them.
- Personalisation allows relationships to be built with influential affiliates.

4. Starting to use social media and PR

This section is for companies interested in exploring digital marketing as a channel to attract new customers. It will focus on the core areas of Google AdWords, social media (paid for and organic), online public relations and a very top-line view of using search engine optimisation (SEO).

I met up with the team at 10 Yetis Digital, which are behind marketing campaigns for clients such as Superdry, Made.com, Confused.com, etc. Together, we discussed some of the best examples of how to get digital marketing to deliver for you quickly.

Key takeaway

- 'News-jacking' is the most cost-effective way of raising awareness of a company or brand after an initial launch.
- Social media, specifically an influencer-led campaign, can be one of the most cost-effective ways to grow a new brand, attract new customers and build a newsletter database.[1]
- The likes of Google AdWords and social advertising are good for drilling down and targeting a specific demographic, but can be more expensive when going through the learning stages of understanding what keywords and profiles will work best for your company.

[1]Tomoson, (2015) 'Influencer Marketing Study', *http://blog.tomoson.com/influencer-marketing-study/*.

The advice

Pay per click (PPC)

The most popular type of PPC is Google AdWords, but you can also buy PPC from a raft of other providers. PPC is a way in which a company advertisement can be triggered and presented to a potential customer when that customer types a certain phrase or keyword into the search engine.

There are entire textbooks available on just the technical aspect of how to set up Google AdWords and, as such, it would be difficult to explain in just one chapter.[2] The following should act as a good overview of the opportunities that Google AdWords presents for start-up companies that are trying to attract new customers.

This is an example of how (in very simple terms) Google AdWords works:

1. A brand that sells a range of shoes has a Google advert prepared that showcases its range of 'shiny red shoes' when the phrase is typed into the search engine.
2. The brand sets out how much it is willing to pay for someone to click on its advert in the advert settings.
3. The consumer types 'shiny red shoes' into Google.
4. The brand advert is displayed.
5. The consumer clicks on the advert.
6. The brand is charged for this click.

The price that a brand pays when the consumer clicks on its advertisement is dependent largely on the competitive nature of the industry in which it operates. The more competitive the sector, the higher the cost of the click.

---

[2] Our company recommends the following book: *Google AdWords for Dummies*, Howie Jacobson, http://www.amazon.co.uk/Google-AdWords-Dummies-Howie-Jacobson/dp/1118115619 (Note: our company has no commercial or vested interest in recommending this book).

Brands have a choice of how their ads are triggered and these are based on the kinds of keywords that they select. These are:

Exact match: the advert is displayed only when the consumer types in an exact phrase, e.g. 'shiny red shoes'.

Broad match: this is the default setting in Google AdWords. If the brand selected *broad match* on 'shiny red shoes', then it would display the advert when the user typed in variations on this search term that Google felt were relevant.

Modified broad match: when a + symbol is added at the start of the chosen keywords, e.g '+shoes', then Google knows that the advertisement should be displayed only when the consumer types a phrase that contains that term.

Phrase match: the advertisements are triggered when a search query contains the words for which the brand wants to appear, in the order that they have selected, but can include words before or after the required search terms. For example, if 'red shoes' are the keywords that a brand wants to use to trigger an advert, *phrase match* would show advertisements triggered by searches including phrases like 'cheap red shoes' or 'red shoes size 11'.

Brands can also choose if they want their advertisements to appear in both Google's Display and Search Networks. The Display Network is where site owners, big and small, sell space to Google to place adverts. Even the likes of *The Guardian* and some of the biggest news websites and portals in the world offer display advertising.

The Search Network is Google's own search engine website. Brands can choose to advertise on just one of these networks. Our experience tells us that a start-up brand trying to attract new customers is better served by using the Search Network, as consumers on here are more likely to be in a buying mode, rather than those on the display network who will be, at best, in research mode.

Now that the most confusing area is out of the way, it is time to look at some Advertising101 best practice for getting the most from adverts. The number one rule of an advert is to have a clear 'call-to-action'. Examples of calls-to-action are; 'call today', 'buy now', 'sign up here', etc.

If the number one rule is to include a call-to-action, the number two rule is 'solve a problem'. Advertisements that give a solution to an issue that a consumer faces are going to get more clicks than a more general advertisement.

Google AdWords also gives the advertiser the opportunity to use a display URL. A display URL is the web address that Google shows to customers for the advertisement. It can be different to the actual URL that is associated with the advertisement and, essentially, makes the advertisement more attractive.

Going back to the red shoes example, the URL that consumers will be taken to may be ShoeCompany.com/red-shoes/1011.html. This is not a visually attractive URL. The display URL could be ShoeCompany.com/RedShoes and this is far easier on the consumer's eye. The user still would be directed to the unattractive URL, they just would not see it as part of their journey to the site.

The final point to address is ensuring that the 'landing pages' of where the traffic is being pointed to by the advertisements are optimised. It is important that the landing pages are relevant to the advertisements that consumers are clicking on. Some brands create dedicated landing pages for their advertisements with multiple calls-to-action including buying and sales messaging and also encouraging visitors to sign up for company newsletters and information.

Whilst creating dedicated landing pages is not essential, it is best practice and is also another way in which you can measure the success of a Google AdWords campaign.

Social media

This section will give an overview of how a brand can use social media to attract new customers. The social platforms that this section will focus on are Twitter, Facebook and Instagram. These three are in the top six most popular social networks globally.[3]

---

[3]Moreau, E. (2015) 'The Top 25 Social Networking Sites that People are Using', http://webtrends.about.com/od/socialnetworkingreviews/tp/Social-Networking-Sites.htm.

The three social networks not included from the top six are Google+, YouTube and Pinterest. These are all clearly successful and influential platforms but not ones that, in our experience, deliver as successful results as Twitter, Facebook and Instagram for start-up brands trying to attract new, long-term, customers.

It is also worth mentioning Snapchat, an image-based mobile messaging application. This platform launched in 2013 but has yet to go mainstream with consumers. It is a hugely popular platform with Millennials and, typically, a younger demographic. At the time of writing, there is no way for brands to advertise on the platform and it is virtually impossible to track interactions that lead to sales. Once this functionality becomes available to brands, it is our agency's belief that this platform will overtake Instagram in terms of popularity and mainstream take-up.

As a starting point for a business, it is very important that social media accounts are set up on as many channels as possible. Even if the brand decides to go on and concentrate on only a few core channels, it is best practice to have secured the brand name on every platform, where applicable, in order to prevent others (competitors, for example) from doing so in the future.

When the reader has reached the end of this chapter, it should become clear that one of the common traits of what works well on social media is the creation of high-quality content, such as professional imagery and well-thought-out and shot video snippets to support a status update, tweet, or Instagram post, be that of a sales or non-sales variety.

One of the key ways to attract new customers in a cost-effective manner is to piggyback on hashtags or national awareness days. Hashtags will be explained later in this chapter, but national awareness days are events like British Chip Week, National Ice Cream Day and more specific ones like National Small Business Day.

Brands can piggyback on these national awareness days by creating bespoke, branded content that fits that particular day. This content can then be deployed on all of the social media platforms outlined in this chapter, along with using the supporting hashtag.

Another common theme across all social media platforms is the emergence of 'influencer' campaigns. The true definition of what an 'influencer campaign' really means is still being debated by the wider social media industry. As we see it, an influencer is someone who says something that creates an action by those who follow them.

In days gone by, our parents were the original influencers because, if they gave advice or instruction, their followers (i.e. us, their children) would listen and act. In today's social media terms, influencers are seen as individuals or organisations with experience and credibility in their industry and, more often than not, a large following.

Influencer campaigns can result in big returns; however, they do not happen overnight. Brands need to take their time and build up relationships with key influencers and can, in fact, become influencers in their own right over time.

The first stage in these campaigns is to identify exactly who are the influencers in the target industry.

There are many platforms out there that assign a score for an individual's Twitter, Facebook or Instagram account in order to allow brands to see who has supposed influence, but, more often than not, these results are flawed and it is easy to see who is trying to 'game' their influence score. For example, someone may have bought Twitter followers to make them look more influential, but a quick review of their accounts can often point out if this is the case because of a lack of engagement with the content that they share. This is just one, very basic, way to investigate influencers.

The best way to identify influencers is via the brand's own industry knowledge of who is who and who are the leaders in its sector. Similar to real-life, on social media it is important to build trust and form one's own opinions on who should be listened to and who commands respect. Direct engagement and the building of a relationship is the most effective way of getting to know influencers and, eventually, having them share a brand's content or speak positively about that company.

Whilst brands cannot buy influence, they can buy mentions from influencers. Often, this is in the form of a blog post from an influencer talking about a brand, through to a tweet, Facebook status update or Instagram post. In accordance with Advertising Standards Authority guidelines in the UK, influencers should declare when they have been paid to post something on behalf of a brand.

The following is a breakdown of our experience on how to use the three social media platforms that will be focused on in this chapter.

Facebook

As well as having the ability to set up company 'pages' on Facebook, brands can also use it as an advertising platform. Similar to Google AdWords, describing the technical details of how to set up adverts on Facebook would take longer than one chapter and the following is a comprehensive overview.[4]

Facebook advertisements to promote a business take the form of three core areas. The first is to promote the company page. The second is to promote a call-to-action from the company page, such as 'buy now', 'click here' or 'sign up'. The third is to promote or boost an individual post on a company page.

Facebook advertising has become hugely popular with brands because of its ease of use and also because of the level of targeting that can be achieved. For instance, if a brand wanted to target its advertisements around a set demographic, or a common interest (or even both), it can. This targeting can be set up for all three forms of Facebook advertising.

The brand goal for using Facebook is to attract 'likes', with those likes being from an engaged audience, interested in the brand, product or service, that will then lead to sales. Creating great content that attracts people to take the time to like the page is the key. Many brands have made the mistake of trying to fast-forward the number of likes on their Facebook page by running competitions or even buying likes from third-party providers.

---

[4]Facebook guide for brands advertising on its platform, www.facebook.com/business/ads-guide.

The issue with this is that the brand is left with an unengaged, un-interested follower base. Facebook has its own algorithm that can detect when a brand page is not getting good engagement from its audience and penalises the brand by not giving content from that page a good organic 'reach'. Reach is a Facebook term that shows how many people have viewed or interacted with a piece of content or status update.

This is another reason why it is very important that brands constantly strive to post engaging and thought-provoking content. At the time of writing, Facebook has said it is giving extra focus on content that is placed on the platform using its 'Facebook live' video streaming.

This is where a brand can stream video footage live to its Facebook page via a smartphone or a tablet device. For example, a brand could film the launch of a new product or service, have a senior member of its management team talk through an aspect of the business or maybe something fun, like a company sports event or challenge.

Brands can also take advantage of trending hashtags on Facebook, although it is worth noting that this should be done with care and it is best practice never to jump on the back of a trending hashtag that surrounds something sensitive or would cause upset.

A hashtag is the # symbol and is something that Facebook users, brands and individuals, use to share their thoughts on a common event or theme. For example, when the Budget is being announced by The Chancellor of the Exchequer in Parliament, many people comment on this story and they would use the hashtag #budget. If a user was to click on the word #budget, they would see all of the updates that contain that term.

An opportunity for a brand to piggyback on this term could be a company that maybe offers a mobile app that helps track or log personal finances. The company could push out branded content related to the budget and use the hashtag #budget to make sure it gets in front of people who may be interested.

Although this is the section on Facebook, it is worth noting that hashtags first appeared on Twitter and can be used in exactly the same way over on that platform.

Here are some top tips for brands on getting the most from using Facebook to attract customers:

- Use attractive imagery, preferably professionally shot, to support brand status updates.
- Try and use more engaging and immersive content when posting a status update, such as video.
- Facebook is a 'pay to play' platform for businesses. This means you will need to pay to boost posts in order to get higher levels of interaction. This is a great way to kick off the launch of a great piece of content that a brand may have on its website, that it wants potential customers to see.
- Plan what the brand will be saying on Facebook in advance and create the supporting content in advance. Our own agency plans its content three months in advance, but one month is also sufficient time to plan social campaigns.
- Make sure that the brand page on Facebook is optimised for driving traffic to the company website, getting newsletter sign-ups or even selling. There are multiple shopping platforms that a brand can place on its Facebook page using a tab, with one of the most popular being Shopify.[5]
- Monitor emerging trending hashtags and engage with them, where possible.
- Facebook is good for testing out new product ideas or for running mini focus groups for research purposes. A brand could set up a secret Facebook group, invite its most devoted customers and then post information about new product ideas and received feedback straight away.
- Do not just continually run competitions to grow page 'like' numbers. The people who enter these competitions often are not truly interested in the brand and just want a chance to win a prize. A competition every now and again is fine.

Twitter

Twitter is a social networking platform that allows people to communicate using 140 character tweets. Similar to Facebook

---

[5] Shopify is not a client of 10 Yetis Digital.

and Instagram, Twitter has its own advertising platform. Also similar to Facebook, Instagram and Google, explaining the technical aspects of its advertising would take longer than one chapter. Here is a good guide that has been created by Twitter: https://business.twitter.com/.

Twitter facilitates two main ways to advertise on its platform. The first is to promote a tweet that the brand has written and issued or a dedicated tweet for use in an advert. The second is to promote an account on Twitter. As with Facebook advertising, a brand can deploy advertisements that are targeted around a very specific audience, interests, age/demographic or all of these combined.

It is important for brands to realise that Twitter is not just a proactive marketing tool, but it is also a great discovery and listening platform. Consumers increasingly are turning to Twitter for customer service and product/service information issues. Consumer-facing brands often set up a secondary Twitter account that deals exclusively with customer service issues.

Hashtags are a core part of the Twitter experience. The previous Facebook section outlines how hashtags work. In addition to piggybacking on trending topics, brands can use Twitter to try and engage with journalists who are looking for information around a story or products. The fastest way to find a journalist in need of help on Twitter is to monitor the hashtag #journorequest. A brand can do this simply by typing #journorequest into the search box on Twitter.

Here are some top tips on brands getting the most from using Twitter to attract customers:

- Use professionally shot images to support messages being deployed on the platform.
- Do not just pump information out. Listen to and engage with the audience that is being spoken to.
- Do not just run competitions to try and swell follower numbers. The audience attracted to these competitions will not be engaged with the brand. It is ok to run competitions every now and again.

- Put together a campaign plan in advance and begin creating content in advance.
- As well as having a core brand account, consider having accounts for the more charismatic senior people within the organisation. People buy from people and are more likely to engage with a person than a brand account.
- Make sure that a company Twitter account has a strong visual presence and makes the most of its header and profile images.
- Tools like Buffer enable brands to schedule content in advance. This is a handy tool to have when planning content campaigns.[6]
- When following lots of people, it can become difficult to keep an eye out for tweets from key people. Brands can set up lists, publicly or privately, on Twitter. Add the people that are important to keep track of, competitors or industry peers to these lists.
- Do not be afraid to ask for retweets of important content.
- Get to know and engage with influential people within your industry so that they are more likely to share your content.
- Look for opportunities to carry out branded, random acts of kindness. If a company spots an influential potential new customer or industry influencer requesting something that the brand can help with, the brand could help them in the hope that they get a positive mention on social media in return.

Instagram

Instagram is a smartphone-based image-sharing app that allows its users to take a picture, shoot a short video or use a previously shot video or picture and then add a filter to slightly change its appearance and share on its platform. The key area for brands to remember with Instagram is that they need to use visually stunning images in order to build their audience and get engagement.

Understanding the use of hashtags on Instagram is key to a brand growing its follower numbers. There is no limit on the

---

[6]Not a client of 10 Yetis Digital: Advance scheduling tool for social media: https://buffer.com/.

number of characters that a person or brand can use when typing text to support an image they are posting. This means that multiple hashtags can and should be used. Using the example of a red shoe shop posting an image of a pair of new red shoes they are selling, they may want to support the image with some of the following descriptive, funny and helpful hashtags to make the post more attractive to those searching for shoe-buying inspiration:

> #RedShoes #WomensShoes #ShoePorn #CheapShoes #Affordableshoes #ShinyRedShoes

Brands should also try to attract and win new customers by carrying out hashtag searches for topics that relate to their industry. It will then be easier for them to identify the hashtags that they should be using. Doing so is also an opportunity for the brand to go and 'like' or 'comment' on images that they feel fit with their own brand in order to try and grow its follower numbers.

Although Instagram does offer the opportunity for brands to use advertisements, it is one of the last social media platforms where branded content does not necessarily have a 'pay to play' requirement. A brand can freely use and grow its audience on Instagram without having to buy advertisements, although advertising can speed up that growth, if done correctly.

Instagram is owned by Facebook and, as such, its advertising is powered and controlled by Facebook's own advertising platform. A guide to the technical specifications of setting up Instagram advertisements can be found here: https://business.instagram.com/advertising/.

It is worth noting that, at the time of writing, Instagram allows users to post only one clickable weblink and that is on the user profile page. Users cannot post clickable links in the text that they use to support an image or video.

Here are some top tips on brands getting the most from using Instagram to attract customers:

- Use professionally shot images where possible.
- Plan content campaigns in advance and create the required content in advance.

- Get to grips with industry hashtags, as these are key to growing an engaged audience.
- Give 'likes' and leave comments on relevant content. This is the fastest way to grow an engaged audience.
- Consider unique ways for the brand to use Instagram. For instance, can a senior member of the team take over the account at an event or to showcase a launch or similar?

Search engine optimisation (SEO)

Search engine optimisation is a longer-term way to find and attract new customers. SEO campaigns do not show immediate results, *but* over time, SEO, deployed correctly, can transform a business.

SEO is the way in which a brand tries to get its website to appear as high as possible on search engines for terms that it knows its potential customers may use when looking to buy or research a product. For example, a car insurance company would want its site to appear as high as possible on a search engine for the term 'cheap car insurance'. There are a number of factors that can affect where the insurance website may appear.[7]

Google is the most used search engine in the world and, as such, the information in this chapter relates to this platform only. It is also worth noting that SEO has a number of key elements that are too complex to cover in one chapter. The website Moz.com is the platform that our agency recommends for clients wanting to get a more in-depth understanding of modern SEO tactics, explained in a really simple way.[8]

Top SEO tactics that a brand can use to attract and win new customers include the following:

- Attract links that go from popular websites back to the company website. This is explained from a media and news perspective in the next chapter.
- Ensure that the company website loads in the web browser as quickly as possible. A key way to ensure this is to make

---

[7]Not a client of 10 Yetis Digital: https://moz.com/search-ranking-factors.
[8]https://moz.com/.

sure that all images shown on the site are as small in file size as possible.

- Ensure the content that is written for the company website is unique (not copied from elsewhere), well written and explains the necessities in a strong way.
- Make sure the titles of the pages are relevant to the content on the page and user terms that potential customers may input when using Google.
- Make sure that the onsite content contains the words that customers may search for when using Google. For example, if a brand wants to appear high in the search engine for the term 'cheap car insurance', this must appear multiple times on the website pages and in the website page titles. Do not overdo it, though!
- Make sure that the website displays correctly in every browser and on mobile phones and tablet. This is called 'responsive design'.
- Make it easy for Google to be able to 'index' the website. Index is where Google goes through a site to make sure it sees every page. Think of Google as running water; make it easy for it to flow throughout the site. The best practice is a site-map that is a page that shows every page on a site. Typically a site-map is designed in a way that is similar to an actual map.
- Make sure pages are optimised to keep people on the site and interested. Google knows if someone lands on a page and then leaves immediately because they could not find what they needed, and penalises a website for people not staying on a page for a time that it deems suitable.

Online public relations (PR)

The team at 10 Yetis believe that online PR can deliver the best return on investment in terms of the time spent by a brand managing and deploying campaigns, compared to the wider marketing efforts of that brand.

Online PR is the way in which brands can engage with highly influential journalists and encourage stories to be written about their services or products that are then shown to a mass-market audience. A story in a national newspaper or on an international website can get a company in front of millions of readers.

Not only is the story visible to millions but, if a clickable web link is included in the story, then this also delivers potential customers to the company website and gives a great boost to the brand's SEO campaign (see Chapter 1 for more information on the benefits of this). In addition, being able to showcase the mention that a brand has had in the media is another marketing opportunity, helps with credibility and can be shared on social media platforms.

The typical way in which brands secure online media coverage is to issue a press release about a pre-agreed company story to journalists. Brands should have a regular proactive campaign plan of stories that they wish to share and that can be written in advance. Press release topics could include: new product launches, new senior level appointments, reaching business milestones, product innovation or commentary on industry goings-on.

The latter (commentary on industry goings-on) is, in our opinion, the fastest way to grow a brand's industry credibility, demonstrate thought leadership and get links from authority websites back to the company website. This is commonly known as 'news-jacking'. The brand is, essentially, piggybacking on an ongoing, existing, news story in order to raise its own profile and put its own point across.

As with a press release, news-jacking needs the company to have built up a list of key journalists to whom it can send its news. Using a media database to find the right journalists to target can help with this. Our preferred media database supplier is ResponseSource.[9] If that is a budget stretch too far, the brand could read the titles and websites that it is interested in contacting and then use Google to find the journalists' names.

Quite often, a journalist's email address is freely available on the website for which they write or the news outlet's email string is made clear, e.g. firstname.lastname@Newsoutlet.com. In addition, most modern-day journalists and freelance writers have a Twitter account that you can follow and engage with.

With regards to news-jacking, time is of the essence. The fast-paced nature of the modern media is such that journalists have

[9]Not a client of 10 Yetis Digital: http://www.responsesource.com/.

very little time to work on a story and need input very quickly. Brands need to react to breaking news immediately in order to stand a chance of getting their comment used.

Monitoring emerging hashtags on Twitter is a great way to spot opportunities, as is simply having one of the TV news channels on in the background of day-to-day office life. Being fast is not the only factor, though.

It is vital that a brand makes what it wants to say as interesting and colourful as possible. In the same way that a person never wants to get stuck next to a dull person at a party, a journalist does not want a dull quote. Journalists look for controversy and a brand can give this via a more engaging and fun comment, where appropriate.

Top online public relations tactics that a brand can use to attract and win new customers are:

- React to everything your organisation can give comment on that is breaking in the news.
- Be fast to react.
- Make statements and comments interesting.
- Use a media database to speed up the process of finding key journalist contact information or use Google or Twitter, if budget is an issue.
- If a brand gets a write-up or a comment in a news outlet, do not be afraid to ask for a link back to the company website.
- Build relationships over time and try to get to know the key industry journalists – get out and meet them.
- Make sure, when pitching a story or press release, that the journalist being spoken to actually writes similar stories.
- Following up a press release with a phone call to a journalist increases the chance of the story being used, but never ask if they got the release (journalists' number-one pet hate) and keep in mind that journalists have very limited time.
- Think bigger than just a press release. Create videos for the media, concept images of futuristic products or similar, web-widgets or common interest quizzes that the media may want to share with its audience.

- Many news outlets encourage brands to share on social media the write-ups that they have given. Brands that can demonstrate a large following could be viewed more favourably by a journalist.

Lessons for you

- Monitor and react to the hashtag #journorequest on Twitter to find media opportunities direct from journalists, freelance writers and influential people on social media. This is the fastest brand growth-hack there is.
- Where appropriate, piggyback on national days on social media (for example, National Pie Day, National Chip Day) and create relevant branded content that can be shared, and use the relevant hashtag.
- Remember to include calls-to-action in all of your campaigns, such as 'buy now', 'click to read more', 'sign up to our newsletter' or something as simple as 'please share this'.

Recommended actions

- *Short term/quick win*

  If you are not already doing PPC yourself, start with that. That will give you a benchmark of relative success, then hire a PPC agency, hold them accountable for their ROI so you can justify their fees. Make sure you have them teach you what they are doing, how they are doing it – so you can take over later.
- *Medium*

  What social channels are your customers using? Sign up to their advertising service and start testing it.
- *Long term*

  Map all journalists/writers that cover topics linked to your business, start following them on social media, reach out to them individually with your best angle for a story. Remember, they are not interested in writing an advertisement about your company, so think, instead, of a trending topic or theme that you have expert knowledge about and offer your help/commentary.

4.1 Deep dive: from social listening to predicting

Can we move from simply observing past customer actions to a world where we can predict them? That is possible, according to Startcount, a social intelligence agency founded and backed by Edwina Dunn and Clive Humby, which previously created Dunnhumby (for more information, visit: www.starcount.com).

For most companies, transactional data will never be able to show retailers the personalities, passions or motivations of their customers. This level of insight can be found, however, using connections on social media. The complex networks around customers provide a rich understanding that brands can use to take audience understanding into the next generation.

Social media can be used in one of two ways. It can be used as a customer service channel and social listening tool and, historically, has been limited to this. Or it can be used as the world's richest and furthest-reaching research tool. The many connections surrounding each individual form networks that can unlock the passions, motivations and habits that drive customers. Retailers now have the opportunity to understand the people behind transactions, and this level of audience understanding should be used to inform strategy and customer engagement across the business.

Until now, audience understanding for most retailers has comprised either demographics or trying to replicate the Tesco Clubcard model with analysis transactional data. However, few retailers enjoy similar transactional patterns or volumes to supermarkets and, as a result, using the same method to understand customers will not yield the same level of audience understanding. By understanding the connective networks around audiences on social media, brands are now able to surpass this level of understanding. They are able to understand a person's interest in their own industry, but also their interests in all aspects of their lives.

- Despite the many claims by the media, browsing behaviour and transactional data will not be able to build the detailed customer profiles that brands desire to know of their audience. For retailers with additional challenges, such as cash transactions or low loyalty scheme engagement, this problem is amplified.
- To understand a person, we must look to their 'social persona'. Most customers regularly use some sort of social platform and form complex networks around them by connecting with the profiles that represent their varying passions. Analysing these gives us a 360-degree view of audiences.
- Content produced by the 13 per cent of users who actually post often is deceptive or selective and an inaccurate or incomplete image of the individual. To understand 100 per cent of users, without bias, we must look to what they consume, not what they talk about – who they follow.
- Understanding from social media is not restricted just to selected audiences, but to the entire market. This wider view provides the opportunity to understand the competition and a brand's position in the community.
- The combination of rich market understanding and detailed customer profiling allows brands to segment their audience with precision and create customer-centric strategy.
- The real-time nature of social media means that strategy can be adapted and improved continuously.
- Understanding social data gives a global opportunity to even the smallest businesses, who now have access to a worldwide research and communications tool.
- Companies who are able to recognise the potential of social media will be able to have unparalleled audience understanding. Accurate understanding will inspire exciting and creative strategies.

Twenty years ago, a revolution took place in retailing. Tesco launched Clubcard and leapfrogged Sainsbury's to become the UK's biggest grocer in the space of 18 months. Much of the credit for this huge transformation is attributed to the detailed understanding of customer behaviours that Tesco obtained by analysing data collected by Clubcard for every customer.

Historically, audience understanding has been formed using demographics and retrospective purchasing patterns. In a time where demographics can no longer be indicative of life stage – a 25-year-old could be married with children and a 35-year-old working or studying – audience understanding is a more complicated task. The rise of the ever-present internet that enables customers to analyse a huge range of products (and prices) in their hand wherever they are, has resulted in the decline of brand loyalty and, as such, the decline in loyalty schemes traditionally used to harvest customer data.

Today, this detailed analysis of customer transactions and web browsing behaviour is promoted as a panacea to all retailers. Deep insights into customer behaviours theoretically offers retailers the ability to step change their relationships with customers. However, for most retailers, the ability to benefit from insightful transactional customer data will forever be out of reach.

Grocery is a very distinctive type of retailing; where customers return every week and buy the same or similar products and, even amongst infrequent shoppers, the retailer will see the customer 8 to 12 times a year. Nearly all other retailing is so very different from this. Most retailers will have large numbers of customers who make fewer than four purchasing visits a year, do not engage in loyalty schemes or simply choose to shop with cash. For these customers, building up an accurate image simply is not possible using only a retailer's own data.

Even for the small group of regular customers, the story is much the same. Understanding the role that the retailer plays in its customers' lifestyle is much too difficult from the 15 to 25 items they happen to buy. The truth is that, even if companies have huge amounts of transactional data, this rarely tells you anything about the person making the transactions, why they did so or what they may be likely to do next week.

The answer to this lies in their 'social persona'. The vast majority of customers use some sort of social media platform and leave a detailed fingerprint of their interests and passions open for analysis. This social fingerprint can unlock more than how a customer has spent their money historically; it can give insight about the passions that motivated the people to behave this way, it can bring personality to the data. Social data can show the media consumed, influencers followed and brands engaged with. If this cultural understanding of motivations and aspirations is gained, retailers will be able to see themselves through their customers' eyes. Until now, social media mainly has been used to provide another form of customer service or for social listening to understand the mood of a select few customers. The much bigger opportunity to understand not just vocal customers, but the whole market, has been overlooked.

This is coupled with the rising expectation of customers for a bespoke and personalised service to provide retailers with a new challenge around audience understanding. Most customers now consider themselves to take part in some form of data exchange; cookies and shopping online are just some of the examples that most people come into contact with on a regular basis. The exchange is accepted. However, in return, people have come to expect to be understood by the brands to which they give data. There is mild outrage now at receiving an email about unrelated or inappropriate products. This expectation means that even large and traditionally data-rich retailers must use other resources to further their understanding of their audiences. The largest, most comprehensive and under-used of these resources is social media.

The way people use social media can be described in two ways: projective and consumptive. Projective social media involves posting content that is usually a carefully curated gallery of the best parts of a person's social life. It is the highlights and usually is deceptive, showing only a tiny portion of a person. However, this is the shiny version that the person wishes to portray themselves as, not how they really behave. If they are interacting with a brand, usually it is to give (negative) feedback or get something free, and cannot give much indication as to how the person really sees the brand or any of their other interests. To see how customers behave in 'real life', brands must look to what they choose to consume instead.

On consumptive platforms such as Twitter, the majority of people tend to be silent. Analysis by Starcount shows that only 13 per cent of users on Twitter regularly tweet. The rest of the audience are characterised by following a high number of influencers and brands related to their passions from which they can consume content. These connections tend to be one-way relationships and result in profiles with huge followings, for example Katy Perry who has 84 million followers globally. The audience use these platforms to create a portfolio of profiles that keep them immersed in their varied passions.

You could be a financier getting market updates, following top chefs for restaurant ideas, getting the lowdown on the newest cycling gear, following your football team and indulging in that guilty pleasure of *Daily Mail* gossip. Each 'follow' enriches the picture built of a person and shows the technicolour image of the individual. No person can be defined by one label, and is interesting to different brands for different reasons. The complex network of connections sheds light on these reasons and it is these connections that are essential to understanding the silent majority, the 87 per cent who do not regularly tweet or post content.

For each individual, the complex network they create by connecting with the profiles in their portfolio is the key to understanding what makes them tick. Starcount has identified 750,000 popular accounts ('stars') in social media that account for over 85 per cent of content consumed and codified the genre, themes and topics these accounts represent. The combination of these popular accounts a person follows can show us the different passions and motivations of the individual. These combinations show us who a person really is, not what they project. For many people, if they are asked whether they are interested in celebrity gossip, they may answer with something along the lines of, 'No, well maybe sometimes for a joke.' To answer this question accurately you just have to look at the huge volumes of people following celebrity gossip stars; it may not be something a person is particularly proud of, but it does tell a lot about the way they may respond to certain media campaigns or celebrity endorsements.

The connected networks can be expanded and brands can use the social universe to view the entire market, not just the part they inhabit. For retailers, the UK Twitter base of 13.5 million active users can be tapped to create profiles with a level of understanding that takes demographics and purchasing habits to the next level. Similar methods can be applied on other social networks.

Using social media as a research resource allows retailers to understand the wider market place. Traditionally, companies have been restricted by the limitations of their own transactions; it is one thing to understand why a customer shops with you, but why they do (or do not) compared to someone else, brings the understanding to the next level. The connections joining each user and star build up highly intricate networks. By having a view on the entire network, retailers are able to see where in the market they fit. This shows brands how they are seen by their audience in relation to the wider community.

The view on the wider community gives retailers the ability to analyse the size of the market place and the opportunity for growth. The knowledge of the size of the prize, who the prize is and what they are driven by has, heretofore, been unknown. Exploiting this can inform the best use of resources when creating a strategy. In particular, for brands with more limited resources, this can inform the difficult decisions when deciding budgets and strategy.

The social universe allows retailers to understand who the competition is and what their audience looks like. Brands will be able to find out why certain brands are their competition and what their attraction is to the audience. They will even be able to analyse the size of their audience and how they differ to their own. The desire to understand competition is nothing new. However, until now, it has been a dark art, with very little hard data to support it. This has left the understanding open to being highly subjective and difficult to prove. The scale of social data can help to validate and evolve the perception of the competition.

Once the market is understood, this context can be used by brands to enrich the understanding of their audience. Stars on social media include media titles, brands, celebrities, influencers and many more. The variety of stars from every industry imaginable creates a complete picture of the individuals who make up audiences. We are no longer just left with the idea that a Nando's customer likes chicken, chips and a diet coke. Now we are able to see that this Nando's customer loves music, their favourite musician is Professor Green and another favourite restaurant is Pizza Express. They do not follow fast-food outlets such as KFC and do not view Nando's as fast food. The differentiating passions of audiences and the brands/influencers that they consume show us the person behind the purchase.

These profiles can then be combined with market data and used to shape strategy. Once a customer segment has been defined, retailers can understand their appeal to the segment and the benefits they offer. They can also understand the tone of the audience, if they are deal-driven or excited by the new thing. To be noticed by these people, do you need to be cool, reliable or can you attract people with deals and offers? The research and resulting actions should not be restricted to social media strategies. Instead, it should be used at the highest levels when decisions are made on customer engagement strategy.

Using the profiles built by the segments to form strategy allows retailers to begin a cycle of understanding. This can be developed to create sustainable and scalable growth. The feedback from the strategies can be used on each segment to further enrich the understanding. In turn, this can drive ever more precise and innovative strategies. Precision strategy allows brands both to appeal strongly to the relevant audience and to target people, not just modelled types. It also enables brands to avoid overwhelming and annoying the inappropriate audience, those who will never be customers and may resent you for bombarding them. The knowledge of who not to target saves money and effort and allows brands to spend more on rewarding campaigns. The real-time nature of social media means that this evolution of strategy can be continuous and instant.

In an ever globalised market place, being able to trade internationally is a fantastic opportunity for retailers. To do this has, traditionally, been risky and required huge amounts of capital investment. As such, it has been possible only for larger companies. Social media has opened the door for smaller businesses who are now able to create awareness abroad and to get an idea of where and how they should begin trading internationally. The global nature of social media means that retailers are now able attract customers from far and wide and understand markets across the world. Social media offers large potential audiences globally; which people in Asia are Anglophiles and like to follow English heritage brands, key UK celebrities and the like?

These huge volumes of users allow retailers to compare their existing and potential audiences in different regions and tailor their strategies accordingly. Furthermore, it can help retailers to gain an understanding of foreign market places before the launch of a new product. An understanding of local culture and the nuances of a new community prevents brands from entering the market with little research.

Social data is open to everyone, and brands of all size finally have the ability to reach and read the whole market. Gone are the days when only large multinationals could afford volumes of focus groups or scale up IT/CRM systems. In the present day, even the smallest businesses are able to analyse the market, understand their customers and create precision strategies to gain new ones. This poses a challenge and opportunity in equal measure; it is the companies who take advantage of the insight and use this very personal understanding of audiences to make innovative strategic decisions that will come out on top.

Companies have long known that social media is a reserve of data they should be tapping. However, using it just to listen to and occasionally speak with noisy customers has distracted from the full potential of this incredible resource. Using social media as an understanding tool opens up the realms of possibility for the next generation of customer insight and customer-centric strategy. We can now understand who a person is, not just what they have bought or said. Real-time analysis of audiences combined simultaneously with transactional and market data will enable brands to create increasingly creative and detailed strategies and will, ultimately, result in improved customer experiences.

The brands that can take advantage of this understanding and provide the best value to customers will reap the rewards. Big data and precision customer understanding will not be the end of creativity; it will be the fuel to fire a new generation of thinkers and inspire innovative and exciting strategy.

In summary

- Using only transactional or demographic data to understand customers builds an incomplete picture of a brand's audience.
- In the UK alone, there are over 8 million active users on Twitter, each user following an average of 363 profiles. This vast, connected network can be used to map out the passions of each individual, giving an unprecedented level of customer understanding.
- Precision audience understanding should be used to drive customer-centric strategy at the highest level.

4.2 Case study: Björn Borg

Email marketing is one of the most effective ways to reach the target audience, according to the Direct Marketing Association. They found that ROI from email rose from £24.93 in 2014 to £38 in 2015. But, this ROI becomes relevant only if the emails are relevant to the audience and consistently make their way to the recipient's inbox.

With Björn Borg sending out such a high volume of messages to subscribers, Noelia Guinón, ecommerce manager, recognised the need to make the email messages relevant, if they were going to be effective at capturing the attention of the customer in a short space of time. Poor email deliverability was causing the email channel decline, both in growth and revenue. She knew that the only way to achieve this would require a better use of their customer data.

Key findings

- Within the first six months, Björn Borg saw positive results. Newsletter deliverability rate increased by 75 per cent, click rates increased by 83 per cent and there was a 66 per cent increase in email-generated revenue, as a result of a more personalised and relevant approach.

Interviewee

Noelia Guinón has been ecommerce manager at fashion label Björn Borg for over two years. Previous roles have included marketing manager for fashion brand Halens and online marketing manager at Consortio Fashion Group. She has over 15 years' experience in online marketing.

About Björn Borg

Founded by the international tennis star of the same name, Björn Borg is a fashion underwear and sports apparel brand based in Stockholm, Sweden. Initially established in the Swedish fashion market in the first half of the 1990s, it was relaunched as a premium sports fashion brand in 2015. It also sells footwear, bags, fragrances and eyewear through licensees.

Björn Borg products are sold in around 30 markets, of which Sweden and the Netherlands are the largest. The Björn Borg Group has operations at every level from branding to consumer sales in its own Björn Borg stores.

Its online retail strategy

Björn Borg's business spans multiple channels and uses a variety of messaging strategies. A large proportion of these messages were based on discounting. The brand was founded in Stockholm, Sweden and expanded to become a leading fashion underwear business in the Nordics and Benelux in the early 1990s. In 2015, the brand successfully relaunched as a premium sports fashion brand and is distributed in around 30 markets worldwide.

Part of Björn Borg's online retail strategy is currently to send out nearly 20 million marketing messages a year to 200,000 email subscribers across 12 markets.

The key projects for the next 12 months are to expand its email marketing campaigns to encompass basket abandonment, post-purchase outreach and product recommendations within its improved brand unified email messaging framework. A major part of this is its ongoing effort to move its messaging away from its focus on discounting.

The Case

The problem

The company wanted to unify the brand under one umbrella to improve sell through and become the number-one sports fashion brand. The business recognised that the way to achieve this was to engage customers with more personalised communications that were more focused on being a part of the Björn Borg tribe.

The solution

Björn Borg decided, ultimately, to go with the email platform provided by Bronto Software. The brand already used Magento's Enterprise ecommerce platform and the solution needed to integrate easily with the existing ecosystem. The project first launched in May 2015 and, in the first six months, Björn Borg saw good results in the execution of its email marketing.

Creating a consistent brand experience

With a variety of messaging strategies spanning multiple channels, Björn Borg knew that improving brand affinity and recognition were key to unify the brand's position. This was especially important as the brand worked to take its messaging beyond being based largely on discounting. Guinón explains: 'We believe that the way to reach our goal is to engage our customers with more personalised communications that are more focused on being a part of the Björn Borg tribe.'

A key part of this, in addition to updating its marketing emails, was to reinvent the brand's transactional emails. 'We know these emails are the most opened ones, so why not use them to establish a better brand experience?' The project has enabled Björn Borg to deliver messages with a 'spot-on' brand feeling. 'Our customers instantly recognise our order confirmations, building our brand awareness even further.'

More engagement – better personalisation

The improvements also enabled Björn Borg to import three types of data into their email marketing platform to enhance their emails, basic address and customer information, product data and images and order history details. 'We only get a person's attention for a very short time, so we need to deliver a message they feel is directed at them personally.' The new functionality allowed the brand to create more relevant and personalised emails.

In addition to this, the brand was looking to ramp up the reliability of their email marketing deliverability. 'The primary objective was to invest in a platform with rock-solid deliverability. Previously, we encountered a variety of issues, including a high bounce rate that hurt our delivery rate.'

Results

Within the first six months, Björn Borg saw impressive results. Newsletter deliverability rate increased by 75 per cent, click rates increased by 83 per cent and there was a 66 per cent increase in email-generated revenue, as a result of a more personalised and relevant approach.

To encourage new customers, Björn Borg also introduced an email welcome series, which is also delivering sizable results. In fact, the performance of the welcome series has exceeded the standard marketing emails. The click rate is 232 per cent higher, conversion is up by 21 per cent and the revenue from the welcome series is up by 217 per cent.

Three more campaigns, focusing on basket abandonment, post-purchase outreach and product recommendations are already in the pipeline.

Lessons learned

If you want to move away from mass marketing and get more personal, email marketing is an incredibly powerful channel. The results of Björn Borg show just how powerful it can be, if it

▶

is approached in the right way. Gaining brand alignment across all types of emails is extremely important to keep customers engaged and grow sales. Whether you are building a premium brand or not, having a smart email strategy in place will prove an important investment. As brands, we get a person's attention for only a very short time, so the message needs to be relevant so consumers feel it is directed at them personally and will encourage them to respond accordingly.

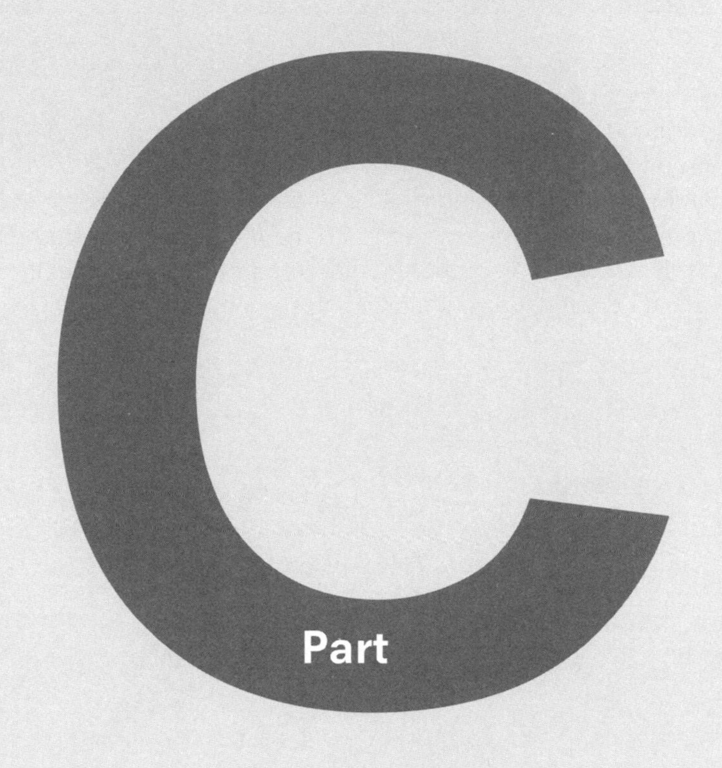

Part C

Selling more

5. Presenting products and services online

The more relevant you make your website for each visitor, the longer they will stay, the more they will do, the more they will spend and the more they will tell other people.

I met up with the team at Red Technology, an ecommerce solutions provider, combining ecommerce agency services and authoring an ecommerce platform. For more information about them, visit: www.redtechnology.com.

We discussed how the theory of personalising your ecommerce makes sense to everyone, but that most retailers do not really know where to start and what to do to get the best results. In fact, 98 per cent of respondents surveyed by eConsultancy saw personalisation as critical to success, but only 22 per cent had implemented it in some form or other (Davis, 2015).

Key takeaway

- It is often thought of as the preserve of huge, multinational retailers and not available to the mass market due to its cost and complexity. Not only that, many retailers often suffer from paralysis when it comes to the idea of trying to implement anything but the most basic forms of personalised content and promotions on their ecommerce sites and emails. They are unsure of where to begin, whether they already have or need to buy the technology required to do it, how to justify any time and expense and how to prove the results.

▶

- Retailers may display very basic recommendations, such as the items a user last looked at or what other users purchased when ordering a certain product, but little else. Most businesses tend to adopt more of a generic 'one-size-fits-all' approach, so are missing out on the huge potential that even basic personalisation can offer, including increased conversions, orders, average order value and customer loyalty, as well as a reduction in cart abandonment and bounce rate.
- The capability exists to customise entire user experiences down to an individual user level – serving unique content, pricing and promotions to each, but the resources, effort and cost required to do this properly in such microscopic detail means it is unlikely to happen for all but the largest retailers. More achievable is the scope for delivering content (in the form of onsite advertising, products, offers and promotions) to more generic groups of users and providing a degree of personalisation that those remaining 78 per cent of retailers still will not be delivering.

The advice

1. Product recommendations

Often, the first, and most basic, step for the majority of retailers in delivering some form of personalisation is the use of product recommendations, which can be delivered by almost all ecommerce platforms nowadays. In fact, personalised product recommendations can help generate around 10–30 per cent of ecommerce site revenues (Agrawal, A. 2015). Depending on the sophistication of your ecommerce system and the data you have available, these may be delivered manually, via automated algorithms and metrics or a combination of both.

Types of product recommendation

There are at least three different types of product recommendations to consider, all of which can serve personalised content aimed at increasing the user's likelihood to buy.

Similar: items that are similar to or can be substituted for the ones being viewed. These might be slightly different versions, different brands/makes or have more/less advanced features and a higher/lower cost.

Complementary: offering additional or complementary products to those being viewed. Often advertised under guises such as 'Complete the look' or 'Customers also bought' trying to upsell and increase basket size.

Recently viewed: what other items a user has recently looked at (most likely session-specific – but more advanced versions can remember users from previous visits, either via account login or using cookies).

Many ecommerce sites deliver only one of these three types of product recommendations across their entire website. Increasing the types you offer can help target different customers, with different buying requirements and habits, at the same time, whilst also providing the capability to upsell.

Placement of product recommendations

Another thing to consider with product recommendations is their effectiveness on different pages in the purchase cycle. For instance, tempting users with last-minute or special offer items on the checkout page can encourage impulse buys, whilst giving them alternative options (potentially more advanced or more expensive versions of what they are looking at to drive an increase in your average order value; you could create an algorithm that will not show an alternative product of a lower value, for instance) may work better on the product pages during their browsing and research phase.

By beginning to personalise the output of these recommendations, using more than one type of recommendation at the same time, and thinking about the most effective place on your website to put them, you should expect to see significant increases in conversions.

When you have mastered the more generic use of product recommendations, you can move on to displaying items specific to individual users based on the data you have gathered and profiled, such as demographic, interests and behavioural.

When done well, product recommendations tend to use a combination of technology and manual input for best results. As you develop, and more information is gleaned to populate product recommendations, the more personal you can get. You can begin to use customer data, such as demographics, interests or website interaction, alongside manual input from merchandisers, product experts or stylists.

Due to the time involved when trying to manually populate your product recommendations, particularly when you start, you may need to heavily rely on automated systems. However, do not let that stop you from having some human input and watch out for the following common failings with some automated systems:

- Product recommendations being the same across all products, and thus often unsuitable, regardless of the product being viewed.
- Seasonal items being displayed after the event – no real point showing people Christmas decorations that somebody bought before Christmas, in January, as they are unlikely to be relevant.
- Recommendations being exactly the same item as that currently being viewed.
- Recommending other colours or sizes of the same product (these variables should always be shown on the same product page).

2. Target content

Onsite targeted content is a method of displaying some information to your users in specific areas of your website. Most often, it takes the form of advertisement (image), but could also be some product recommendations, flash content, a video or plain text and tends to sit in a pre-defined place on each page.

Types of targeted content

There are two basic forms of targeted content both with advantages and disadvantages, as shown in the following table.

Table 5.1

Inline content: appears in an area or areas within a web page and are, possibly, less likely to attract the user's attention, but are also less likely to annoy them. These tend to be more commonly used and more appropriate in most situations.
Pop-up content: appears in a lightbox above the page and either will require user action to remove, or will have a time limit to disappear automatically. Very likely to catch the user's attention, but can be used really only once during a user's visit before they begin to annoy.

Placement of targeted content

The placement of content is key to its success. As the areas available for it are likely to be defined during your initial site build, it is important to consider where you want them and how easy they are to change. Delivering the right content, in the right form, at the right stage of the user journey and purchase cycle could be the difference between converting and not. For instance, last-minute bargains on the mini-basket and checkout pages can encourage impulse buys (particularly on low-value items), whilst a flash sale could be highlighted across all pages, so it is shown during their browsing phase. Most catalogue and transactional pages across your ecommerce site should contain the scope to include targeted content, whilst ensuring that they are easily visible to the user.

Customer and display conditions

Having established the types of targeted content, and the different pages and places where you can put it, the next stage is understanding when and who to display it to. It is this that will set your website apart and help to begin personalising what you display, ensuring it is delivered to the right people at the right time. Most ecommerce sites will display the same content to everybody across their entire website, but there is scope to be much smarter than that. Some techniques will require knowledge of who your customers are, whilst some can be delivered with little or no knowledge of them. The following section is an example of one way to use targeted content on your site for people using your onsite search.

Onsite search

When a user conducts a search on your ecommerce site, immediately you get an idea of exactly what they are looking for and thus can begin personalising what is displayed to them, based on that search. For example, their search query could trigger the display of an advert based on that particular search term.

You can also build up a search bucket of other similar search terms that would trigger that same targeted content, rather than creating different things for every single search term, which is unrealistic. By examining your website analytics to see the specific search terms that people are using, you can begin to build up a series of targeted content based on those, starting with the most popular. You can also check that any misspelt searches automatically return the right results and, thus, the right targeted content, too.

As the display of such targeted content is completely created and defined by you, you could choose to show ones directly related to a search term or decide that, if they are already looking for something in particular, show complementary or auxiliary products related to their search. If your web pages allow it, you could show multiple pieces of targeted content and complementary items. Remember, targeted content does not always have to be promotions or offers, it can also take the form of more generic information.

By starting with a few pieces of targeted content and then increasing the quantity and sophistication of it, you can begin to build up a portfolio based around your most popular search terms. Through rotating, testing and analysing, you can also begin to see which techniques produce the best results.

That is just one example of how to personalise advertisements, but there are loads more that you could consider, including:

- The contents of their current basket – drive up average order value by prompting users to take advantage of bundle offers if they have not met the full criteria, or display complementary products to what they have added.

- *The value of their current basket* – free delivery over a certain value is quite a common promotion, so prompting users to meet those thresholds via targeted content is a common and successful tactic.
- *The offers applied to their current basket* – if you have the capability to layer multiple promotions, then using targeted content to deliver them all is a great way to ensure users keep on taking advantage of them and driving up their basket value.
- *Geographic location* – even if you are not offering your customers completely localised sites, you could use GEO IP to identify international users and target them with localised content that may pertain to specific events in their country, like Thanksgiving in the USA or Bastille Day for your French customers.
- *Source (referrals)* – display different targeted content to different users based on how they have reached your site. They could be different for PPC visitors, third-party referral sites like Quidco or from your own email marketing.
- *Device types* – the advent of responsive web design means you can target users with different targeted content based on their device type. This may be particularly prevalent for mobile devices where users are potentially on the move and could be targeted by omni-channel retailers trying to drive them to stores.
- *Time and date* – great for flash sales or, with increased customer knowledge, for delivering personalised content such as individual offers for a user's birthday.
- *Specific customers/customer groups* – assigning users to common groups based on demographics, interests or previous behaviour is a great way to segment and personalise content, i.e. different targeted content could display to all loyalty card members or people who have bought certain products.
- *Wish lists/gift lists* – if you know what items are on a user's wish list, you could deliver targeted content to prompt them or use offers to convert them, specific to those products.

3. Promotions

The clever use of online promotions can help drive the conversion phase of your ecommerce customer's lifecycle, encouraging users to order via your website rather than one of your competitors' and also encouraging them to order items they had not originally intended to purchase, and thus drive up average order value, too.

Types of promotions

Online promotions can take many forms and often you will be restrained by the technology they use as to what types and complexity of promotions they can deliver, but even the most basic ecommerce platforms should be able to deliver a few different promotions options and you should experiment with as many as possible to see which convert the best.

Typical options may include:

- percentage off an order;
- percentage off a product(s);
- money off an order;
- money off a product(s);
- fixed price product;
- free products;
- free shipping;
- get cheapest free;
- bundles (e.g. buy 2 get 1 free, 3 for £10);
- coupons;
- buy X get Y free;
- free gift/sample;
- tiered spend and save discounts.

Placement of promotions

Promotions themselves are not tangible, so are not really placed. They need to be delivered with a targeted content delivery tool to inform users of the details of any offer and try to engage and convert them. It is similar to a physical store where the actual promotional details and calculations will be held in the till system, but the posters and on-shelf labels will be advertising those offers to customers. As such, promotions will depend on the use of a system to deliver targeted content and the placement of that content. As they are so heavily linked to targeted content, there is also similar scope for managing them. You can:

- schedule offers to run at certain times or dates;
- personalise them based on the source of the visitor;
- automatically trigger them based on a user's action (like adding something to their basket, or completing a review) or session;
- include or exclude certain products, brands or customers;
- limit the number of uses both individually and site-wide.

Delivering promotions is an art form. Ensuring that the right offer reaches the right customers at the right time requires strategic planning and customer profiling. A personalised approach to promotions and content is proven to engage, and re-engage customers, increasing average order value and loyalty.

4. Emails

The final tool to consider is email marketing, which is linked primarily to the re-engagement phase of the ecommerce customer lifecycle. The re-engagement phase of your customer cycle is vital to the ongoing success of your ecommerce site. Everybody knows the statistics about the cost of acquiring new customers versus existing ones and email plays a vital role in re-engaging users and driving them back to your website.

There are three specific types of email, each having the capability to be personalised to some extent:

- *Bulk/blast emails* – general marketing emails delivered to everybody or specified groups based on demographics or other segmentation.

- *Transactional emails* – individual emails with account, ordering and fulfilment information.
- *Automatic/triggered emails* – automatically sent to individual users based on behaviour.

Bulk/blast emails

Whilst most retailers will be sending out bulk/blast email campaigns to their customers, the capability to personalise them is an opportunity not to be missed. Campaign emails can be segmented using all of the traditional demographic information, as well as using previous transactional data to target existing users who have purchased a certain product, range or brand with other complementary items or services.

Transactional emails

For transactional-type emails, there is further scope to personalise by adding recommendations or offers to these emails based on what items have been ordered at that time. For instance, adding cross-sells to an order confirmation email or incentivising users to re-order on a delivery confirmation email can be effective methods for re-engagement.

Automated/triggered emails

Triggered emails take the re-engagement phase a step further by automatically targeting users based on their behaviour, including things like what they buy, whether they order, how much they spend, whether it is their first order and much more.

These campaigns can be set up in advance and delivered on an individual level, making them ideal for things like abandoned basket campaigns, re-ordering reminders (for items that require regular purchasing) or welcome emails. They deliver true personalisation with a minimal amount of work, as, once you have created the campaign, you can set it up to work automatically for each user that meets the criteria. They are great for increasing customer loyalty and conversion and have a significantly higher open and click-through rate than generic bulk emails.

Recommended actions

- *Short term/quick win*

  Use a few of the more basic ideas that you feel are easier and cheaper to implement and prove they work. These may not require as much effort, money or complicated technology as you think; you may be able to do them relatively quickly with the resources you currently have. This will help you gain buy-in from other stakeholders, improve confidence in what you are doing and, potentially, help secure investment for more sophisticated systems in future, if required.
- *Medium*

  Continually test and optimise your strategies to improve their efficiency and see what works well and not so well. Ensure you use analytics to provide facts, rather than relying on instinct or opinion, as this combination of data and knowledge can help when further increasing your personalisation output and applying other techniques.
- *Long term*

  Once you have proved it works and seen the results, start to expand your personalisation strategy in terms of both quantity and complexity to increase its effectiveness. Think about tying all of the four tools together to harmonise everything and shape your user's journey, remembering the key phases of engagement, conversion and re-engagement.

▶

References

Agrawal, A. (2015) 'Ecommerce Marketing: 5 Tips to Boost Product Sales', Customer Think. Available at: http://customerthink.com/ecommerce-marketing-5-tips-to-boost-product-sales/ [Accessed 7 March 2016].

Davis, B. (2015) '17 ways to personalize ecommerce for four types of customer', Econsultancy. Available at: https://econsultancy.com/blog/67211-17-ways-to-personalize-ecommerce-for-four-types-of-customer/ [Accessed 7 March 2016].

5.1 Case study: The Board Basement

A passion and love for snowboarding and a decision to approach retailing differently gave birth to The Board Basement, www.theboardbasement.com.

This case study will show you how a small online store developed into one of the UK's top independent snowboard retailers by selling via more channels.

Key findings

- Simple, targeted adjustments to broader order management can generate impressive improvements.
- Efficiency comes from identifying the right areas on which to focus.
- Customers want to feel supported, whether online or instore.

Interviewees

Two friends, Luke Martinez and Stuart Tait, have spent the last seven years passionately growing a specialist online retailer of winter sports and snowboard equipment, clothing and accessories. Founded on Martinez's 20+ years' experience in snowsports and surf retailing and Tait's background in digital marketing, the two of them decided to take a different approach to traditional high-street retailing.

Like any successful example of entrepreneurship, The Board Basement's story has humble beginnings. The company was started with an investment of just £3,000 and born out of a simple idea – to help lovers of winter sports fight against the growing cost of enjoying their passion.

The pair's journey has been different from most in the retail industry. The Board Basement was founded during the last recession when external investment in retailing was minimal and retailers were cautious of adapting their business models to meet the needs of the modern consumer.

Martinez and Tait perceived these challenges as an exciting growth opportunity and the chance to provide customers with quality equipment at affordable prices. The Board Basement achieves this by putting its customers first, whether that be passing on deals the team has found in the marketplace, selling stock from past seasons at a reduced price or buying the latest in-season equipment.

About The Board Basement

The Board Basement sells across multiple marketplaces including eBay, Amazon, Rakuten, its own online store and, due to customer demand, its own physical retail space in Exeter, Devon. Its broad product range includes everything from snowboards to boots and helmets, as well as streetwear, footwear, luggage and bags and other specialist items.

Since The Board Basement was founded, the company has grown fourfold with an annual revenue of £1 million in 2015 and a staff count of six full team members, all of whom are keen snowboarders, skaters and surfers.

The Case

One of The Board Basement's founding principles was to treat customers as the team would like to be treated themselves.

This drive for excellent customer service and a desire to meet the expectations of customers led Martinez and Tait to assess how a business in their sector should support its customers. They applied the lessons they learned during their time in a traditional retail landscape to ecommerce and started to build the business.

Part of delivering on these promises meant the company needed precise marketplace management across each channel and throughout the entire sales process. Furthermore, because of the company's commitment to selling previous seasons' product lines as well as in-season, there was an added layer of complexity in terms of order management and fulfilment.

▶

For example, a customer's purchase instore, on eBay or on the company's online shop front, would need to be reflected instantly on other marketplaces, as well as in the company's warehouse and its physical store.

The problem

With the company growing rapidly – in the last four years, turnover grew from £250,000 to £1 million – understanding how to solve this challenge was a major strategic initiative for Tait and Martinez.

Seasonality, competitive cross-border sales tactics and supplier demands also added to the challenges facing the team. Another lesson has been how to adapt the company's business model to drive growth whilst countering European retailers that have capitalised on a weaker euro in recent years and undercut heavily on price.

This led the company to extend its product range to include popular equipment from past seasons. Customers often grow fond of a certain brand or product line, but find it difficult to purchase equipment elsewhere due to other retailers focusing only on the latest equipment. The Board Basement has addressed this requirement by providing a comprehensive range of in-season and previous season products.

This enthusiasm for supporting customers over the long term translates to the company's wider shopping experience. Customers can now buy online or, unusually, in the context of ecommerce, visit a physical store for buying advice, equipment support and a shared appreciation of winter sports.

In fact, the opening of a physical store reflects the customers' growing desire to ask questions to an expert, as well as the winter sports sector's sense of community and how customers need to be nurtured throughout the entire sales process.

The solution

The growth of The Board Basement's physical store proved to be the turning point for The Board Basement. For example, a customer would choose an item, be served and then a sales representative would have to log into each online marketplace to adjust the stock accordingly.

At that moment, Tait and Martinez recognised the potential value of a solution that could offer a centralised overview of the entire order and sales fulfilment process. Manual workflows were just too laborious and time-consuming. There had to be a simpler way that would prevent both founders being pulled away from their strategic role of growing the business.

At this point, Gustaf Antti, The Board Basement's website director, joined the company from Oliver Sweeney and, along with Tait, started on the project. They began by assessing how technology could help and what options were available. There were three strict criteria to be met. Any solution would have to be efficient, deliver the control the team was searching for and be future-proof.

To the duo's initial dismay, they found that many solutions were overly simplistic, quickly outdated, or offered minimal support in how to implement the solution into The Board Basement's own operations.

Eventually, this led to Volo Commerce (www.volocommerce.com), which provides online merchants and brands with the tools, knowledge, confidence and sense of community they require to succeed in key ecommerce marketplaces.

From the outset, the implementation had the desired effect, as the team started to automate key components of its existing sales and order processes.

The team began with stock visibility across each marketplace to ensure everyone was spending less time on general control processes and more time on sourcing and selling great products.

The Board Basement then assessed how to use the service to improve customer communication. A common challenge was with equipment sizing and ensuring that customer questions were answered in a timely manner. The team worked closely with its service provider to improve the quality of its product listings in an effort to cut repetitive inquiries.

The team have also applied the lessons learned from day-to-day liaison with its service provider to other operational areas. This includes automating product packing, shipping and customer communication around fulfilment, and overall internal logistics within the warehouse and the physical store.

Once the immediate challenges were solved, the team moved on to leveraging its new partnership to drive growth in new marketplaces. This included expansion into cross-border trade on both eBay and Amazon to face domestic and international competitors head-on without any negative impact on business or operational efficiency.

Results

New internal efficiencies and rapid sales growth have made The Board Basement's initiative a major success for a number of reasons:

- Revenue of £1 million last year, an increase from £250,000 four years prior.
- Sustained expansion into new marketplaces and international channels.
- Ongoing success for physical store (the largest independent in the South West of England).
- Simplified order, sales and operational management.
- A strong, growing reputation in the global sector.
- Impressive staff productivity that prevents unnecessary hires.

Everyone in the company was on board with the new system and willing to endure short-term, small-scale disruption for the sake of the long-lasting benefits possible.

Critical success factors

Because of the service provider's unique revenue share model, the capital investment required by The Board Basement was minimal. Both companies are able to grow together and, due to the partnership relationship, The Board Basement has gained numerous team members without any extra costs, in turn releasing the existing team to focus on marketing and selling products.

The Board Basement is simply better at what the company promises to do and deliver to the customer. The team received a service that the business needed, not just the latest tool, and one that is growing with the business.

Lessons learned

This focus on value was critical for The Board Basement and Tait, as he concludes:

> 'This kind of project can be daunting at first because all the possibilities are in front of you and you see all the things the system can do. **Start slowly, focus on what's important, be patient, and you will get to use all of the things you saw at the very beginning of the project**. For us, at the end of the day it's all about your data and seeing what your data can do. Now all our customer touch-points are integrated, regardless of the channel they come through, with the reporting at the back end. It has been phenomenal.'

Recommendations

- Start slowly – rushing ahead creates mistakes.
- Focus on what is important – not everything is an urgent priority.

▶

- Be patient – results often take longer than first thought.
- The goalposts are continually moving; keeping up with changes is paramount.

5.2 Reducing shopping cart abandonment

Billions of pounds in revenue can be recouped by addressing shoppers who exit a website and leave behind unpurchased goods in their digital shopping cart. Techniques commonly employed by ecommerce retailers may be high-cost quick fixes; however, there are practical solutions that are being overlooked.

I met up with the guys at Spot Studio, a digital marketing agency and technology company, to explore this topic further. For more information, visit: www.spotstudio.net.

In the event that an online shopper does not proceed to buy goods that have already been placed in their e-shopping cart, the cart is said to be abandoned. When statistics resulting from 31 studies into abandoned carts are averaged, the median rate at which carts are abandoned stands at 68.53 per cent ('33 Cart Abandonment Rate Statistics', Baymard Institute). Placed against the accepted understanding that ecommerce brought in approximately $1.7 trillion ('B2C E-Commerce Sales Worldwide 2018 – Statistic') globally in 2015, it becomes clear that abandoned carts are a massive source of potential revenue for ecommerce vendors.

Key takeaway

- Projections carried out by industry experts place ecommerce revenues at $3.551 trillion by 2019 (Lindner, 2015), a twofold increase that makes abandoned carts an even more pressing concern for vendors. Currently, ecommerce sales make up 7.3 per cent of a total of $22.822 trillion in retail purchases, a figure obtained from Emarketer.

- Narrowing the field to the UK, e-shopping brought in around £93.89 billion in 2015, which means that the cost to retailers of abandoned carts in the UK alone is also in the billions – and, more than that, is set to increase exponentially.

The advice

The top eight reasons for cart abandonment

Carts are most often abandoned due to one of the following, says a recent study:

1. The cost of mailing an item.
2. Mailing would take too long.
3. The cost of the item.
4. The original intention was browsing rather than purchase.
5. The customer questions the trustworthiness of the retailer.
6. The website prevents the customer from making payment in the manner they wish.
7. Making the purchase is overly convoluted.
8. The customer prefers to purchase with a discount.

What most retailers do about it

The four key methods we will be focusing on in this section are:

1. Exit intent technology.
2. Retargeting shoppers via email.
3. Retargeting shoppers online.
4. Storing purchases as cookies.

This data is based on answers from 50 leading UK retailers, supplemented with visual observations from the 60 retailers with the most visitors (SimilarWeb, 2016) and the top 200 SMEs, as determined by Trustpilot.

1. Exit intent technology

Tracking the tempo and patterns of mouse use through exit intent technology can result in accurate anticipation of cart abandonment by e-shoppers. Pop-ups can then target the shopper and incite them to follow through with their original intent to purchase.

However, this method is not being used commonly to address cart abandonment by leading etailers. Just 2 per cent of the 50 most popular online clothing vendors and 1.64 per cent of the 60 most popular sites resorted to exit intent technology as a tool.

Instead, discount vouchers offering 15–20 per cent off original prices were being offered to prompt shoppers into completing their purchases.

The mark-up of mark-downs

The use of discount vouchers directly hurts revenue to the tune of £1.33 billion in the UK and is not a supportable business tactic. This figure is calculated considering the UK market of £52.25 billion, consumers who only buy on discount 17 per cent of the total, and the typical voucher offering 15 per cent savings. The number of online shoppers who do not buy at all if a voucher is not present is rapidly mounting, increasing by 70 per cent to 17 per cent ('Are UK Shoppers Getting Savvier?') of all shoppers. A further 16 per cent customarily search out discount codes, which means that regular users of online discounts now make up 33 per cent of the market altogether. These figures should be taken with a grain of salt, considering that they come from a voucher website. The consistent upping of the numbers are, nevertheless, quite revealing of the general tendency.

What is more, cunning shoppers are manipulating ecommerce algorithms to benefit from discounts offered in response to abandoned carts, as evidenced by testimonials across message boards and websites offering online shopping advice ('Abandon Your Online Shopping Basket And Unlock Secret Discount Codes').

This is a further sign that discount vouchers should not be considered long-term solutions to the problem of abandoned carts.

Back to exit intent technology

SpotStudio put exit intent technology into action on an ecommerce website and tracked action with the thought to provide another, more substantial option to the use of discount codes. In this experiment, exit intent technology was used to encourage customers to preserve the contents of their shopping carts by caching them into email. At the end of three months, 9.43 per cent of users had opted to receive these emails; 68 per cent of emails were opened, resulting in a click-through rate (CTR) of 22.05 per cent.

Although this is not as high as the usual abandoned cart email, this may be down to differing levels of engagement on the part of the shopper at this point. An advantage of using exit intent technology to prompt shoppers to sign up for emails, which are the most lucrative tactic for addressing abandoned carts, is that only the email address is needed instead of all the fields of the standard form. The vendor has the option to remarket to these shoppers also, with 94 new entries on mailing lists per 1,000 abandoned carts.

Because the rate that the CTR translated into sales stood at 10.2 per cent, altogether 1.53 per cent of consumers who opted to receive their abandoned carts via email when prompted via exit intent technology went ahead with their purchases, at prices unaffected by discounts.

2. Retargeting via email

Abandoned cart emails (ACEs) cue shoppers back to the purchases they have left behind. In order for an ACE to be sent, customers must be signed into the retail website; this is essential for any company selling goods online.

Systems can be programmed to send ACEs at very little cost, taking into account individual user preferences and buying tendencies. Interestingly, a relatively low percentage of 22.95 per cent of the leading UK ecommerce vendors (Next, Argos and Asos among them) sent ACEs, and just 26 per cent of the leading UK clothing vendors did so. In contrast, 29.5 per cent of the leading 200 SMEs and 34 per cent of the leading 50 utilise ACEs.

This is especially important when looking at the statistic that 44.1 per cent of ACEs are opened, with a median CTR of 11.61 per cent. Of these, 29.9 per cent lead to sales. Remarkably, shoppers purchasing after prompting by ACEs escalated their average order value (AOV) by a mean of 14.2 per cent. Taking this into consideration, each series of ACEs brought in a median of £5.20 ('Basket Abandonment Emails: Why You Should Be Sending Them').

The following table clarifies the loss to online businesses that do not utilise ACEs, estimating that businesses retain contacts and information from 40 per cent of online shoppers:

Average Order Value	**Open Rate**	**CTR**	**CTR to Sale**	**Lead to Sale**	**Conversion Rate**	**Conversion Rate per Any User** Assuming we have contact details for 40% of users
£36.62	44.10%	11.61%	29.90%	3.47%	1.39%	0.56%

Source: Spot Studio (www.spotstudio.net).

3. Retargeting shoppers online

Through software that detects online user footprints, vendors can remarket themselves to shoppers who venture to other places on the internet after abandoning a shopping cart. Consumers who are targeted with remarketing efforts are 75 per cent more inclined to engage with a promotion than those unfamiliar with the vendor. Thus, remarketing initiatives are much more effective than the usual PPC promotions.

Google and Facebook (FBX) remarketing were considered in this study, as shown in the following table.

Segment	Do They Remarket Via Google?	Do They Remarket Via Facbook?
Top 60 Shopping	78.69%	9.84%
Top 50 Clothing	78.00%	24.00%
Top 50 SMEs	54.00%	12.00%
200 SMEs	47.50%	8.50%

Source: Spot Studio (www.spotstudio.net).

As seen above, again the leading clothing online vendors are the most ambitious, with 24 per cent working with FBX compared to only 9.84 per cent of the top online shopping companies. Surprisingly, the number of leading SMEs using FBX is higher, at 12 per cent. The percentage of the leading 60 online shopping companies and the leading 50 online clothing vendors utilising Google for remarketing is similar at 78.69 per cent and 78 per cent respectively.

Remarketing via Facebook means access to the broadest online market in the world. Specifically, this means approximately 936 million dynamic users per day; 798 million dynamic mobile users per day; 1.4 billion dynamic users per month; and 1.25 billion dynamic mobile users per month, all figures as of 21 March 2015 ('How Facebook Retargeting Increases Advertising Conversions'). Although not every user can be reached via remarketing, the potential is there and can be expanded upon with the utilisation of existing technologies.

Not only that, AdRoll has stated that retargeting efforts via FBX resulted in a quarter over quarter increase in CTR of 1.3x; in conversion rates of 1.7x; and in ROI of 1.1x in a case study conducted in 2015 ('All-in-one advertising for all-in-one apparel').

As for Google, not only does its Display Network offer contact with 10 per cent of the web, according to its marketing materials, but efforts can be aimed directly at what Google terms 'shopping basket abandoners'. Looking at case studies reveals that retargeting efforts via Google resulted in cuts in cost per acquisition (CPA) within 25–67 per cent, also according to marketing. AdWords dividends also went up by 30 per cent.

4. Storing purchases as cookies

With persistent carts, the customer will find their intact basket in just the same place when they click on the website again. This tactic, possible through the use of online cookies, is widespread among all types of online retailers considered in this study. Consider that 90 per cent of the leading 50 SMEs, 89 per cent of the leading 200 SMEs, 93.75 per cent of the leading 60 online vendors and 96.72 per cent of the leading 50 clothing vendors are utilising it.

The small percentage who do not employ persistent carts are practically asleep at the switch; their rationalisation may be that cookies are optional and they wish to avoid confusing the sales process. They may be convinced when they see that, according to the SpotStudio investigation, more than half (56 per cent) of online shoppers intended all along to purchase another day; 28 per cent extend the buying process longer than a day, 21 per cent by 3 days and 18 per cent prefer to leave it for a week or longer. Furthermore, when Internet Retailing took a look at buying patterns, it found that online shoppers in the UK habitually stretch purchases of electronics, health and beauty products over a median of 6.69 days (Skeldon, 2015).

Let us now look again at cookies. When online businesses retain carts, how long do they keep them for? Surprisingly, the study shows that it is a matter of hours for 42.6 per cent of etailers and of days for only 31.7 per cent. Evidently, numerous sales are being lost due to this oversight.

Lessons for you

The leading 50 online clothing vendors set a standard for the rest of the industry, adopting a variety of innovative and accepted techniques to address abandoned carts. Looking at findings by group, the leading 60 online shopping vendors are not far behind the clothing retailers, with occasional overlap between the groups. Even taking into account varying budgetary considerations, techniques that are relatively quite inexpensive with high potential returns often are being overlooked.

SMEs often are not utilising Google remarketing; this may be due to the cost. We postulate that many are just not retargeting shoppers with abandoned carts elsewhere on the internet. Interestingly, a higher percentage of SMEs utilise ACEs in comparison to the leading 50 clothing retailers.

Although the cost of remarketing via Facebook is low, not many of the top 200 SMEs or top 60 online retail companies were using this technique. Admittedly, FBX remarketing results in a lower sales conversion rate than Google remarketing; however, this is because users targeted on FBX are in a different mindset about purchasing than those using Google. The use of this technique by clothing retailers implies that more companies should be considering it, especially given the low cost.

Although honing in on discounts and remarketing (often pricey) as solutions for abandoned carts may result in momentary gains, the often forgotten ACEs are inexpensive and effective in the long term for companies and their committed customer bases.

It is worth bearing in mind that consumers habitually stretch the process of making an online purchase over five days. This important window of time allows the company to contact the shopper and encourage them to buy. All ways in which retailers are able to do so, especially the low-cost ones, should be fully considered to maximise earnings.

Recommendations

Thought and care should be given to search out suitable long-term solutions to abandoned carts and secure real customer loyalty. The consequences of band-aid solutions that mask long-lasting problems with fast sells should be looked at with clarity. Focusing on discounts and spending more on remarketing will affect the entire industry negatively, if continued to be implemented indiscriminately.

References

'33 Cart Abandonment Rate Statistics', Baymard Institiute, 14 January 2016: www.baymard.com/lists/cart-abandonment-rate, 2016 [Accessed 16 March 2016].

'Abandon Your Online Shopping Basket And Unlock Secret Discount Codes', This is Money, 2015 [Accessed 16 March 2016].

'All-in-one advertising for all-in-one apparel', AdRoll, 2015 [Accessed 16 March 2016].

'Are UK Shoppers Getting Savvier?', Voucherbox.co.uk, 2015 [Accesssed 16 March 2016].

'B2C E-Commerce Sales Worldwide 2018 | Statistic', Statista, 2016 [Accessed 16 March 2016].

'Basket Abandonment Emails: Why You Should Be Sending Them', Econsultancy, 2016 [Accessed 16 March 2016].

'How Facebook Retargeting Increases Advertising Conversions', CyberInnovation.com 2016 [Accessed 16 March 2016].

Lindner, M. 'Global e-commerce sales set to grow 25% in 2015', Internet Retailer, 2015 [Accessed16 March 2016].

SimilarWeb, 2016 [Accessed 16 March 2016].

Skeldon, P. 'Indecisive Shoppers And Cashback-Savvy Brits Among Unexpected Mobile Buying Habits Across Europe – Internetretailing', InternetRetailing, 2015 [Accessed 16 March 2016].

5.3 Case study: STA Travel

With the increasing expectations of consumers for a personalised digital experience, STA Travel knew that its new online customer account area had to provide a relevant cohesive experience across channels. And, by doing so, it was able to increase cross-sell, upsell and loyalty amongst its customers.

Key findings

At the outset of the project, it established a key performance indicator (KPI) framework that would allow it to measure the outcomes of the project against the business objectives. The ultimate focus was to improve cross-sell and upsell from existing customers and, as a result, increase customer lifetime value and average transaction values.

STA Travel used a combination of Google Analytics and internal sales reporting to create a reporting dashboard that allowed it to measure the following results:

- 15 per cent above target for mobile app downloads;
- 35 per cent above target for active users of the customer account area;
- 323 per cent increase in social sharing.

Interviewee

For businesses to survive in today's digital environment they must be nimble, experimental and intimately connect with their customer to encourage repeat business

John Constable recently celebrated his 10-year anniversary with STA Travel. CEO of STA Travel since 2012, he joined the company as managing director for the UK in 2006. Constable has been a driving force behind the company's growth and has played a lead role in repositioning the brand to appeal to a broader group of customers with a business vision, global store refresh, new website and savvy digital presence.

About STA Travel

STA Travel is the world's largest student and youth travel company. Started by two students in 1979, every year it sends more than two million passengers on life-changing adventures. STA Travel has more than 2,000 employees in over 200 stores in 11 countries.

Its online sales strategy

A deep knowledge of its Millennial customers and a passion to deliver them the best adventures that money can buy is at the heart of STA Travel's online retail strategy.

Since 1979, STA Travel has continuously adapted to the ever-changing needs, aspirations and behaviours of its core audience – youth and student travellers. And, during the last three years, it launched a number of new initiatives to make it easier for Millennials to find and enjoy adventures around the globe, through their channel of choice.

STA Travel connects with its audience through contextual content – bite-sized targeted entertainment. It creates exclusive, relevant and original content, with a strong focus on music, video, STA Travel's own travel experts and customers' real travel stories. This content is woven throughout its social channels – YouTube, Facebook, Twitter, Instagram, Tumblr, Snapchat, blogs and, soon, WhatsApp – as well as screens across its global retail network, digitising an historically offline environment through real-time social feeds.

Millennial customers are social and are online 100 per cent of the time. They expect to connect with brands on any channel, at any time. That is why STA Travel has adopted a 'mobile first' mindset and continues to make significant improvements to STA Travel's mobile sites worldwide. The company is trying to make it easier for customers to find and buy the right flight, insurance, destination or round-the-world adventure whilst they are travelling.

Recently, STA Travel digitised its global brochure suite, championing a paperless world and giving its customers access to rich, interactive content on mobile and tablet. Last month, it became the first global travel agency to offer a meta-search capability for adventures and tours that brings the same level of expertise and product choice that customers are used to receiving in its retail environments.

STA Travel is bringing peace of mind to its travellers. All customers can now access their itineraries and personalised recommendations, plus last-minute deals on MySTA, an online customer account that can be accessed via the website or the STA Travel App. And, if they run into problems, they can always reach STA Travel on Twitter through @STATravelCares. Its people are available 24/7 to deliver customer service and answer questions from any corner of the world.

STA Travel understands that music and travel are intrinsically linked and, in 2015, it launched STA Travel Sounds – a digital platform to showcase young, unsigned musical artists from around the world. STA Travel Sounds illustrates the adaptability of the brand to hone in on the needs and wants of its audience, who favour 'experiences over stuff'.

The company's innovations are underpinned by STA Travel's core value of being experts in student travel. Its BlueTicket – exclusive student and youth fares to under 30s – and price-beat guarantee contributed to a double-digit increase in online sales in 2015 and 2016.

The future of the STA Travel online retail strategy is firmly about bringing together an omni-channel approach and continuing to personalise the customer experience. Its aim online is to offer tailored content and expertise to help customers choose the best adventures and give them ownership over their itinerary, still with the knowledge that they are in the safe hands of a trusted brand.

The Case

The problem

STA recognised that the experience expectations of its target audience had changed significantly. Ubiquitous mobile access, social networks and an on-demand/convenience culture had resulted in customer journeys that were more complex than

▶

ever before as customers move between channels and use multiple devices to accomplish their goals.

They expect their experiences to be consistent across channels and contextually relevant and personal to them. Whilst the company had always been able to offer that in its retail stores, it also needed to be able to provide that personalised experience online to both its new and existing customers.

Consumers want to be able to leverage the benefits of each channel and choose whichever different platform they wish for different tasks, e.g. discuss a destination with a travel expert and book flights instore, read peer reviews of hotels on mobile and then purchase hotels and adventure tours for their trip online.

To enable that to happen, the company needed to create an online customer area that understood who the customer was, what they had purchased and what else they may need before, during and after their trip.

The background

In order to capture the younger target audience and achieve growth in its online business, the company needed to invest in its digital offering to bring together a disconnected digital real estate and move forward towards a single customer view.

Some of their competitors already provided an online customer area to view existing orders, but they were not using that opportunity to enhance their understanding of customers. And, as a result, were not able to provide the personalised experiences that customers are expecting.

STA wanted to provide an online experience that differentiated it from its competition and that resembled the type of personalised experience and brand tone of action that customers receive within its retail stores.

The company knew that delivering a seamless and integrated experience across channels would require it to bring together the data from all its systems and third parties into a single customer view. Without it, the company would not be able to provide the personalised customer experience it needed. But, doing that would require integration with a range of back-end systems, different data silos and third-party APIs.

The company considered the option of a large-scale IT re-platform, but the significant costs and long leads made the option unviable.

By delivering a personalised experience within the customer account area, the company expected a range of overall business performance improvements:

- *An increase in online revenue per customer through upsell and cross-sell:* by displaying associated products and services that were tailored to a customer's profile and related to their upcoming and in-progress trip, the company expected to be able to grow attachment rates to different products and the overall customer value.
- *An improvement in customer retention:* alongside improving cross-sell and upsell, STA expected personalisation to increase customer advocacy and retention.
- *Help to provide more effective marketing:* with the volume of content, products and services available, the company knew that its marketing would have better cut through if it was targeted to each customer's individual needs.

As a consequence, STA also expected to achieve operational efficiencies through decreased calls into retails stores and the call centres querying previous purchase information.

The solution

STA chose to leverage its in-house teams and partner, Rockpool Digital, and the STA Travel online customer account area is today available on web, iOS and Android apps across its four key markets (USA, UK, Australia and New Zealand). It gives customers the ability to control their bookings and travel documents in their own personalised itinerary. It offers up personalised, location-based cross-sell and upsell suggestions for

▶

hotels, activities and tours and allows users to share their travel plans with friends and family.

Making interaction easy and social

The social take up and convenience expectations of its target audience meant that STA wanted to use social media login for the website and the mobile app. By allowing customers to use its social media login credentials to sign in, STA provides convenience for them and the ability to personalise the online experience, based on their social graph information. This includes being able to provide a different online experience for group bookings in the future.

Social media logins also make it easier for customers to share their travel plans with friends and family, which was key for helping with the acquisition of new customers and facilitating group travel.

Bringing the data together

By bringing all the data together into a single customer view that is used across digital platforms and instore, the company can use a number of different signals to create personalised and tailored digital experiences:

- the *device* or interface they are using;
- their *location* and *environment* to understand where a customer is in the world geographically and provide localised information;
- their current *situation* and need state, including relative elements such as time zones to provide timely messages before, during and after travel;
- their *behaviour*, which includes historic interaction, personal data, browsing behaviour and social graph.

This also provides a better ability to track customers and their communications across different channels, enabling more consistent and continuous conversations as customers traverse channels.

Continue to understand the customer

The company also wanted to use the platform to continue learning about its customers. So STA made it possible for its customers to provide additional information about themselves, their travel preferences and how they wanted us to communicate with them. This was coupled with analytics information to build a more complete view of each and every customer.

Provide what they want

By understanding each customer, the company was then able to interlace its online itinerary with tailored content, products and services that were relevant to the customers, their travel plans or their friendship groups. The unique customer experiences that this creates demonstrates to its customers the value it places on understanding them and anticipating what they need, when they need it.

Continuity across channels

STA knew the digital experience had to work seamlessly across all channels, so it ensured that the technology choice supported that. It used a bespoke version of the Umbraco content management system for a responsive design across desktop, tablet and mobile web. The team at STA then integrated the new customer account area into both the iOS and Android mobile apps to allow customers to go from web to mobile seamlessly.

Delivering at speed

By working in 2-week sprints, the web platform was turned around in an ambitious timeframe of 16 weeks, with both mobile apps following just 6 weeks later. Achieving this speed to market was ambitious and challenging for both STA's internal team and its partners.

The future

STA's next round of optimisation aims to give customers a direct channel to its instore Travel Expert to discuss their personalised Travel Wish List. They will be able to pin to this whilst browsing STA's wealth of online content and access it at any time through their online account.

▶

Results

At the outset of the project, STA established a KPI framework that would allow it to measure the outcomes of the project against its business objectives over time. The company's ultimate focus was to improve cross-sell and upsell from existing customers and, as a result, increase customer lifetime value and average transaction values.

As stated at the start, STA used a combination of Google Analytics and internal sales reporting to create a reporting dashboard that allowed it to measure the results.

Lessons learned

Speed to market was a key driver for the project and, so, what made the project a success was the ability to deliver a personalised experience across different channels so quickly. The company's initial expectations were that it would take 6 to 12 months to deliver the new platform, but, working with its partners, it was able to do it in a fraction of that time.

The agile delivery approach also allowed the company to respond easily to the inevitable changes that arise in such a complex project. By all teams and suppliers working closely together, STA was able to accommodate new requirements and deliver an experience for the customer that matched the original expectations, releasing something that outperformed its competitors.

Recommendations

- Make sure that the customer experience you are trying to create is consistent across different channels.
- Take every opportunity you can to personalise the experience for your customers to create 1:1 interactions.
- Focus on an implementation approach that allows you to accommodate inevitable change, deliver quickly and then learn and iterate, based on the results.

6. The checkout journey

Businesses invest hugely in product selection, merchandising and great pricing – plus more on advertising and marketing, but this does not always translate into a high volume of online sales. Even more frustratingly, online retailers might note that people are visiting their web pages in large volumes but either they do not look for more than a few seconds or they abandon their shopping carts without converting and disappear into the ether as previously discussed.

I met up with the team at Commerce Futures, the organisation that brings together a 'real world' community of ecom practitioners to discuss 11 ways the checkout journey can be optimised further. For more information about Commerce Futures, please visit: www.commerce-futures.com.

If businesses want to ease frustration and increase online sales, retailers must follow these rules of the road. Online retailing is not rocket science, but, in 2017 and onwards, it is definitely all about detailed planning, testing and measurement.

The advice

The need for site speed

As already discussed, page load speed on online retail websites is hugely important to visitors. This may seem obvious but, if a website is relatively newly deployed, it is probably taken for granted that it will load quickly for visitors, even when the volumes of visitors are high.

Consumers are busy people. As a result, companies can end up fighting for attention among numerous competitors and distractions. Research throws up varying figures for how fast web users actually expect pages to load, but every result is 'very fast'.

As web traffic starts to grow, retailers must think about all of the factors that influence page speed: the weight of graphics (and ancillary software plug-ins) on each page; the proximity of the servers hosting the website to its visitors (especially for those with a large overseas customer base); whether the website needs to be cached and replicated using a Content Delivery Network or similar.

So businesses should forget the performance results they got on their last site relaunch and start testing every part of their sites, optimising pages across all platforms.

Which browsers do you really, truly support?

It is becoming common knowledge that mobile browsing has taken over from desktops, laptops and tablets. However, the same is not necessarily true when it comes to conversions. So websites have to look good and perform well on all the major browsers, on all key platforms, even some older browser versions. Retailers must examine visitors by device and browser type – and then decide, as well as communicate clearly, which browsers their website is designed to support.

A website simply must be optimised. It is unforgiveable to leave it untouched once it is live, especially when consumers are moving forward.

Is your website really responsive?

Websites that recognise and respond to the format of the device the consumer is on will, undoubtedly, perform better today than those that do not.

Consumers cannot be forced to transact on their small format devices (mobile, tablet, etc). Some simply feel more comfortable using a PC for financial transactions. It is important, however, that people can find retailers' websites when searching on their mobiles and are able to view the business products and services intuitively, no matter what platform they are on.

Consequently, it is imperative that a website is fully responsive. If it is not, businesses will be penalised by Google when users search on their mobiles, and that is not good for site traffic.

In addition, a business will, almost certainly, want to present its information in a different way on smaller screens. So, if it has not been addressed already, start now – business may depend on it.

Test, test and test again

A/B testing takes the guesswork out of optimising a website. It provides validation to any suggested changes by showing exactly what effect those changes have on key performance indicators. Where changes do not prove to be positive, learnings can be drawn from them.

A testing strategy needs to be exhaustive when done but not so overbearing that a company can fail to do some of the other optimisation tasks at hand.

Remember the nervous customer

There will always be potential buyers out there who are either nervous of buying online completely, or lack confidence in buying from a website they have never visited, or a vendor they have not heard of.

If retailers want to sell to this audience, they need to make it very clear how safe and easy it is to purchase from a company website. Many territories favour listing 'web safety' logos and features upfront on their websites, so businesses should be aware of international customers also. Do not wait until they have made the critical decision to add a product to their basket or made it to the checkout. Chances are they will not get that far. Instead, tell customers on the home page and on every single page on the site.

Nobody is saying this is straightforward or simple. However, if a customer does not identify the company site quickly as one they can easily buy from, the rest will not matter.

By now, the testing strategy should be in place, therefore try out various combinations of homepage and checkout page at the very least. Just remember to try it on all platforms because the solution will not be the same for each one.

Payment and delivery – upfront and everywhere

A business needs to ensure that the key issues of secure payment and efficient delivery are brought to the fore on every page of the website. Amazon is driving the online experience forward with the myriad of delivery options that are offered – businesses should keep in mind that consumers expect the same experience of smaller vendors.

There are few things more irritating than filling in a form, only to find out that payment is not accepted via a specific or preferred method, or delivery is not available. Take a first-time visitor this far and it is unlikely they will come back again.

Conversely, a wavering user may turn into a conversion if they are positively surprised by how easy it is to pay or get delivery. Online retailers should remember to factor mobile into this. Keep payment really simple for mobile users with solutions such as PayPal Express.

Keep USPs in mind

Before launching a website, there will have been a driving force behind it. The business's purpose needs to be communicated clearly and in a compelling manner to all visitors. The unique sales points (USPs) are fundamental to that process.

It may be hard to differentiate a product from that of a competitor, especially if it is selling the same thing at more or less the same price. But where a business can win sales is by offering specific benefits, such as free delivery, more attractive guarantees or payment options, recycling or price promises.

To make the benefits work, retailers should shout about them well before checkout – if not generally across the site, then at least on individual product pages.

Use content to personalise the company website

Content is the new battleground when it comes to the web experience. What started as a way of bringing a business up in the organic search rankings has now formed an industry all of its own. It is safe to say that every user has a unique set of expectations from a business. The content they see can wildly impact their behaviour.

New users may need more encouragement to buy and more information about payment and delivery options early in their visit. Existing customers may find too much of this sort of information annoying and see it as clutter rather than encouragement, but may be encouraged to buy, or buy more, if they see other messages or linked products.

Personalised content at the various stages of the buying cycle is a technology that is coming fast and is a broad subject. An organisation needs to consider the user journey for many types of consumers and consider how it can improve and personalise this on a page-by-page basis.

The checkout – the moment of truth

Most online retailers live with the fact that over 90 per cent of website visitors leave at the end of a website visit without buying a thing. When time and money has been spent on creating website traffic, a business should be motivated in every possible way to look for new methods to try to achieve the highest possible conversion rate. The following checkout tips are neither exhaustive nor prioritised – but they are from first-hand experts who trade on websites each and every day:

- Do not make users register on a website if they do not want to, and always offer an anonymous or guest checkout capability. By all means, tell them why it is a good idea, but do not force it on them.
- Make it easy for customers to enter their address by offering an address finder based on entering a postcode. Make sure this is tested for usability to ensure the solution really is helpful and accurate.
- Always make it clear how far visitors have got through the checkout journey, as each website is different and checkout processes still vary. Customers view the checkout process as the same as queuing instore and, if the process takes too long, then you risk abandonment.
- Validate every single field as a customer moves through the completion of a checkout page; do not wait until they have clicked 'submit' to list all of the errors that have been made in the process.

- Before the transaction is completed, present customers with a clear, unambiguous list of exactly what they are paying for, including delivery dates, times and guarantees, and tell them what will happen next. This will help to minimise returns and avoid abandonment.
- Keep in mind that customers may well need to change their mind at various stages – and 'step backwards' in order to complete their purchase. A business needs to make this process simple and intuitive.
- Speed. Checkouts must be light, fast and uncluttered. Remove every single distraction on these pages that you can see and get help from people who do not use your site today.

Remember, your customer has the remote!

It is easy to think that consumers buy in the same way as a business. However, this simply is not the case. As the number of people making mobile payments is increasing, remember not to force the channel on a customer.

If there is any chance that a customer may have questions about the product or its purchase, let them get in touch by phone and make it easy. If it is not easy, another company will make it easy and some users may be prepared to pay a premium to know that they are buying the right product and/or can buy it over the phone straightaway.

Putting the gloss on

Remember to look around for new ideas constantly. Here are more ideas companies may want to consider:

- Customers who do not want to buy immediately need to be nurtured. Creating a wish list feature for those who are shopping but not yet buying is a great idea.
- Make form filling easier using technologies such as HTML5, for example. Use placeholder text to explain what needs filling in and swap to a numeric keypad for phone number and other purely numeric fields.
- Integrate PayPal and PayPal Express on mobiles, with preloaded forms to minimise keystrokes and increase conversion. Many retailers are seeing mobile account for almost 50 per cent of sales in early 2016, so this is critical.

- Offer promotions in the basket, such as service options and extended guarantees.
- Always provide help and support, such as telesales, live chat and/or video chat. Do what is needed to get them to complete the purchase.

Recommended actions

- *Short term/quick win*

  Reduce the number of steps required to complete the purchase. Do not force them to register to complete a sale; create an account for them automatically.
- *Medium*

  Offer your customers a complete range of payment options, not just PayPal, but also things like instalment finance.
- *Long term*

  Add chat to the checkout process so customers can ask you questions at any stage in real time without having to feel the need to abandon the purchase.

6.1 Expert commentary: make it easy to buy

I met with Larry Brangwyn, head of user experience at PCA Predict, to talk about how a retailer can help its customers to complete their purchase with the aim of increasing the number of successful transactions.

Despite the constant evolution of ecommerce technology, the checkout journey is often problematic and unnecessarily complicated for online shoppers

PCA Predict is a technology company that helps businesses capture accurate customer data, with clients such as Trip Advisor,

Dow Jones and Oxfam. Brangwyn has a background in digital marketing and online creative media and is a seasoned UX strategist who has worked with a variety of top agencies. For more information about PCA Predict, please visit: www.pcapredict.com.

Brangwyn explains that, despite the constant evolution of ecommerce technology, the checkout journey is often problematic and unnecessarily complicated for online shoppers. As with bricks and mortar shops, the best option is to reduce barriers to purchase by making products easily visible, clearly labelled and not repeatedly asking customers if they need help.

Online shopping has made it increasingly easy to find what we are looking for and has eliminated the concept of queuing by promoting self-service. The checkout, however, remains the transaction-heavy part of the experience where almost all the information exchange occurs.

The key to making this process delightful lies in one of the basic tenets of behavioural economics. Reciprocity is one of the more powerful psychological triggers and empathising with the dilemma of what personal information you provide versus the service you receive can positively impact basket abandonment as well as customer satisfaction.[1]

Do not force users to register straight away

Surprisingly, many online retailers still don't offer new (and possibly one-time) customers the opportunity to checkout without registering all their personal details. However, according to Larry, the key is knowing when to ask for these details, so as to maintain their motivation.

Consumers are wising up to the fact these details are mainly used for marketing opportunities. In fact, an Econsultancy survey showed that 25.65 per cent of customers abandon their shopping if they are forced to register.[2]

---

[1]Fehr, E. and Schmidt, K.M. (1999) 'A theory of fairness, competition, and cooperation', *The Quarterly Journal of Economics*, 114, 817–68.

[2]Moth, D. 'Basket abandonment: case studies and tips to help improve your conversion rates', Econsultancy, https://econsultancy.com/blog/11182-basket-abandonment-case-studies-and-tips-to-help-improve-your-conversion-rates/.

Annoying customers before they have completed their purchase will lose you sales and useful data. However, giving the option to register towards the end of the checkout process means that they will not feel as pressured, are more invested in the process and information gathering does not seem as invasive.

Stick to a clear, linear process and set expectations

Ensuring that the process is defined and linear is crucial. Some steps, like delivery details and card address, are a must, but using a simple interface element, such as a progress bar, gives the user a clearer idea of what is required from them and what the next step of their shopping experience will be. It also helps shoppers to get an idea of how long it might take to complete checkout.

Delivery estimates are another place this works well. Capturing an address pre-checkout is a great way to give the customer some useful information that might help them when deciding whether to purchase in exchange for data you need. It also means that, when they come to enter their shipping details, you already have this information and they can skip a step.

Optimise data entry for speed and accuracy

Accurate data is critical to retailers. The key is not to put too much pressure on the user, as this can result in frustration. Making elements of the form as easy as possible to complete will reduce this, as well as the amount of time required to fill in details.

Do not assume your work is done

Even if your checkout is doing well at the moment, do not assume that you do not need to do anything to improve it. There is always room for improvement.

Brangwyn reminds us to make sure to test new ideas if you want to stay up to date with changes in technology and reassess customer behaviour. Keep users involved and remember to use evidence to support decisions rather than relying on design fads, no matter how tempting this might be.

I had a chance to catch up with Michael Rouse, CCO of Klarna, to talk about why the checkout journey on mobile devices is particularly complicated. Klarna is an online payment platform used by 65,000 online retailers, including Samsung, Disney, Spotify, etc. To find out more about Klarna, visit: www.klarna.com.

Although mobile sales are growing three times faster than desktop sales, historically, mobile commerce has suffered from low completion rates

This is mainly due to the friction of the mobile shopping experience: there are too many steps to completion and performing tasks, like entering credit card numbers or passwords, is more annoying and time-consuming on a phone's small virtual keyboard. This friction means only 3 in every 100 sales begun on a mobile device are completed. However, there are ways to improve these conversion rates significantly.

Rouse explains that merchants must make mobile payment as simple as mobile browsing – delivering convenience and removing barriers to getting the product into customers' hands, without sacrificing security. By reducing the number of steps to purchase completion and eliminating the registration process altogether retailers can boost mobile conversion rates by up to 60 per cent.

The simpler it is for a customer to confirm a purchase, the higher conversion rates climb, and the lower basket abandonment rates sink. Customers tend to return to sites which simplify purchases, so first movers will profit from increased retention. The standard checkout process has led to an abandonment rate of 71 per cent across tablets and 81 per cent on mobile in 2014. 'The amount of monthly sales abandoned each year totals just over $4 trillion', says Rouse.

Although simplicity is key for a modern payment solution, the consumer wants more than *just* simplicity. For example, does the payment technology provide a process where the customer can complete the purchase in seconds, then pay for their goods at their leisure, regardless if that means right way, later or in instalments?

Especially when dealing with distractable, time-poor customers limited by small on-screen keyboards, retailers should be looking to see what payment technologies can, additionally, provide for customers. Using sophisticated algorithms, it is now entirely possible to get an instant answer as to whether or not a customer should be provided with the option of paying after delivery with an invoice or in instalments. Once you have the answer to this question, there is no need for the customer to then input four pages' worth of information at the point of purchase.

With a mobile-first approach and a clear focus on simple checkout solutions – with a variety of payment methods allowing the customers to decide exactly how and when they want to pay for their goods – retailers will be able to boost conversion rates and solve the problem of the abandoned shopping basket.

I was also able to catch up with John Slater, lead UX designer at EKM, to try to understand why he does not think that one-page checkouts is the holy grail. EKM is the largest UK-based ecommerce provider, offering a fully hosted, all-in-one ecommerce solution. For more information about EKM, visit: www.ekmpowershop.com.

It turns out, though, that one-page checkout is not the saviour of the ecommerce checkout. It actually causes more issues than it fixes

Slater tells me that he remembers, back in his early days at EKM, one of the most requested features was a one-page checkout. At the time, it was going to be the saviour of the ecommerce checkout – it would take away the need for customers to navigate from page to page and wait for pages to load.

'It turns out, though, that one-page checkout is not the saviour of the ecommerce checkout. It actually causes more issues than it fixes,' says Slater.

The issues with one-page checkout

In EKM's research, it found that customers faced with large numbers of fields are put off. In an alarming number of cases, it would put off the customer enough for them to leave the checkout and site entirely.

The primary selling point of one-page checkout was that a customer could start and finish purchasing a product without having to wait for pages to load. In practice, though, this meant that every field that was needed, in order to complete the checkout, had to be output on one page.

'A customer visiting this flow can become overwhelmed by the number of fields they're required to fill out, and rethink whether they want to continue with the purchase,' says Slater.

Another issue the company found with the one-page checkout was that, even though shop owners knew there were only one or two steps to complete a purchase (depending on which payment method was selected), the customer did not. At first glance, they could be lead to believe that this huge list of fields was the first of, potentially, many more steps.

Slater's current best advice is that the checkout is a multiple-page flow that varies between four and five steps, depending on the shop set-up:

- customer login (optional);
- delivery and billing details;
- order summary;
- payment;
- order complete.

Data retention

As a customer fills in their information, the checkout should retain their data so, when they navigate from page to page or back a page, all previously entered information is kept.

Customers should be able to go back to previous steps both with on-page buttons and the browser back button. Even some of the biggest ecommerce websites are failing to meet this customer expectation.

Visible progress

You should also show your customer the progress they are making, how many steps there are to go until they have made a purchase.

6.2 Case study: Carpet Underlay Shop

This case study will look at how improvements made to the checkout journey for Carpet Underlay Shop significantly increased its conversion rates. Using best practice guidelines and UX research, removing distractions, improving field validation and altering the structure of the journey, Carpet Underlay Shop was able to significantly improve its conversion rates.

We will look at:

- problems with the original checkout;
- application of new checkout;
- how the checkout journey changes impacted the conversion rates.

Key findings

- Forty-one links leading away from the checkout journey were removed as part of the improvements made.
- Comparing conversion rates in the seven days before improvements were made and the seven days after improvements were made, there was a 30 per cent increase (from 1.88 per cent to 2.44 per cent).
- Comparing conversion rates in the 28 days before improvements were made and the 28 days after improvements were made, there was a 30 per cent increase (from 1.55 per cent to 2.44 per cent).

Interviewee

David Teague is the general manager for Texfelt UK. Having been with the company for over three years, Teague handles the day-to-day manufacturing and retail operations for Texfelt UK, which includes managing its online B2C retail outlet, Carpet Underlay Shop.

About Carpet Underlay Shop

Carpet Underlay Shop supplies carpet underlay, carpet fitting tools and flooring supplies to both trade customers and consumers. Carpet Underlay Shop acts as the retail arm of Texfelt UK, a manufacturer of carpet underlay and flooring accessories.

Established in 1992, Texfelt UK was initially a business-to-business (B2B) operation, selling its products to carpeting retailers and fitters worldwide, but never selling directly to the public. Whilst carpet retailers had followed the digital trend and taken their full product ranges online, very few underlay specialists had done the same. There was also a lack of products of this type in the multinational marketplaces, like Amazon, which led Texfelt UK to identify this absence as a potential gap in the market. In 2007, it opened Carpet Underlay Shop, a business-to-consumer (B2C) site, allowing consumers to buy not only products manufactured by Textfelt UK, but also other underlay brands, as well as the tools and accessories a consumer would need to fit underlay. Being in such a niche industry online has rewarded them with relatively few direct competitors and, the fact that the company manufactures a portion of the products it sells online has allowed it to be highly competitive when it comes to pricing.

The Case

The problem

The checkout before 2016

As is the case for many retailers, much of the work done to Carpet Underlay Shop's online operations aimed to increase the number of sales on its online shop. Whilst also looking at traffic coming into the site through SEO work, one of its main focuses was ensuring that visitors who found the products they required had a higher chance of actually completing their order on Carpet Underlay Shop's online store. This coincided with work that its ecommerce provider had scheduled to improve the checkout process for the platform as a whole, introducing new conversion rate optimisation (CRO) practices into the checkout process.

Carpet Underlay Shop has been hosted with its current provider since 2007 and, for a majority of this time, the checkout was presented in a standard one-page layout. This style of checkout presented all of the steps required to complete the checkout (i.e. billing information, shipping information, payment method) on one page, rather than spreading the same number of steps across several pages.

The one-page checkout process was widely favoured over a multi-page layout during this time, as it reduced the number of steps an end user had to go through from a product page to a completed order. There were, however, some inherent issues with the one-page checkout process that, potentially, lowered the conversion rate of its online retail operation.

Problems with the checkout before 2016

Distractions

The first issue with the checkout experience of Carpet Underlay Shop was the number of distractions the end user encountered whilst checking out. The one-page checkout process was presented within the main site's page navigation framework, meaning that an end user was able to navigate away from the checkout process at any time. Whilst this increased the potential for a higher value order, by allowing end users to add more items to their order, it also increased the likelihood of cart abandonment. Distractions are unavoidable to an extent, as the end user can always be distracted by external factors beyond the control of the site owner (for example, a ringing telephone), but onsite distractions should always be minimised. During testing conducted by the Baymard Institute:

▶

> '... some of the test subjects directly mentioned that they'd like to see the navigation gone, while others mostly complained about clutter and were at times distracted during checkout (in part due to the constant presence of the standard navigation). On those sites where the navigation was hidden, no test subject complained about it being missing from the site.'
>
> (Appleseed and Holst, 2013)

Minimising distractions will help the end user stay focused on the checkout process itself and decrease the amount of time between starting the checkout process and completing their order.

Field validation

The second issue with the one-page checkout experience was the limited degree of validation in place for the fields that the end user was asked to fill out. The one-page checkout process had validation on certain fields, such as the email address field, which informed the end user when the field had been correctly filled out, but this was not present on all fields. It also marked required fields with an asterisk. However, the fields were not checked until the end user attempted to proceed to the payment stage of the payment process. This meant that, if an end user had accidentally failed to complete a required field, they were not informed of this until they attempted to proceed to make payment. This delayed form of validation had the potential to cause frustration for the end user, which, in turn, could cause them to abandon their order.

Structure

The final issue with the one-page checkout process lay within the structure of it. Whilst the one-page checkout style was the industry standard for online shops until around 2012, the layout of a majority of one-page checkouts led to long pages that required the end user to scroll down the page to see a large proportion of the checkout process. To quote Danny Halarewich, co-founder and CEO of the popular ecommerce professionals' blog LemonStand:

> 'The problem with a single page checkout, if you have a number of fields, is that the design and layout start to look cluttered. You're basically trying to cram 3-4 pages worth of form fields into one page. This could actually backfire and turn customers off.'
>
> (Halarewich, 2015)

There were common practices that aimed to reduce the length of a page, such as reducing the height of fields or using a two-column format for the billing details and the delivery details – but these practices were not without flaws, increasing the complexity of the checkout process and reducing its overall usability.

The solution

The application of the 2016 checkout

In 2016, the ecommerce provider applied its new checkout process to Carpet Underlay Shop's online store. The new checkout process had been designed with both industry best practices and shop owner requirements in mind. It aimed to deliver a cleaner, distraction-free checkout experience to end users to help improve the conversion rates for all shops hosted on the platform.

In the development of the new checkout process, the ecommerce provider used research combined with in-house usability testing to determine the potential pitfalls in its existing checkout processes and create viable solutions to these pitfalls. The new checkout process then went through three rounds of internal testing, involving members of staff from all departments within the company and a round of beta testing, conducted by shop owners. In addition to this, the ecommerce provider also collected post-release feedback from shop owners and used this to inform further amendments to the checkout process.

Distractions

In the old checkout journey used by Carpet Underlay Shop, there were 41 separate links presented to the end user during the checkout process. A majority of these links led to other categories

▶

or products within the online store, whilst others linked to information pages and offsite resources, such as social network pages for the business. Each one of these links had the potential to take the end user away from the checkout process, with some links taking the end user away from the online shop entirely. Whilst there was some benefit in maintaining the site's navigation and overall aesthetics during the checkout process, the main benefit being increased customer confidence in the retailer, the potential distraction provided by these links outweighed this benefit heavily.

The new checkout removed the site navigation menus and other links within the checkout journey to reduce the time taken to complete the checkout process and decrease the likelihood that the end user would be tempted to leave the checkout flow. It still retained the overall look and feel of the online shop, with the logo and colours from the standard shop pages being used in the checkout process. This visual consistency, combined with security indicators within both the browser (the HTTPS padlock browsers display to show transmitted information is secure) and in the checkout process itself, meant that end users of the website felt confident in the security measures in place within the checkout process. This, in turn, made them less likely to abandon their order.

Field validation

Carpet Underlay Shop's old checkout process suffered from the previously outlined potential aggravations most commonly caused by limited field validation. The issues caused by the lack of validation were also exacerbated by the mechanics of the one-page checkout process, to some extent. One example of this is a link that allowed the end user to copy their billing address over to the delivery address fields. This in itself is a useful facility for the end user, as it allows them to complete the checkout process more quickly and so increases the likelihood of a completed order. However, if the end user failed to complete a required field within the billing address section, then copied this over to the delivery address, then attempted to proceed to the payment stage, the error given to the end user would inform them of only one missing required field. If the end user then completed this field in the billing details section, it would not be copied automatically across to the delivery address and, if the end user did not spot that this was also missing within the delivery address, they would be prevented from progressing through the checkout for a second time, increasing the chance of them abandoning their order.

The new checkout also improved the validation of the fields within the checkout process. Correctly filled out fields were clearly marked with a green tick, whilst required fields that had been missed were marked with an amber warning sign. Industry research by the Baymard Institute has found that indicating correctly entered fields is important, as it keeps the end user's experience positive, as described in this quote:

> 'When implementing inline validation, it's important not just to show errors, but also to show when fields are entered correctly. Otherwise you're only telling your customers what they are doing wrong. Instead, make the experience positive and show them how they are progressing nicely with green check marks next to the fields they've entered correctly.'
>
> (Appleseed and Holst, 2013)

This validation was all inline and instant, so, if an end user clicked into a required field but did not enter any information and clicked into another field, the amber warning sign would display instantly in the required field that lacks input, highlighting to the end user that further input is required.

Structure

In the case of Carpet Underlay Shop's checkout process, the potential issue caused by the length and complexity of the one-page checkout style was compounded by the site's navigation being displayed within the checkout process. The menu took up valuable space above the fold, forcing more of the checkout process below the fold and out of the end users' view when first arriving at the checkout process. The layout the company's

▶

ecommerce provider used for its one-page checkout flow followed a two-column layout for the billing and delivery details, which went some way to reduce the length of the checkout page. However, Carpet Underlay Shop added to the length through custom fields within the checkout, which asked the end users for additional delivery information. These fields helped improve the overall experience offered by the retailer to its customers, but they also extended the length and complexity of the checkout process, increasing the potential for cart abandonment.

The new checkout process broke up the input fields into a logical, staged process. The new checkout process also added visual progress indicators to show end users how many stages of the checkout they have completed and how many stages they have left to complete, making end users more confident in their ability to complete the checkout process quickly, which, in turn, increases the likelihood of a successful conversion.

Results

With the one-page checkout process in place, Carpet Underlay Shop had a conversion rate of 1.55 per cent in the 28-day period before the implementation of its new checkout process, and a conversion rate of 1.88 per cent in the 7-day period before the implementation of its new checkout process.

It is difficult to compare one shop's conversion rates against an industry standard, or another company within the same industry, as the differences in traffic sources and perception of the products being offered by each retailer will all contribute to whether an end user decides to complete their purchase. Peep Laja, a leading conversion optimisation expert from ConversionXL, describes this difficulty in the following manner:

> 'Even if you compare conversion rates of sites in the same industry, it's still not apples to apples. Different sites have different traffic sources (and the quality of traffic makes all the difference), traffic volumes, different brand perception and different relationship with their audiences.'
>
> (Laja, 2015)

As such, any comparisons made based on the conversion rates can only truly be compared against historic conversion rates experienced by Carpet Underlay Shop itself.

With the new checkout process in place, Carpet Underlay Shop's online store had a conversion rate of 2.44 per cent in the 28-day period after the implementation of its new checkout process and, in the 7-day period after implementation of the new checkout process, its conversion rate was, again, 2.44 per cent. When comparing these figures to the conversion rates measured in the 7-day and 28-day periods before new checkout implementation, there was a 30 per cent improvement in conversion rate for the 7-day period and a 57 per cent improvement in conversion rate for the 28-day period.

Whilst it cannot be denied that other factors, such as seasonal flux in sales and general retail trends, may have influenced this increase to an extent, the increased usability and distraction-free nature of Carpet Underlay Shop's new checkout has, undoubtedly, had its own impact on the increase in conversion rates seen by Carpet Underlay Shop.

Lessons learned

By taking into account best practice guidelines for the industry and the needs of the end user, relatively minor changes to the checkout journey can lead to significant increases in conversion rates for any online retailer. However, before embarking on such work, there are a few points worth keeping in mind:

- *Know your audience* – best practice guidelines are extremely useful and can help identify potential areas of weakness within a checkout journey. However, they need to be backed up by individual research looking at the specific audience a site is performing to. For example, an online store that gains a majority of its orders from repeat custom will likely require a very different checkout journey to an online store that gains a majority of its orders from first-time purchasers.

▶

- *Experience the journey yourself* – the owners of online shops rarely need to experience their own checkout. However, it can be very useful when looking to make improvements to a checkout flow to experience it first-hand. Sitting in the end user's seat can be eye-opening and help in spotting issues with the flow that would be difficult for an end user to describe.
- *Watch other people experience the journey, too* – there are many services online that will allow you to gather commentated videos of users going through set activities on a website. Using such services can give great insight into any frustrations caused by a checkout process.

Recommendations

- Always use your own customer experience research to tailor the best practice guidelines to your specific needs.
- Experience the checkout journey for yourself so you understand the potential frustrations from an end user's point of view. Back this up by watching others go through the journey.
- If using conversion rates as your variable of improvement, do not try to compare your business with other businesses; you can only try to improve your own conversion rate each month.

References

Appleseed, J. and Holst, C. (2013) 'E-Commerce Checkout Usability: Exploring the customer's checkout experience', Baymard Institute. pp. 24 and 93.

Halarewich, D. (2015) 'The Great Debate: Single or Multi-Page eCommerce Checkout?' Available at: http://blog.lemonstand.com/the-great-debate-single-or-multi-page-e-commerce-checkout/ [Accessed 8 March 2016].

Laja, P. (2015) 'What's a Good Conversion Rate?' Available at: www.conversionxl.com/whats-a-good-conversion-rate/ [Accessed 8 March 2016].

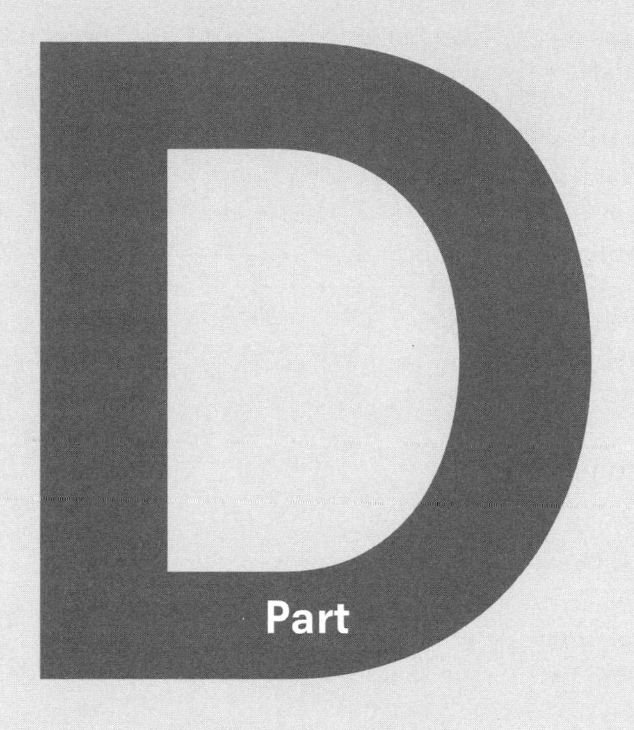

Part D

Surprising customer service

7. Make your brand your customers'

When you deliver excellent customer service, you get great reviews. Customers are becoming more accustomed to checking reviews routinely before buying and are happy to return the favour to future customers by sharing their own experience after completing their purchase. In other words, reviews are fast becoming the new currency for anyone selling online. Companies without reviews look unprofessional; a company with many bad reviews will struggle to turn their luck, whilst companies with good reviews seem to do better and better – encouraged by the response to its good behaviour.

Why do people rely so heavily on the words of others? Does it make a difference beyond warm words and good feelings? Well, to understand the impact of a good review, we turn to search engine rankings.

An SEO advisory firm, Moz.com, analysed the actions of 1,000 people in terms of their search engine behaviour. When the team asked how far down the results people looked, 36 per cent of respondents said that they looked at the first two pages and beyond. However, their actual behaviour showed a different pattern. Data shows that people are more likely to look at less than 2 per cent of searches below the top five results on the first page. This shows us that people are not only unaware of their behaviour, but also much more discretionary in their decision making than they understand. What it did show was that people were prepared to look at both the first and second page of the Google search results, but only under test conditions. That means that they are unlikely to display these behaviours when working in their own time or carrying out 'normal' searches.

How do reviews impact on this?

Since search engines now include review ratings as part of their ranking algorithms, good companies tend to show further up, as the search engine deems them to be more recommendable businesses. Moz.com went back to its test group to ask how important online reviews were in terms of online purchase decision making. The research showed 67.7 per cent of respondents' purchasing decisions were impacted by online reviews. More interestingly, more than half of the respondents (54.7 per cent) also claimed that online reviews are fairly, very or absolutely an important part of their decision-making process.

Not only will positive rankings generate the possibility of a potential customer finding your review before they find you, but a healthy number of positive reviews can help counteract any negative reviews you might get.

Some people are just never happy, though

The best thing you can do as a brand owner is to engage directly, by replying to negative feedback particularly (but also positive, just to say thanks). This is your chance to not just put things right for this particular customer, but, perhaps more importantly, show your prospective customers that you are a responsible business owner that always tries to put things right on the rare occasions things do not work out as planned.

Moz.com's research showed that almost a quarter, 22 per cent, of customers will reconsider when one negative article is found by users thinking about buying a product. If three negative articles are found in one search, the potential for lost custom jumps to 59.2 per cent and a massive 70 per cent of customers will have doubts if they find four or more negative reviews.

How can you minimise the impact of a negative article?

Check the first two pages of Google searches, and other search engines, for negative reviews. Negative reviews are more likely to generate clicks and so will climb the rankings faster than positive reviews. This is a regular check and one that should be done in conjunction with taking the temperature of the online world. Are they feeling warmly towards you or are you getting the digital equivalent of a cold shoulder? Make a list of review sites important to you and your industry and review them.

The answer to counteracting negative reviews lies in increasing the number of positive reviews and it often falls to a brand's digital team to ensure that they have control of the messaging contained in the reviews – not trickery, simply ensuring that your brand experience is up to scratch and driving your users to review.

How good are good reviews?

Good reviews increase customer conversion. Stats reveal that 47 per cent of Britons have reviewed products online. According to Reevoo stats, 50 or more reviews per product can mean a 4.6 per cent increase in conversion rates. Sixty-three per cent of customers are more likely to make a purchase from a site that has user reviews.

Customer Strategy Consulting and think tank organisation thinkJar conducted research showing that 55 per cent of consumers are willing to pay more for a guaranteed good experience. thinkJar CEO, Esteban Kolsky, highlights the word 'guaranteed', saying that customers are no longer satisfied with just being promised a good experience.

How do I start to get (good) reviews?

The first thing that you can do is to shake off the idea that you are imposing on your customers. If 67 per cent consider reviews in their purchase-making decision, it demonstrates that they are receptive to the idea in some way. There is a core of sensible approaches that can help you target the good reviews you have worked so hard to generate:

1. **Ask the right people**

   Do not wait for the unhappy customers to start reviewing you; approach those you think have no reason to dislike you and ask them for help. If you are struggling to get anyone to say anything nice, you have to address their feedback in your offering to put a stop at least to future reviewers that are unhappy about the same thing.

2. **Timing is everything**

   Knowing when to ask for a review is as important as knowing how to ask nicely. You need to capture both their imaginations and their comments when their experience is fresh in their minds.

   There are several smart touchpoints that you can use to collect reviews:

   - just after their last visit or transaction;
   - when they have passed a certain value spend or time loyal to the brand;
   - when you invoice them;
   - when they interacted with you or your team for any reason.

3. **Do not put words in their mouth**

   Be transparent but not dishonest. When you ask them if they would like to review your product/brand/service, it is crucial to make sure that you do not try to sway their opinion in any way. Do not ask them for a good review or even a positive comment. Simply ask them for their honest opinion – it is perfectly fine to say that you use their reviews as an opportunity to improve your business, but it is also a chance to develop a trusting relationship with your clients. Yes, they will tell you what they do not like, and so they should, but they will also be able to tell you what they did like. Bear in mind that, often, it is harder to get a positive response from someone than a negative one.

4. **You can ask more than once**

   Often, people genuinely want to support your business through a review, but finding the time might be a little trickier. Whilst your marketing software, like MailChimp, may show you that emails have been opened, it will not capture the intent of your customers. You may have caught them at a bad time and then they forget about it as it drifts down their inbox.

   Instead of sending the same thing out to the same people, simply segment the list into two and prompt the openers to have another go at your review. Send the same email with a different subject line to the non-opens. Just maybe, they will like this one better.

5. **Manners cost nothing**

   When your customer has been kind enough to submit your review, make sure to have some way of monitoring what they said. Then, get back to them with a thank you for a good review. For a negative review, it may need a little more consideration. It is rarely a totally lost cause and how you respond to a negative review can turn the situation on its head.

6. **Use a third party**

   Strategically, this is a clever move. Whilst that sounds mercenary, it is not. The objective is to secure as many reviews as you can and hope that they are more positive than negative. Using a review provider means that your customers are talking to an independent, third party and are more likely to be honest, than in a situation where they have to talk to you directly.

   People are increasingly getting used to dealing with these sites and may well have some form of trust with the third-party review provider. Review providers have also been finessed to make it as easy as possible for someone to leave a review. This means that you can leverage the investment that the review provider has made in their system, when you have an easy-to-use system.

Lessons for you

There is also an element of courage needed to seek reviews online, but, if you have your brand ducks in a line, this should be easier to bridge. As reviewers grow in strength and publishing prowess, it is likely that the power of the review only will increase as time goes on.

If reviews can increase sales and brand loyalty, the question must, then, surely, be not 'If I decide to ask for reviews . . .', but, rather, 'How soon can I start?' and 'What format shall I use?'

Recommended actions

- *Short term/quick win*

  Create an account with the review site that seems to have the biggest clout in your industry. Complete your profile and start to invite individual customers you think have had a good experience.

- *Medium*

  Whenever you get reviews, good or bad, be quick to respond to thank them or offer a solution to put things right. This shows your future customers that you are taking them seriously.

- *Long term*

  When a customer has received their goods or service (and are at their happiest), make sure you automatically send everyone an invite to review you. Sometimes, an entire review is too much effort for customers, so just ask them, at the very least, to let you know how likely they are to recommend you to a friend on a scale of 1–10 (see Google NPS for more details).

7.1 Expert commentary: Bazaarvoice

I met up with Prelini Udayan-Chiechi, vice-president marketing EMEA at Bazaarvoice, a marketing leader with over 20 years' experience from SAAS, Software, IT, Telco and the finance sectors. She's an accomplished public speaker and thought leader on social, marketing and customer experience specifically. Over the years, she has held senior positions with a range of high-profile organisations, such as Lithium, Adobe, IBM and Lotus Software among others. We talked about how profound the importance of consumer feedback has become and how it can affect not only a brand's image, traffic to a website or online sales, but also offline results, such as instore purchases.

Bazaarvoice powers a network that connects brands and retailers to the voices of their consumers. Each month, more than 700 million people view and share authentic opinions, questions, and experiences about tens of millions of products in the Bazaarvoice network. The company's technology platform amplifies these voices into the places that influence purchase decisions.

Network analytics help marketers and advertisers provide more engaging experiences that drive brand awareness, considerations, sales, and loyalty. Headquartered in Austin, Texas, Bazaarvoice has offices across North America, Europe, and Asia-Pacific, Bazaarvoice has over 4,000+ customers globally.

Online reviews driving instore purchases

As the lines between online and offline platforms continue to blur, it's crucial for both brands and retailers to understand the profound importance of consumer feedback and how it can affect not only a brand's image, traffic to a website or online sales, but also offline results, such as instore purchases. As an example, according to a recent study Bazaarvoice conducted, 54 per cent of online buyers read online reviews before purchase, while 39 per cent of instore buyers read online reviews before purchase. Similarly, 31 per cent of online shoppers share recommendations and reviews with friends and social-network connections about what they bought, while consumers surveyed trusted the opinions of strangers online over those of friends and family.

Prelini says that authentic customer feedback has huge potential to positively influence buying intent and audience opinion. Acquiring more authentic consumer-generated content (CGC) will help businesses achieve higher conversion rates and create lasting, valuable relationships. It is important to note, as experiences have become richer, so has the need for richer content in the form of photos and videos. Thus, when we think of content that consumers are engaging with, and how organisations need to interact with their consumers, they need to evolve and use content that their customer base is using, whether that is text-based, visually enhanced or both.

It is crucial to remember that consumers have a fundamental right to trust the content they encounter, and it is a business's responsibility to ensure authenticity of content at all times

Therefore, sharing authentic content is essential to building customers' trust, particularly with today's growing informed and connected consumers. A step a brand should consider towards earning this trust is displaying a trust mark along with the review, as it can demonstrate the brand's commitment to authentic consumer feedback. In fact, in a research commissioned by Bazaarvoice, 84 per cent of consumers stated that they would feel more trusting of reviews if they knew the reviews were screened for fraud, moderated and displayed by a neutral, credible third party.

Contrary to business sense, brands still fear negative customer feedback; they consider it a threat to their image and reputation. This is because they simply cannot see the great value behind displaying and engaging with negative content, and treat these as insights and opportunities to improve their offering; CGC is a precious form of R&D for brands and retailers, as it can provide valuable insight that can inform better business decisions, lead to innovation and ameliorate the customer experience. Furthermore, there is also a lack of education among internal stakeholders on how to gather, respond to and leverage that feedback, which requires more of a paradigm shift to be accomplished, a change in the brand's mentality about CGC as a whole. Additionally, given the cost involved and the technology required, some businesses may be reluctant to build a CGC-related strategy – that is why it is crucial to be properly informed about the ROI of investing into CGC.

When it comes to measuring a campaign's success, it is no longer about traditional marketing results. Several forms of ROI manifest at different levels of interaction, extending beyond conversion increases to drive search traffic and reveal product improvement suggestions. As products continue to build volume of CGC, over time we have found that the conversion lift is just phase one of the cross-business benefits. Conversion rates see a steep incline as reviews stack up, and continue showing incremental increases well past 1,000 reviews. The SEO value of fresh CGC continually grows stronger as volume increases, even into the several hundreds and thousands.

As an example of this, Bazaarvoice have worked with Sealskiz and GHD. Their aim was to provide impartial information to make it easier for consumers to select products and improve conversion. GHD has experienced a 30 per cent uplift in conversion as a result of having ratings and reviews content on product pages in the UK, and even more in secondary markets in other countries, where they're seeing anywhere from a 35 per cent to 127 per cent uplift in conversion when people interact with reviews. With Sealskinz, they worked to increase shopper-purchaser conversion and use input from customer reviews to learn about new customer demographics to target. As a result, in December of 2014 alone, Sealskinz saw a 102.6 per cent lift in conversion from visitors who engage with reviews compared to those who didn't.

7.2 Case study: Gopak

British furniture manufacturer and retailer Gopak reveals how increased competition on page one of Google and the lack of 5-star ratings within search results led to a major new digital strategy and website project that included:

- the development of new ecommerce SEO and PPC strategies;
- the selection of an independent review platform to meet Google's technical requirements for displaying Rich Snippets reviews in organic search results and ad seller ratings in paid search results;
- reviews migration, launch and ongoing management.

Key findings

- Adding 5-star ad seller ratings to PPC ads increased click-through rate by 29 per cent.
- Ecommerce PPC revenue increased by 44.69 per cent year on year after launch.
- Ecommerce SEO revenue increased by 96.88 per cent year on year after launch.

Interviewee

Diane Ponting is the sales and marketing director at Gopak. She joined the firm in 1984 and, over the last 32 years, has pioneered the adoption of innovative multi-channel sales and marketing strategies. Having been selling online for more than a decade, Ponting recently launched Gopak's new ecommerce website with enhanced online marketing and business system integration capabilities.

About Gopak

Gopak is a British manufacturer and retailer of furniture, specialising in folding tables. Established in 1947, the original design included an innovative table top with steel folding legs that could be constructed without the need for screws or fixings. From humble workshop beginnings, Gopak's range of over 6,000 tables, stacking benches and storage trolleys are now sold UK-wide with clients such as the BBC, Pinewood Studios and hundreds of schools.

Its online retail strategy

The Gopak online retail strategy is part of a wider multi-channel strategy that includes ecommerce, partner and catalogue sales. Therefore, the online retail strategy needs to support and work in tandem with the other sales channels to create a cohesive omnichannel customer experience.

Over more than a decade that Gopak has sold online, the online marketing channels that drive eCommerce sales have been continuously tested, honed and developed.

Whilst initially starting with marketing investment in niche directories, PR and advertising targeting specific segments of the market such as schools and universities, the Gopak ecommerce marketing channels now include Google AdWords pay-per-click campaigns, Google Shopping campaigns, Bing Ads, SEO, content marketing and email marketing.

In recent years, new market entrants with considerable online brand authority, such as Amazon, Tesco and Ikea, made online trading conditions through search engines considerably more challenging and competitive.

With search marketing being a major source of online revenue, a significant investment in a new website with enhanced search engine friendly functionality and improved user experience for all sources of traffic was launched.

As part of this project, a brand new ecommerce SEO strategy was devised to combat the increased page-one competition in Google for high-traffic volume terms such as 'folding tables'.

The new search marketing strategies deployed included identifying a wider selection of more audience-relevant keyword terms with higher buying intent and less competition such as 'school folding tables'.

This led to constructing a completely new website architecture and URL structure to enable every type of new and returning visitor to arrive on the most appropriate page for their search, reducing the number of duplicate versions of pages in Google's index and increasing both ecommerce SEO and PPC conversion rates.

After implementing the new website and correctly redirecting old pages using Google's Webmaster Guidelines, new visitors who do not yet know the Gopak brand that are making category searches such as 'school folding tables' and returning visitors who know the brand already and are making more specific, longer tail searches such as 'Gopak contour folding tables' can find the Gopak website on page one of Google's search results.

For the next 12 months, the expansion of the online product optimisation strategy is key. Product innovation is central to how Gopak established itself as a market leader and, therefore, ensuring integrated marketing communications of the existing and new product inventory across all channels will be the top priority for continued record-breaking ecommerce revenue.

The Case

The problem

Having previously experienced significant traffic and revenue from both the SEO and PPC channels, Gopak's ecommerce SEO and PPC performance was suffering due to increased

▶

competition, together with an old website that was slow to load and not particularly user friendly.

Gopak had recently seen an explosion of competition on page one of Google from online supermarkets and market places, like Amazon and Tesco, offering low-cost folding tables for consumers, as well as third-party websites selling Gopak-branded products. Therefore, Gopak needed to protect brand terms as a priority to dominate the search engine results pages for product keywords, as well as increase brand awareness with new B2B customers.

As an established British manufacturer and retailer of folding tables for over 60 years, Gopak already had an extensive number of customer reviews on its website – many more than its new search competitors. However, Gopak's 5-star ratings were not appearing in Gopak's organic or paid search results.

As a result of this, Gopak wanted to launch a brand new ecommerce website in July 2014 that built on previous SEO successes as well as devising new ecommerce SEO, PPC and content strategies to be integrated within the site from launch to increase ecommerce revenue and conversions as soon as possible.

Background

Developing a new website presented Gopak with the opportunity to gain first mover advantage by displaying customer reviews within both organic and paid Google search results.

At the time, Gopak's competitors, including Tesco, Ikea and Amazon, were not displaying 5-star customer reviews within their folding-table-related search results.

The advantages of including the customer reviews within organic search results were:

- increased organic click-through rate due to attracting more attention than listings without any star ratings;
- increased organic traffic to product pages which are more likely to have a higher conversion rate;

- increased organic conversion rate due to independent verification of the brand in other customers' own words;
- increased organic revenue as a result of all the above;
- increased organic rankings due to increased Google listing interaction and landing-page engagement.

The advantages of including the customer reviews within paid search results were:

- increased paid ad click-through rate due to attracting more attention than adverts without any star ratings;
- increased paid clicks to product pages that are more likely to have a higher conversion rate;
- increased paid conversion rate due to independent verification of the brand in other customers' own words;
- increased paid revenue as a result of all the above;
- increased paid positions and reduction in average pay-per-click cost due to an increased Google AdWords quality score that rewards increased Google ad interaction and landing-page conversion.

The major challenge for Gopak with enabling customer reviews to display into both organic and paid search results was that Google's technical requirements were different for both SEO and PPC channels.

Gopak's existing customer reviews published on their website were not being shown in the organic search results as they were not contained within the correct 'Rich Snippets' format that the Google search engine robots recognised.

However, even if the new website was coded in a way that the search engine robots could understand Gopak's existing online reviews, these 5-star ratings would still be shown only in organic search results and not be shown at all within pay-per-click ads. This was because reviews published via Gopak's own website were not independently verified by a Google-approved third-party review platform and therefore did not meet Google's PPC requirements for reviews.

▶

Whilst implementing a third-party review platform had the potential to display 5-star ratings in both SEO and PPC search results, this would still include only new reviews via the new platform from launch onwards and exclude all the existing reviews that had previously been provided via the website.

The solution

Ultimately, Gopak wanted to be found in both Google's organic and paid search results with gold 5-star ratings, as well as presenting online shoppers with all of their historic reviews already published via their website.

Ecommerce SEO and PPC strategy

Gopak's specialist ecommerce SEO and PPC agency, ThoughtShift, assessed the independent review platforms on the market to deliver the best solution for Gopak's new ecommerce SEO and PPC strategies, which also met all of Google's requirements and could work in conjunction with the existing website reviews.

Independent review platform strategy

Feefo was selected as the review platform because it provided Gopak with the features it was looking for.

Ecommerce SEO reviews strategy

As part of Gopak's ecommerce SEO strategy for the new website, existing customer reviews were migrated across into the new website content and new independent third-party reviews

Table 7.1 Summary of review platform options

Review platform type	SEO 5-star ratings	PPC 5-star ratings	Existing reviews included
Own website	Yes	No	Yes
Third-party platform	Yes	Yes	No

were incorporated into the new product page design by Gopak's web design agency, Lightmaker.

This was achieved by using a tabbed user experience so that customers would be able to switch between their choice of customer reviews, including organisation names that they may recognise and/or independently verified reviews where 100 per cent of reviews are guaranteed to be published. From the search engine's perspective, both types of review content for each product is on one page, as the URL remains the same, providing Gopak with an extensive number of reviews per product page.

Rich Snippets markup was added to the schema code for all product pages containing parameters such as 5-star ratings, review comment, product price and product stock availability.

Rich Snippets code was then tested using the Google Structured Data Testing Tool available within Gopak's Google Search Console to ensure the 5-star ratings were recognisable by Google and had the potential to be displayed in organic search results when deemed relevant by Google.

Where in the old web design there previously had been three different product URLs per product, these were combined into one product URL with the old variations being permanently redirected to the new master URL. This would reduce the number of similar pages within the organic search results, enable all of the disparate SEO equity that each separate URL had to be accumulated into each new product page and also display all the disparate reviews into one master set of reviews per product to further increase the amount of social proof.

The permanent 301 redirect server protocol for the new website architecture restructure was used for SEO migration best practice. This meant that search engine users finding existing organic search results would be automatically redirected to the new location and Google would transfer the accumulated

▶

authority of the old pages across to the new pages, rewarding the improvement with increased organic rankings, leading to increased SEO traffic and SEO revenue.

Ecommerce PPC reviews strategy

Due to 30 independent reviews being required by Google before the 5-star ratings are included within PPC ads, Gopak began setting up the new review platform processes months in advance of the new website going live so that the new ecommerce PPC campaigns would include the Ad Seller Ratings immediately from launch.

The new eCommerce PPC strategy for Gopak included researching new keywords that Gopak's Google AdWords ads could appear in paid search results for, especially promoting products with independent reviews so that the gold 5-star ratings would be shown within the adverts.

Research techniques included analysing the voice of the customer identified from new and existing review comments, as well as product keywords proven previously to drive PPC revenue using data from Google Analytics.

New PPC ads were created featuring a combination of proven revenue driving keywords and new keyword gaps where the language matched that of previous customers that had left reviews. The new AdWords ads also included as many Google Ad Extensions as possible, such as Ad Seller Ratings, which not only increases the visibility of the adverts to increase click-through but is also a proven technique to increase Google AdWords Quality Score and grow PPC ROI.

Product Listing Ads (PLAs) were also created to display the 5-star Ad Seller Ratings within Gopak's Google Shopping campaigns.

Reviews migration and launch

Before launch, tracking code for Google Analytics, Google AdWords, Remarketing, Bing Ads and Google Search Console was added to the website code to ensure that current ecommerce traffic, revenue and conversion rate results were benchmarked and future performance could be measured.

The ecommerce SEO and PPC reviews strategies were implemented and, as the number of reviews and independent reviews grew, ongoing adjustments were made to maximise the visibility of the gold 5-star ratings within Google's organic and paid search results.

Results

The new ecommerce SEO and PPC review strategies launched at the end of July 2014 and monthly reports showed the impact as follows:

- AB tests of PPC ads with and without Ad Seller Ratings found the gold 5-star increased click-through rate by 29 per cent.
- PPC revenue for the three-month period immediately after launch between Aug–Oct 2014 increased 10.7 per cent to £113,342, compared to the same period the previous year (£102,378).
- PPC revenue increased 44.69 per cent year on year to £49,559 by the third month after launch (Oct 2014).
- The total paid media spend, including agency management fees for the three-month period between Aug–Oct 2014 was £13,522 and therefore the return on investment for PPC for the three-month campaign was 7.4 per cent.
- SEO revenue over the three-month period between Aug–Oct 2014 (£79,950) was up 96.88 per cent year on year when compared to the same period in 2013 (£40,608).
- SEO transactions between Aug–Oct 2014 increased 70.77 per cent year on year (130 v. 222).
- The conversion rate increased 19.90 per cent year on year when comparing Aug–Oct 2014 to the same period the previous year.

▶

Critical success factors

The critical success factors for implementing reviews that meet Google's complex requirements were:

- a fantastic team who work incredibly hard to continuously improve the customer experience;
- innovative products that deserve great reviews;
- a high volume of lovely customers who are keen to share their experiences;
- new website design investment that presented the opportunities to solve the review problems, whilst increasing user experience and conversion rates;
- specialist ecommerce SEO and PPC consultancy to advise on best practice for migrating existing reviews and adding new Google-approved reviews;
- an independent review platform that automates the ecommerce review process, so Gopak reviews are displayed in both paid and organic search results, on the website and via a third-party directory of trusted sellers.

Lessons learned

Diane Ponting, sales and marketing director of Gopak, sums up the journey:

> 'Jumping through the hoops that are necessary to get the 5-star ratings to appear in paid and organic Google search engine results is well worth the investment.
>
> I would recommend that you certainly need to allow a number of months for the initial planning, redesign of product pages, migration of any existing reviews, set-up of new review processes and creation of newly optimised PPC and SEO campaigns.
>
> Luckily we had a great ecommerce SEO and PPC strategy team to advise us on the pros and cons of the different review options and

how our web designers should best incorporate our existing reviews with the new independent reviews.

Gopak has a fantastic 98 per cent Feefo Review Score from hundreds of reviews, our 5-star ratings appear within many of our organic and paid search results and that, combined with the new website and revamped ecommerce SEO and PPC campaigns, has seen PPC revenue increase 44.69 per cent year on year, SEO revenue increase by 96.88 per cent year on year and our conversion rate increase by 19.90 per cent year on year.

So, ultimately, implementing an integrated ecommerce SEO and PPC review solution has been invaluable, as our customers continue to provide social proof that Gopak is the UK's leading folding table brand.'

Recommendations

- Choose an independent Google-approved third-party review platform that provides product reviews as well as brand/service reviews, as only product reviews can be displayed in PPC ads.
- Find a specialist ecommerce SEO and PPC company with proven experience of implementing reviews for both paid and organic search results.
- Set up automated review processes, where possible, to be able to respond immediately to feedback and continuously improve the customer experience.

7.3 Expert commentary: authentic customer dialogue

I met up with Carl Waldekranz, co-founder and CEO of Tictail, to discuss why offering your customers the option to chat to you is the key to success in customer service. Waldekranz was listed on the 'Forbes 30 Under 30' in the ecommerce and retail category and his company Tictail is an ecommerce platform that makes it easy to build an online store. So far, over 100,000 SMEs have already done it. For more information about Tictail, visit: https://tictail.com.

Waldekranz explains, 'At Tictail we spend a lot of time helping to arm small business owners with the tools they need to best build global brands. Throughout our research, across the board, live chat is the preferred communication channel. Ninety-five per cent of shoppers opt for it when given the choice.'

Large companies like Facebook, WhatsApp and WeChat are giving brands a voice to serve their customers' needs. And this makes sense. We all use messaging as our primary form of communication with friends and colleagues. It is intuitive and real-time. It is asynchronous. It is mobile-centric.

Waldekranz thinks the next phase for online retailers will be to bring live chat functionality in-house. Just as customers hate the feeling of calls being outsourced, so, too, do online shoppers literally give up on a sale if they do not have access to the help they need, when they need it.

First step: mobile integration. By the end of 2015, Facebook Messenger was being used by 800 million active users, the perfect proof point to how friends want to engage with their friends on the platform home to all their friends. And via mobile.

Tictail's own stats confirmed the story we have discussed in this book already: over 60 per cent of all purchases on their system are now on mobile devices, with the numbers only increasing. Mobile is not only a growing sales channel, but a channel where engagement actually multiplies business. According to Waldekranz, they see that engaged mobile buyers are spending 40 per cent more than the average buyer.

Carl continues, one of the biggest assets a small business owner has over huge, faceless companies, is the ability to create a lasting and personal relationship with each and every customer. Whilst Jeff Bezos does not have enough time in a day to reach out to each and every Amazon customer and thank them for their business, small business owners do.

Building these relationships and establishing engagement leads to active consumers. Shoppers that engage with a Tictail brand, for example by liking products, following the store and sending direct messages, are almost twice as likely to make a repeat purchase from the same store.

Recommendation

Waldekranz's recommendation to growing online retailers is to create an engagement tool where shoppers can interact as much as possible with a brand – even before a sale takes place. Furthermore, use that tool as an ongoing log of individual customer conversations. In-app messaging helps to extend a relationship beyond the sale. Merchants can follow up with shoppers to check in and see how they like their product, to offer discount codes and send first-look images of new collections.

Direct chat creates an equally accessible channel of communication from either party: the shoppers who want additional details beyond what is available online, and the small business owner who wants to engage proactively with a shopper regarding an upcoming sale, event, restocking or more.

7.4 Case study: Grabble.com – getting mobile right

Whilst some online retailers are focusing on understanding offline retailing, the founders of the fashion discovery site Grabble.com were busy building an addictive mobile experience.

This is a case about Grabble's mission to make discovering fashion and trends simple. However, Grabble's journey to developing a 'sticky' app to accomplish that was anything but.

Initially having invested over a year into looking to optimise a web-based user experience, Grabble realised that its not-yet launched product was already outdated, as Millennials were flocking to mobile instead.

With a matter of weeks before Angel investment ran out, the company used insights gleaned along the way to quickly develop an app. It was launched to the younger end of its audience first, in the belief that they would be the easiest to convert if marketed to authentically. The approach and plan paid off.

Key findings

Fourteen months on, the social commerce platform has now found its winning formula. It puts the market, not the product, first and is focused on delivering an exceptional customer experience.

- Highly engaged audience – 26 per cent monthly active users.
- Investment focused on delivering customer service and real-time messaging.
- Constant product development to satisfy Millennials' high expectations of being able to access curated content and personalised experiences whenever suits them.

Interviewee

Daniel Murray is the co-founder and CMO at Grabble. A serial entrepreneur, Murray's inspiration for Grabble came whilst working at a daily deals site he co-founded. As one of Drapers' '30 under 30', he represents the next generation of the UK fashion industry.

About Grabble

Founded in 2014 by entrepreneurs Daniel Murray and Joel Freeman, Grabble is a social commerce platform that seeks to change the way Millennials discover fashion online. The app, tipped by Forbes as one of 'London's hottest start-ups to watch,' takes a different approach from the fashion retail industry.

Handpicked by a team of expert stylists led by Cherry Collins (Ex Grazia, Selfridges and Net-A-Porter), the mobile-only app is a daily edit of the best designer and high-street pieces. It allows users to take inspiration, save and buy from curated fashion, lifestyle and beauty collections.

As a young entrepreneur, Murray turned to the Shell LiveWIRE Youth Enterprise programme, which secured him a £1,000 start-up grant. A few months later, he won the annual competition, providing £10,000 in funding. The funding helped with the development and marketing of the app ahead of launch. Within the first two months, Grabble generated 20,000 downloads, trended nationally on Twitter and featured on the iTunes and GooglePlay stores as 'Best New App' in 34 countries.

Within 12 months, Grabble raised £1.2 million from high-profile Angel investors in London and Silicon Valley, and grew from a team of 3 to 20 in a few months.

Hosting products from over 200 brands, such as Topshop, Mango and Zara, Grabble has become popular with retailers because the app integrates seamlessly with their websites and provides a user-friendly way of showcasing products on mobile devices.

Since launching the app in August 2014, 350,000 users have signed up, 'Grabbing' more than 900 million items worth £63 billion. Since adding a native checkout, they have tracked over £750,000 worth of sales. For more information, visit: www.grabble.com.

Its online retail strategy

As brands and technology continue to evolve, it became clear to Grabble that mobile retail is the future for connecting to, and winning over, Millennials. In reality, this meant that the brand's mobile strategy has had to be agile enough to continually adapt to meet the ever-changing demands of its users.

Millennials are a challenging bunch who are very active, typically in transit, and hold down competitive, premium jobs. Mobile is their playground because it keeps them up to date when they do not have the time or inclination to investigate the latest products from major retailers or read magazines.

These audience insights led Grabble to develop a product that would build up meaningful, trusted relationships with users through enhanced user experience, content curation and by providing real-time solutions to their needs. Product development remains an iterative, ongoing process because the audience is both difficult to satisfy and has high expectations of being able to get their hands on curated content and personalised experiences whenever suits them.

Customer service is also crucial to winning the support of Millennials who define themselves by being 'busy', and will gravitate towards companies who create a personalised relationship of trust with them, becoming part of their world.

Grabble recognises that the single biggest challenge to, and impact on, ecommerce in the coming years will be how messenger apps become an essential open platform to communicate with customers. Phone support, waiting on hold and talking to automated systems will become defunct as people expect the ability to message and receive an immediate response. Since launching its live chat option, Grabble has seen the volume of support emails fall by 73 per cent, demonstrating Millennials' strong preference for messaging.

The winners in mobile commerce will be those committed to customer experience, and Grabble is investing in driving this mission forward.

The Case

The problem

At launch, Grabble was operating in what was expected to be a high growth area – social commerce. Social commerce had taken off in the USA but not yet in the UK, so the company believed there was an opportunity to build a product for a Millennial audience. At the heart of their mission was taking a fresh approach to product discovery, in response to the web becoming a noisy place saturated with different brands and experiences.

However, in developing their web-based social commerce platform, there were three insurmountable key issues:

1. Due to the way affiliate marketing operated online, there was a significant delay between being able to track a click and seeing whether the sale had been completed. This lack of real-time understanding of the customer's behaviour

created a real challenge when it came to understanding their journeys, conversion rates and re-engagement opportunities.

2. The customers' mobile journeys were becoming increasingly difficult to track, which left users less able to follow their orders. Poor tracking, coupled with slow loading times on mobile web, meant the churn rate increased due to the ecommerce experience being limited when compared to a native app.
3. By focusing on a Millennial audience, who was rapidly changing its entire user behaviour, Grabble had to adopt a completely different approach to engage and retain it.

Ultimately, Grabble concluded that the web was a great place to publish, and, therefore, its approach to discovery through community curation was a viable concept. Users were satisfied clicking 'buy' on an affiliate site, which opened a new tab for the retailer's domain where they actually purchased.

However, on mobile, this all changed. Users were willing only to consume content rather than participate in creating it, which meant that Grabble had to change its vision of how 'discovery' could be serviced to its audience. Users were also frustrated by being sent to mobile checkouts, so the end-to-end user experience involving purchase in app had to be thought out from scratch.

The background

Grabble had set up to solve the problem of fashion discovery and inspiration for its users. It had spent close to a year, and in the region of £300,000, developing a platform for web that would enable users to save their favourite products, sourced from other sites, and receive sale alerts.

Yet, in the time it took to fully optimise this experience, the question of how to best engage Millennials on web had completely disappeared, as their audience instead flocked to

▶

mobile for discovery. To compound this issue, Grabble had a month's worth of funding remaining. Existing investors were unwilling to reinvest due to lack of traction with the web product and, without seeing evidence of the new mobile concept, new investors were scarce.

The solution

Grabble knew through insight that mobile was the opportunity to fully engage with their audience, and made the difficult decision to cease developing on web. This meant an existential shift of focus towards questioning what made for a 'sticky' mobile app and how to adapt their social commerce mission.

They noted the 'mobile first' user experience was the key, but, rather than ripping up the rule book, they analysed the popular apps – Twitter, Facebook, Instagram, Tumblr, Tinder, etc. – and determined that the strongest feature of these was doing one thing well.

Grabble's web competitors had mostly shut down over the course of the year, which indicated they might be next. However, they could not pinpoint any particularly engaging mobile app that felt like it would be successful.

They instructed their designer and developer to build mock ups in HTML5 with the brief of creating a 'Tinder for fashion'. They then took the concepts to a shared workspace, asking 50 people which they preferred. From observing engagement and responses, there was a clear winner. Research noted that simplicity was king on mobile and would create the 'wow factor' for their audience, providing the company a new, commercially viable focus.

The approach

The new remit was to create an iPhone app that, from an engagement perspective, utilised the 'Tinder' style user experience (UX) of swiping. Grabble had built the technology that enabled it to 'scrape' and, therefore, instantly add products from any other site back onto its platform, giving it an inordinate amount of flexibility when it came to merchandising the product or, rather, filling it with content.

Grabble knew its wider market was the coveted Millennial audience, but, faced with a funding timeline that put it under immense pressure, it decided to attack the younger end of this audience first. Students were the agreed focus and the 'Tinder for Fashion' concept was used to attract them.

Timing for relaunch

With four weeks to go before exhausting their funding, they informed their team honestly of the company's position and that, rather than wind the four weeks down trying incremental marketing tests to attract users, they would go with one big bang to try to make an impact. With two weeks to go, they decided that 'trending' nationally was the only real, obvious way they could have the kind of impact required. They researched and then actioned the key tactics that would have the best chances of helping them gain traction.

Launch marketing

With one week to go, they launched their campaign through Twitter on a cold Sunday night after football and before *X Factor* had started – two golden rules discovered about making an impact on a Sunday on Twitter – the platform's busiest period. Knowing that they would have the best initial impact with a university student market (given the 'Tinder for' aspect), they got in touch with hundreds of Twitter account owners and offered to pay them to tweet (between £10 and £50 for the tweet). To ensure maximum impact, Grabble planned for all the tweets to be published in the same 20-minute window when Twitter traffic was predicted to be

▶

heavy but the nationally popular tweets were less frequent (i.e. football).

To ensure a feel of authenticity, the one specific rule to the tweets was that they did not look like marketing and never mentioned 'download Grabble', which was the fastest way to turn off their target demographic and guarantee zero engagement.

Research showed that, to trend on Twitter, a hashtag or @ was unnecessary, and they launched a number of memes and tweets talking from the account owner's tone of voice, whilst the topic focus was to say something mysterious about Grabble to provoke intrigue. An example was the page 'Lord of the Rings Reactions', which had hundreds of thousands of very engaged followers.

They tweeted a picture of Frodo at Mount Mordor holding the ring, which said, 'That feeling when you finally find that ring on Grabble'. This was retweeted over 10,000 times in seconds, and was one of 200 accounts with similar success. Within 10 minutes, they were trending, and the engagement on Twitter was coming from the general public asking what Grabble was and engaging in a conversation about how everyone was suddenly talking about it.

During the course of an hour, they had seen tens of thousands of tweets come in, causing a huge surge in downloads, crashing their servers, much to their disappointment. However, by the time they got back up, the downloads were still coming in fast and, by Monday morning, they had surged to number 7 in the app store and were featured that week in 'Best New Apps' on the App Store.

The campaign had cost them £5,000 and had been a risk but, following its success, they were able to approach their investors again, who rapidly put money into the company. They swiftly raised £750,000 with a vision of building a mobile company, and began identifying the key hires to achieve that goal. Having previously run their tech from an outsourced team to save costs, they now looked to build an in-house team. Key roles such as CTO fashion director, head of growth (marketing), lead iOS developer, product manager and lead designer were brought into the team to drive value and build at speed.

The team decided on a three-pronged communication strategy; the founders' (Daniel Murray and Joel Freeman) vision on mobile commerce, the fashion director's (Cherry Collins, ex Net-A-Porter and Selfridges lead stylist) profile and taste/experience, and the brand's mission to make shopping on mobile fast, fun, addictive and simple. They sought to use the key spokespeople to build the brand, putting themselves on the front line. They were rewarded with a high-profile investment round from leading angel investors, awards and continued product growth.

However, because mobile commerce is such a new area, there were not really any clear business models or approaches to replicate, and the team tried to execute a traditional ecommerce model focused on lifetime value, forcing consumers towards an industry leading mobile commerce checkout with an 18 per cent conversion rate.

It shortly became clear that this was an impossible focus for their strategy; winning in ecommerce requires driving margin and volume, which is counter-intuitive to how people were comfortable using mobile. Also, to flourish on mobile, the product must be 'sticky', meaning people need to come back regularly enough to not delete the app. If the team focused solely on commerce, they were unable to engage users to return regularly enough. These learnings saw Grabble shift its focus to content, which was a huge success and helped create one of the stickiest products in the market.

Results

Grabble has succeeded where many have failed. It has built a mobile commerce environment that is 'sticky' (users come back

▶

regularly) because it was agile and able to adapt to the market whilst learning on the go. With no prior experience of what the industry key metrics should be for benchmarking in its area – it approached venture capital firms (who see many similar companies) to get a sense of what was deemed 'great' in various known industries on mobile.

Typically, social apps would see 30 per cent monthly active users (MAU) and ecommerce apps would see around 5–10 per cent. Grabble assumed that being both content and commerce, it should aim for somewhere between these figures. At the time of publishing, the MAU is 26 per cent, which certainly contributes to their ability to engage users regularly and build traction and buzz around their product. One of the key ways they tested their proposition along the way was to use net promoter score (NPS) ratings. Whenever preparing to release a new feature or change strategy, Grabble made sure, in a control group of usually 15, that the NPS score was at least 7 to ensure success.

Critical success factors

There are three major factors that Grabble feels contributed to its success:

1. They have operated in a highly agile way, testing concepts that they believed would cause an addictive consumer interaction for their product and therefore drive people back to it every week/month.
2. They have been proactive in driving the product forward – moving quickly on new ideas and strategies and consistently developing an innovative, market-leading product.
3. They have focused on consumer feedback and put customer service at the heart of their business. This has given them an open platform for understanding the voice of their end user, who is, ultimately, the person controlling the success of their execution.

Lessons learned

The key lesson learned after a year was to focus on the market not the product. In spending too long iterating and developing their product they had neglected their mission – to make discovery simple – and the product was ineffectively executed. As such, in year two, they were quick to conceive and test a hypothesis, measure the results and change it accordingly.

By doing so, they produced seven different iterations and 'pivots' of the Grabble mobile app in year two before settling on a content-focused mobile product that began to reap the rewards with cohort data, proving they had finally surfaced the winning formula.

The team also learned about hiring people; having hired successful people who had 'done it all before' at established companies, they realised these people were more fearful of change and set in their ways, which is an inappropriate way to think in a start-up. They opted, instead, to nurture up and coming talent, as these are the types of people who understand how to create change, not resist it.

They have been very passionate on their hiring strategy and follow a mantra to 'hire fast, fire faster' if people have not felt like the right fit for their long-term success. As Daniel Murray said on reflection, 'The people with the best people win.'

Recommendations

- Build technology that is scalable but with the understanding that platforms and operating systems change fast. This ensures you are not overly reliant and your business does not die as these develop. Essentially, there is no perfect solution. Instead, build the right tech at the right time that works, then move on to the next challenge rather than finding perfection everywhere. If the whole question changes, the technology you might have spent so much time on can make you obsolete.

▶

- To succeed in your market area, you need ruthless focus. Are you a consumer- or business-focused operation? If you are business-focused, aka B2B, you will need to solve problems for your retailers/partners that fit into their technical stack properly. If you are consumer-focused, you must ignore any friction with your partners and focus on optimising every part of the consumer journey effectively, and efficiently, fast. This is where many start-ups and companies fail – they try to solve too much at the same time. If you want to be a B2C – make sure you are learning, adapting, innovating and reinventing your product rapidly and regularly based on your learnings, and worry about the other bits later.
- At a very high level, suggest a proposition/concept and rationalise why it makes business sense. Ideally, test the theory with a control group and then build it in a quick, efficient way by building a minimal viable product rather than a full-blown version. If you are wrong in your assumptions, you will find out by tracking the user data and behaviour – and do not be afraid to change tack.

8. Deep dive: global payment alternatives

Online retailers have never been under more pressure to tailor their services to consumers' preferences than now. Delivering a flexible and seamless payments process is fundamental to achieving this, but merchants must be mindful of the hundreds of different payment methods favoured by shoppers around the world.

I met up with Kevin Dallas, chief product officer at Worldpay, to discuss how ambitious retailers must get ready to cater to the world of payment options if they want to keep growing. Worldpay is a provider of payment and risk services, processing millions of transactions every day. The company provides an end-to-end service, including card acquiring, treasury, gateway, alternative payments and risk management, all of which can be provided with a single integration to Worldpay. Dallas looks after the global ecommerce business and his responsibilities include product management across the value chain (gateway, ecommerce acquiring, alternative payment methods, fraud and treasury services), global marketing and demand generation and strategy. Prior to joining Worldpay in August 2013, Dallas was a partner at Bain & Company. For more information about WorldPay, visit: www.worldpay.com/global.

Key takeaway

It is vital to connect with consumers in a way that demonstrates value for money and provides an easy, quick, secure, shopping experience that will convert them and keep them coming back for more. When it comes to online sales, it has never been more important for retailers to match the payments process to consumers' preferences.

However, with hundreds of payment methods in use around the world, this is not easy. Many online merchants assume that credit and debit cards are universally popular, and indeed they are in many markets, but their use varies substantially by region and by shopper, especially online.

In order to sell more goods and services to more consumers, online merchants must offer alternatives to card payments – such as bank transfers, digital wallets, pre- and post-pay options and, in some cases, even cash on delivery.

The insight

Alternative payment methods (APMs) are all of those payment options that do not belong to a global scheme card network, such as Visa, MasterCard, Discover, Diners or American Express. The use of APMs is on the rise. They accounted for 51 per cent of global ecommerce turnover in 2015 and it is expected that 55 per cent of global ecommerce sales will be made via alternative payments by 2019, driven by growth in emerging markets and the rise of mobile commerce.[1]

Of course, the split between cards and alternatives does vary substantially by market. For instance, the majority of Chinese shoppers have been using APMs for years, whilst card use has risen in popularity only recently. The majority of consumers buying goods online in China do so using eWallets like Alipay and, even when they do use a card, it is most likely issued by the country's only national champion bank card organisation (China Union Pay). It is worth noting that China Union Pay is itself aspiring to become a global brand.

[1]'Global Payments Report', Worldpay, 2015.

Even in Europe, where one might expect card dominance is a foregone conclusion, APM use is high in a number of nations and continues to rise. In Germany, currently the world's fifth biggest ecommerce market, a widespread expectation for easy and simple ecommerce purchases has kept real-time bank transfers at the top of the payments totem pole. Tellingly, other non-credit card methods like Sofort Banking, SEPA Direct Debit and Giropay also have major buy-in among German shoppers who prefer these to cards.

The same goes for the Netherlands, where card payments account for only 13 per cent of the country's ecommerce market. Instead, bank transfers via iDEAL, a real-time inter-bank payment method, lead the way. With many major Dutch banks also offering mobile versions of iDEAL, the platform has become available to more than 90 per cent of the population.[2]

In India, where the ecommerce market is expected to quadruple in size over the next four years, consumers (and the regulatory environment) favour online banking and cash on delivery when shopping online. Indeed, card payments among Indian shoppers are expected to account for just 27 per cent of the country's ecommerce sales by 2019.[3]

When viewed as a whole, these regional trends indicate just how important it has become for multi-national retailers to cater to the specific needs of shoppers in each country to which they sell.

Popular APMs: a few definitions

Whilst there are hundreds of alternative payment methods available to consumers, and even more being developed, APMs broadly fall into six main buckets:

1. *Digital wallets*

   Also known as eWallets, digital wallets allow shoppers to make ecommerce transactions directly from a connected

[2]'Global Payments Report', Worldpay, 2015.

[3]'Global Payments Report', Worldpay, 2015.

device. Consumers can choose to pay using stored value uploaded to their digital wallet from a credit card or with funds from any APM linked to their eWallet.

2. *Real-time bank transfers*

   Real-time bank transfers require consumers to pay for goods using their online banking facility, after which they either are redirected to their bank's payment page or they select its name from a list on a retailer's checkout page before finalising their purchase. Authorisations for bank transfers are immediate in most cases, which means merchants can settle their funds quickly and shoppers get instant confirmation that their payment has been accepted.

3. *Offline bank transfers*

   In the case of offline bank transfers, consumers are given a reference number during the purchasing process, which they subsequently share with their online banking facility to complete their payment. Because shoppers can do this at their leisure, however, authorisation is not immediate and, in some cases, the payment is never made. This not only complicates the settlement of funds for a retailer, it also makes it difficult to automate inventory and shipping models if merchants want to avoid sending goods to customers that have not paid for their order.

4. *Pre-pay options*

   Pre-payment options allow consumers to upload a predefined value onto a voucher that can then be used to pay for goods, much like cash but without the need to actually carry cash around. The popularity of pre-payment vouchers is rising, especially among shoppers who are uncomfortable sharing their personal details or who do not have a bank account.

5. *Cash on delivery*

   Cash on delivery (COD) is the practice by which shoppers pay for products or services only once they have been delivered. Uber, whilst not a retailer, is the example, par excellence, of this approach in many developing markets.

When it comes to retail, COD continues to thrive in countries like China, Russia, the Philippines and Indonesia, due to a cultural preference for cash and the rapid climb of online commerce. The Lazada Group, the aspirational 'Amazon of Southeast Asia', counts COD as its most popular payment method in Indonesia. Amazon itself also supports cash on delivery in China for the large proportion of Chinese consumers who favour this payment method.

6. *Carrier billing*

Predominantly used in countries where mobile penetration is high, consumers are under-banked and security concerns deter people from carrying large amounts of cash, carrier billing allows shoppers to make purchases that are charged directly to their mobile phone account. These transactions are relatively quick and simple as carriers can provide user data directly to merchants, although they are also often more expensive to process. It is worth noting that some carrier billing services are also evolving into mobile eWallets; for example, people in Kenya that use M-Pesa can opt to have their salaries paid via their carrier.

Offering a tailored range of payment options

Operating a successful ecommerce site on a global scale requires a more localised approach to paying online. To ensure they never miss a sale, retailers need to support transactions in multiple currencies, accept each region's most popular card and alternative payment methods, and tailor their offering to local purchasing habits.

It is not uncommon for leading online retailers to boast a tailored cashier service, sites in multiple languages and the ability to support dozens of local currencies and alternative payment methods. Not only does this improve the user experience, it also helps ensure online merchants maintain high acceptance levels for the payments they process.

▶

Wondershare, the number one exporter in the Chinese software industry, raised its acceptance rates by 30 per cent by tailoring its ecommerce and fraud policies according to the needs of each market in which it operates. The company is currently looking to build its presence in Japan, Brazil and Russia whilst bolstering its already strong foothold in both the USA and Europe.

As Mr Sun, CFO at Wondershare, puts it:

> 'Online customers have little patience for an inefficient shopping experience, and the changes we've made will help ensure that their interactions with us are as simple and convenient as possible. With our sights set on expanding into a number of new markets, our improved acceptance rates will help solidify our position as a leading software provider on the global stage.'

Etsy, the leading online marketplace for handcrafted vintage goods, has the added challenge of bringing together buyers and sellers from different countries who often transact in their own currencies. The company continues successfully to process hundreds of thousands of transactions, and pay thousands of sellers each year because it has the ability to seamlessly reconcile currency conversions and accommodate its members' preferred payment methods, no matter where they live.

Managing shopper expectations

Online merchants also need to ensure they can deliver on the expectations they set for shoppers in terms of which payment methods they can support. A recent Worldpay study revealed that 60 per cent of consumers would drop out of a purchase if their preferred payment type was displayed on a retailer's homepage but was then not available at checkout.[4] In France and the UK, more than 75 per cent felt this way.

Additionally, almost 40 per cent of consumers globally admitted they would not take the time to look for their preferred payment method at checkout, and would drop out of a purchase as a result. This sentiment is particularly strong in Japan, where

[4]'The Online Payment Journey', Worldpay, 2015.

62 per cent of consumers would not spend time seeking their preferred payment method if it was not clearly indicated.

Put simply, consumers want to know exactly how they can pay online and be assured the process will go smoothly. They do not want to have to search for information or choose a plan B scenario at checkout after a certain expectation was set on a retailer's homepage. Retailers should provide easily visible and consistent information throughout the buying process – from the homepage through to the confirmation email.

The world of online retail is extremely competitive. If you turn a customer away over a poor experience, including a declined payment, it's unlikely they will come back to shop with you again

> 'The world of online retail is extremely competitive. If you turn a customer away over a poor experience, including a declined payment, it's unlikely they will come back to shop with you again. Our ambition isn't just to grow as a company; it is to deliver the best online shopping experience for the people who use our website globally.'
>
> Steven McKiernan, financial controller, Missguided[5]

Adopting new APMs – what to keep in mind

Before integrating any new alternative payment methods, online retailers need to understand all the ways in which these differ from a standard global card scheme and ensure they can deliver on customers' high expectations for service regardless of which platform they choose.

Pricing – consumers expect to pay the same amount at checkout as the value that was indicated to them on a retailer's product pages. Merchants must, therefore, ensure the price and currency they debit a shopper for match the figure that customer has anticipated paying.

[5]'Missguided turns to Worldpay for Global Expansion', Worldpay, 2015.

User experience – many alternative payment methods redirect shoppers to a separate page to enter their personal details, occasionally placing a time limit on the process. Online retailers must clearly explain each stage of the payment process to customers so they know what to expect and are not confused or turned off when redirected to a third-party website.

Payment capture – for some APMs, the point at which a payment is authorised, and therefore at which funds are settled, comes later after a shopper confirms their purchase than for traditional card payments. As such, merchants must have a consistent and transparent practice in place when choosing at which stage to ship orders to customers.

Refunds – when using cards, refunds are automated in so much as a merchant simply can return a payment to the card used for the purchase. Not all APMs can handle automated refunds and, for those that do not, a bank transfer is required to give back the customer their money.

Fraud and chargebacks – in many cases, APMs result in fewer fraudulent transactions than card payments, as consumers often are required to provide more personal credentials at the time of payment. Whilst this certainly benefits retailers and shoppers alike, it also means customers should be made aware of why they are sharing more information up front so they are not turned off by the added requirement. Another benefit for merchants is that many APM providers do not honour chargebacks, therefore lowering risk. Again, shoppers should be made aware of these policies.

Recommendations

Choosing which payment methods to support in each market is a strategic exercise for retailers. It is neither time- or cost-efficient to simply support every payment method everywhere, nor is it desirable for consumers who may be overwhelmed by too much choice. Merchants not only need to establish their customers' preferences by region, they then need to compare the potential return on investment for each payment method available to select those that will help them achieve their local ambitions.

New payment methods also require new commercial arrangements, as acceptance fees often differ from interchange fees for credit and debit card transactions.

In addition, retailers must be tactical about how they process card payments in foreign markets. In the interest of speed and complexity, many companies will choose to process payments 'cross-border', outside the country they are selling in. However, there are usually – although not always – benefits to processing payments in the same country where a transaction has taken place. These include lower processing costs and higher acceptance rates, as payments processed across borders are more likely to be declined by issuers.

A retailer's ability to process payments locally depends on its operating model. For instance, to process payments domestically in Europe, a business needs a domestic entity in at least one EU nation. In addition to the cost of establishing a local entity, retailers should also weigh the associated tax and regulatory compliance issues for each market carefully before proceeding.

Once these elements have been addressed, retailers must then integrate the right APMs into their websites. This process can take from two months to two years, depending on the size and complexity of the site, the types of payment methods being added, and whether hosted payment pages are being used.

It is worth noting that merchants who use global payment processors, such as Worldpay, Elavon or Cybersource (versus going direct to each payment method supplier), or ecommerce business platforms like Demandware, Oracle, IBM, Hybris or Magento, often find it easier to switch on new payment methods, as these platforms come with pre-integrated payment processing functionality.

Shopper preferences continue to dictate the direction retail is headed in, both instore and online, and the changing way in which people pay for goods is, arguably, the most fundamental element of this shift. In countries everywhere, from China to Germany to Kenya, alternative payment methods have become, or are quickly becoming, more popular than card transaction and online merchants are taking note.

However, they must also be mindful of the many factors that dictate people's buying behaviour. A mixture of cultural, geographical and economic considerations combined with varying levels of internet and mobile access add up to different needs among different people in different places.

A modern ecommerce approach that allows merchants to address this level of diversity comes down to three things: making sure shoppers have a variety of options to choose from, ensuring they can pay the way they want to and providing them with an equally seamless purchasing journey, regardless of which payment method they use.

Recommended actions

- *Short term/quick win*

  Establish where you have the most international customers and research what payment options the market leaders in that region are offering their local customers to get an idea of what options you would like to offer.
- *Medium*

  Replace your current payment provider with one that can cater for your local markets more effectively.
- *Long term*

  Offer customers local language versions of your website for at least the most critical sections of your site, e.g. the checkout and payments page.

8.1 Payment checklist

For many online retailers, accepting payments is considered as an afterthought of the shopper journey. In fact, many opportunities exist to take advantage of the payment functionality in order to actively drive revenue. The key to this lies in data. In this section, I will provide a number of metrics and examples of best practices that merchants can adopt to optimise their payments, transforming them from a cost into a revenue-generator.

To get some real data, without disclosing the financial details of a single company, we looked at research undertaken into three different companies that all work with the same payment provider, Adyen. We will call this new entity the ecommerce organisation.

By merging data from these three merchants, we have an ecommerce organisation that is a US-based company with a global footprint and annual revenues of $1.5 billion, roughly half of which is from the US market. Payments accepted by this merchant include debit and credit cards (accounting for around 60 per cent of transactions overall) and a wide range of local payment methods, such as e-wallets, online banking, cash-based methods, and so on (accounting for the remaining 40 per cent). Furthermore, the ecommerce is rapidly expanding and intends to grow market share in the domestic market as well in new markets internationally.

General online retail strategy

The ecommerce organisation is growing rapidly, and has an expansion plan that includes North America, Europe, Latin America and Asia. In order to fuel its growth and increase its efficiency and profitability, the organisation has the following payments-related objectives:

- To optimise its payments and grow revenue.
- To optimise its approach to fraud management. Fraud, in particular, was an issue in areas outside of the USA, with chargeback rates often double those of domestic chargeback rates.

In order to achieve these goals, it has adopted a data-driven approach, focusing on six payments areas in order to evaluate its performance and drive optimisation.

1. Payment method conversion

The right mix of payment methods will drive conversions at checkout.

In most English-speaking markets, credit cards are the most popular ways to make online purchases. But, across Europe, Asia and Latin America, they are far less popular. And, in fact, large sections of potential shoppers in these markets may not even possess an international credit card. Instead, they use a range of e-wallet, online banking and even cash-based payment methods such as Alipay (around 50 per cent of online purchases in China), iDEAL (60 per cent of online transactions in the Netherlands) or Boleto Bançario (15 per cent of online transactions in Brazil).

To reach local shoppers, the ecommerce organisation offers over 40 payment methods around the world besides the major credit cards, including e-wallets and cash-based payment methods in markets where cash still accounts for the vast majority of transaction volume. This is helping it launch fast and provide a localised experience to a critical mass of global consumers – crucial to maintain its hyper-growth curve into new markets.

However, one thing to note is that, somewhat counter-intuitively, offering too many payment methods may also have a negative impact on conversion, for several reasons. A long list of payment methods can create confusion for the shopper, leading them to drop off at the checkout. Also, some payment methods may work well on desktop, but not on mobile. And, finally, some payment methods are more popular for certain industries.

So, rather than simply adding all popular local payment methods for each new market, a better approach is to A/B test a mix of payment methods for the market and, in some cases, even per device type, product line, and so on.

2. False positives

Risk settings must be carefully managed to avoid blocking legitimate customers.

Once a shopper types in and confirms their purchase, the payment journey is far from over – in fact, it has just begun. The next thing that happens is that the payment is captured by the gateway and sent through a security screening – an important part in the fight against online fraud.

For many merchants, stopping fraud is a priority, particularly as they expand to new markets and add potentially risky new payment methods, and the temptation to raise risk checks in these situations can be strong. However, simply raising risk check thresholds can also lead to an increase in 'false positives'

– legitimate transactions that are wrongly identified as fraud and blocked, leading to frustrated shoppers as well as lost conversions.

To combat false positives, many merchants have a manual review process in place. But, inevitably, a significant portion of false positives will not be identified as genuine and, thus, will be a lost conversion for the merchant. Further, for rapidly expanding companies like the ecommerce organisation, the workload associated with manually reviewing every high-risk transaction means a significant drain on resources.

To reduce false positives and minimise manual reviews, the ecommerce organisation adopted a flexible and iterative approach to risk rules, collecting, linking and checking data to implement a sophisticated approach to stopping high-risk transactions. This is an ongoing process – it constantly monitors and fine-tunes these rules based on a wealth of accumulated data making incremental improvements in order to optimise the balance between stopping fraudulent transactions and approving legitimate transactions.

With this approach, the ecommerce organisation saw an overall reduction of fraud by 27 per cent, and it conversely saw a decrease in write-off loss attributed to fraud. Overall savings in this area were nearly $6 million for the three-year study period.

3. 3D Secure impact on conversion

Dynamic 3D Secure will boost authorisations without damaging conversions.

A potentially valuable part of risk management process is 3D Secure, which is an additional security filter aimed at verifying the identity of the shopper.

3D Secure has been dismissed by many as a 'conversion-killer', because it interrupts the payment flow to redirect the customer to an external site that they may not know. This perception has been strengthened by the fact that, over time, many merchants have taken an on/off approach – meaning they either route all transactions through 3D Secure or none at all.

However, there are, in fact, multiple factors that impact the success or otherwise of 3D Secure and, in fact, implementing it on certain transactions can have a positive impact on conversion. These factors include market, card type, order amount, day or time of order, and so on.

With this in mind, the ecommerce organisation took a rules-based approach to 3D Secure, applying it selectively to transactions for which data showed it would have a net positive impact. This included specific markets (including the UK, France, Hungary and Sweden), and other risk and card characteristics to secure the optimal balance between user experience and the reduction in chargebacks. As a result, the organisation saw revenue gains equating to nearly $2.5 million over three years.

It should also be noted that the landscape for 3D Secure is changing dramatically. More and more issuing banks are using risk-based authentication, and the card schemes are leading initiatives to improve the experience for consumers. This means that merchants need not fear the 'conversion killer' as much as before. Further, applying 3D Secure shifts the liability for the transaction to the issuer, meaning merchants are not responsible if the transaction results in a chargeback.

4. Authorisation rates

One-third of declined transactions could be converted into approvals.

A significant pain point for ecommerce businesses is that, on average, 15 per cent of payments are rejected by the issuing bank (that is, the bank that issues the shopper's card). Whilst the majority are refused for legitimate reasons, such as fraud, there remains a proportion which are declined simply because the format of the transaction does not match up with what the issuing bank expects. This, therefore, presents another opportunity to optimise, measure and incrementally improve on payments success rates.

In order to grow its revenue, the ecommerce organisation identified potential areas for improvement by comparing authorisation rates between issuing banks and implemented logic to route transactions through to banks that give the highest authorisation rates. On a small subset of low-performing cards, this approach resulted in an authorisation uplift of 39 per cent and, overall, a 1.5 per cent transaction approval improvement, resulting in an overall revenue uplift of $1.5 million over a three-year analysis period.

5. Local versus cross-border acquiring networks

Dynamically routing payments via different networks will drive authorisation rates.

An acquirer is a financial institution that processes credit or debit card payments and routes them to the issuing bank. Acquiring networks are either international or local. Deciding the network through which to route the payment can have a significant impact on the response of the issuing bank.

In some countries, for example, routing the transaction via a local network will deliver higher authorisation rates. This is the case in Brazil, where a local acquiring network can result in an authorisation rate increase of over 30 per cent, and in India, where the impact can be as much as 40 per cent.

It is worth noting, however, that, whilst local networks often generate the highest authorisation rates, it is not always the most practical option. Sometimes, a local entity is required in order to make use of local network, which has other implications around cost and logistics.

When evaluating cross-border or local acquiring, merchants should consider the following:

- Does the customer have to pay tax on cross-border transactions?
- Is there a need to set up a local entity in order to process via local networks?
- What is the difference in interchange fees for domestic and cross-border transactions?

In the case of the ecommerce organisation, it used real-time data to evaluate market conditions and dynamically routed transactions via whichever network would produce the best possible result at that moment. The result was an authorisation rate increase of 1.5 per cent, leading to a revenue uplift of $1,463,071 over a three-year period.

Businesses operating in multiple countries are likely to find that a mix of both local and cross-border acquiring will generate the best results overall. This all depends on specific merchant business models and the markets in which they operate.

6. Chargeback rates

Prevention is better than cure.

A chargeback occurs when a customer disputes a transaction and secures a refund from the merchant's bank. The most common reason for this is fraud.

The impact on the merchant is threefold. Not only is the payment lost, but the merchant must pay the associated fees and runs the risk of being black-listed by issuing banks, thereby impacting future authorisation rates.

The ecommerce organisation found itself faced with a fraud rate of 3 per cent when operating outside the USA. This was because credit card verification code validation and address verification are not as widely used in other regions. Therefore, other measures were needed in order to bring down the rate of fraud.

As with most things, when it comes to chargebacks, prevention is better than cure. Merchants should devise means of stopping chargebacks before they occur. This can be done by identifying the attributes of a high-risk transaction and either declining it on the spot, routing it via an additional security filter like 3D Secure, or holding it for manual review.

What these attributes are will depend on numerous factors, including the merchant's business model, and industry. It is important, therefore, to benchmark against similar businesses. Here are some metrics to consider:

- *Average transaction value:* merchants should be wary of transactions that have a value that is significantly above average.
- *Transaction velocity:* a series of rapid transactions made using the same data elements, such as card number, email or delivery address may indicate a fraudster testing one or a number of cards.
- *BIN (bank identifying number):* in some cases, merchants have identified a higher rate of fraudulent chargebacks from specific banks.
- *Countries:* some countries are known to have higher rates of card fraud and merchants can reduce chargebacks by routing transactions from these countries via additional security filters.

Of course, as fraud evolves, new methods are developed to circumnavigate risk settings and merchants must, somehow, keep pace. It is recommended, therefore, that merchants use their own payment data to establish rules, monitor trends and adapt settings accordingly. In the case of the ecommerce organisation, it made use of advanced machine learning and multiple data sources to identify and track fraudsters, resulting in a chargeback reduction of 27 per cent.

Recommended actions

Payments are an untapped resource of additional revenue. To unlock this, merchants should:

- identify the key drop-off points in a payment journey.

  Did the customer abandon the payment process halfway through? Was the payment blocked by risk settings that set too high? Or was the payment wrongly declined by the issuer? Understanding why the payment failed is half the battle won.
- make incremental changes based on the findings.

  Once problem areas have been identified, merchants can make adjustments. This might include adding or removing payment methods, altering risk settings or routing transactions via a different acquiring network.
- measure the outcome and continuously grow revenue through incremental changes.

  Of course, nothing stands still. Regulations change, new payment methods emerge and fraud evolves. In order to stay ahead of the game, merchants must constantly measure and evaluate their settings to ensure their processes remain optimal.

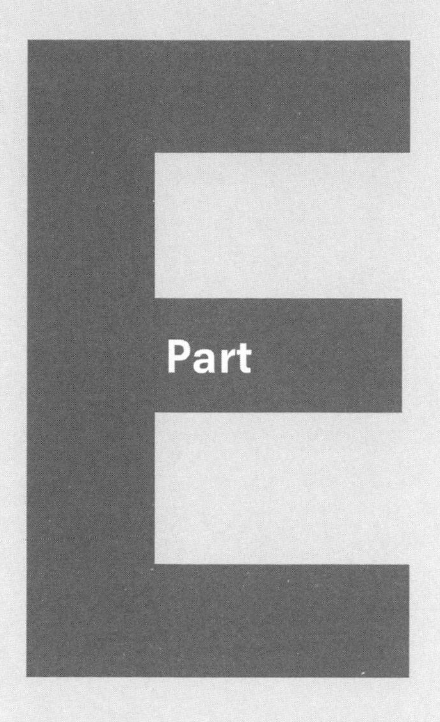

Key opportunities in the coming year

9. Expert commentary: expanding internationally

You are successful in your own territory. You have honed your product or service and know how to make your business a success domestically. Now is the time to expand abroad.

The scale is exciting; get this right and you can turbo-charge your business. So, how do you make this a success?

I met up with Parry Jones, MD of print media at The Specialist Works, to discuss international expansion. Jones specialises in helping ecommerce businesses with just that. The Specialist Works is a customer acquisition media and advertising agency that employs 140 staff with clients such as Photobox, Boohoo and The White Company. For more information about The Specialist Works, visit: www.thespecialistworks.com.

First, you must put customer acquisition at the heart of your decision where to launch. A quick Google search will tell you the scale of each country, both in terms of population and ecommerce penetration (check out www.top500guide.com).

Shipping, storage and local law are key

And understanding the demand for what you offer must be the number one factor. However, none of this tells you how easily you will acquire customers.

Start by looking at where you have been successful domestically:

- How scalable are these channels in the new territory?
- Do your (new) competitors use these channels?

- How do costs differ from what you pay at home?
- How does response rate change by country?

Take the USA and UK, for example. Both are similar in having advanced ecommerce scale (the UK is the third biggest ecommerce territory, yet has only the twenty-first highest population). Media pricing in the USA and UK is relatively low, but so are response rates. You may think you are getting a 'good deal' whilst paying above market pricing. But not all channels within a country are priced the same. German print-media costs a lot more than in the USA and UK, whilst TV advertising costs about the same as in these countries. Make sure you use a media partner that understands these nuances.

Understand your enemy

Each territory comes with its own set of invaluable tools to better understand the competition. Read your competitors' accounts, understand where they are advertising, (roughly) how much they spend and even the creative they use.

Of course, do things better. But learning what has fuelled competitor growth can inspire your own. Plus, they know what works and what does not in their local market.

Localise your proposition

Retain what makes your business successful whilst ensuring it appeals to each new territory. McDonald's famously mixes global and local marketing strategies. Ask yourself why domestic customers buy from you and whether international customers think the same.

Graze and Hello Fresh needed to understand US food culture when expanding to the USA. They have mixed a tried and tested model, with local knowledge, to maximise launch success.

You must understand the buying habits of any new territory. Ecommerce is driving an increasing 'coupon-culture' across Europe; but this is nowhere near as developed as the USA. Use local, direct response specialist creatives to get this right.

Decide whether your national identity is a help or hindrance

French fashion brand Petit Bateau is sold in boutique fashion stores in London; hop over the Channel, and they are stocked in supermarkets. They have taken advantage of how British people perceive French fashion, targeting a different audience in the UK.

Whether you play on your national identity or not, *you must produce local language advertising*. People engage with advertisements in their first language.

Colloquialisms mean that you should use local experts (Americans, Australians and Brits do not speak the same language).

So, which media channels should you prioritise?

Search, social and affiliates can be turned on quickly and are relatively low risk. Transactional inserts work in core ecommerce countries. Use TV when you are ready to scale your business seriously.

Get all these things right, nail your creative and proposition, and you are well on your way to expanding successfully!

9.1 Deep dive: selling to Chinese consumers

I met up with the team at Global-E, a provider of cross-border retailer solutions. They enable retailers to transact locally with customers in more than 200 destinations worldwide, offering a localised, international customer experience. We reviewed the current state of the market through a study of the UK's top 150 online retailers. Using the research findings, we are here making recommendations for UK retailers looking to break into the lucrative Chinese ecommerce market to increase their international revenue.

Key findings

- Today, more than two-thirds (71 per cent) of large UK etailers ship internationally and over half (55 per cent) ship to China. However, the quality of the shopping experience offered to shoppers overseas varies wildly.
- Just over a quarter (26 per cent) of retailers that ship to China offer shoppers the ability to pay in yuan and present prices in local currency.
- Furthermore, only 22 per cent of retailers that ship to China offer Chinese shoppers the ability to pay using local payment methods.

Introduction

China is undergoing massive change. Home to 1.355 billion people, China has now overtaken the USA as both the world's biggest economy and the world's largest ecommerce market.

In spite of China's economic growth slowing in recent times, the country's ecommerce market is continuing to expand at record pace. This year alone, the Chinese are set to spend more than $911 billion online; an increase of 35 per cent or $239 billion on 2015.

> Within the next two years, China's ecommerce market will top $1 trillion, making it bigger than the ecommerce markets of the USA, UK, Japan, Germany and France combined

Within the next two years, China's ecommerce market will top $1 trillion, making it bigger than the ecommerce markets of the USA, UK, Japan, Germany and France combined.

Online shopping in China is largely being fuelled by greater internet and smartphone penetration, an expanding middle class with higher disposable income and greater consumer confidence, with over half of Chinese internet users having now made a purchase on the web.

Rising demand for foreign products is also spurring growth, with China tipped to become the world's largest cross-border ecommerce market by 2020. Driven, in part, by fears over the scale of counterfeit or poor quality goods on sale domestically, China's rapidly growing ecommerce market offers great opportunity for trusted international retailers to grow sales.

However, with online retailers in China improving logistics and mobile platforms, and leading players such as Alibaba launching initiatives to combat counterfeiting, UK retailers must act quickly if they are to encourage preference for their own products and ecommerce services.

So, what can UK retailers do to win over shoppers in China?

Market trend: counterfeiting fears drive international ecommerce sales, as shoppers seek out authentic goods

Counterfeiting remains a major problem in China. The country is reported to be responsible for the production of more than 70 per cent of all counterfeit goods globally, according to the UN Office on Drugs and Crime, and ecommerce has presented an easy target for counterfeiters to exploit.

Figures released by state news agency Xinhua in 2015 revealed that more than 40 per cent of goods sold online in China in 2014 were fake or of bad quality. In the same year, it is estimated that Chinese shoppers may have spent as much as $177 billion online on counterfeit or inferior products.

Furthermore, China has been hit by a number of high-profile counterfeiting scandals in recent years. In particular, 2008's milk scandal, which saw more than 300,000 babies drink infant formula contaminated with melamine, sent shockwaves around the world. Whilst more recently, the discovery of more than 20 fake Apple stores and a fake Apple factory in China has highlighted the scale of the problem that counterfeiting presents in the country today.

Chinese marketplace Alibaba has also been criticised by the US trade office for enabling the sale of counterfeit goods in

China. The marketplace is reported to have spent more than $160 million to combat the sale of fake goods, with founder Jack Ma previously referring to the problem as 'a cancer that we have to deal with'.

Faced with such uncertainty when shopping both online and offline, a growing number of Chinese people are choosing to buy from online retailers based outside the country, that are perceived as being more trustworthy.

A recent report commissioned by PayPal reveals that 52 per cent of Chinese internet users plan to make purchases from international etailers this year, with retailers in the USA, Hong Kong and the UK among the most likely to benefit. The top three drivers behind this trend are desire for greater quality, authenticity and value.

State of the market: UK retailers failing to offer fully localised shopping experience for Chinese shoppers

Today, more than two-thirds (71 per cent) of large UK etailers ship internationally and over half (55 per cent) ship to China. However, the quality of the shopping experience offered to shoppers overseas varies wildly.

A study of the UK's top 150 online retailers, commissioned by Global-e in January 2016, found that just 1 in 10 (10 per cent) retailers that ship to China offer shoppers a Mandarin-language shopping experience. Since the majority of people living in China do not speak English fluently, shoppers are likely to feel unconfident about making a purchase if they are expected to use and translate an English-language checkout.

Just over a quarter (26 per cent) of retailers that ship to China offer shoppers the ability to pay in yuan and present prices in local currency. In the rest of the cases, retailers are leaving shoppers in China to estimate for themselves how much products will cost to buy, which means shoppers could be hit by sudden currency exchange fluctuations or fees from their bank.

Furthermore, only 22 per cent of retailers that ship to China offer Chinese shoppers the ability to pay using local payment methods, such as e-wallets and bank transfers (like Alipay or Tenpay), which account for more than 80 per cent of ecommerce payments in China. Of retailers that do accept Chinese payment methods, 42 per cent offer a single option, barring some prospective customers from making a purchase.

Whilst more than 40 per cent of Chinese shoppers prefer to pre-pay all taxes and duties in advance, when making a purchase online, according to Global-e customer data from 2015, very few UK retailers currently offer this functionality. Almost all (98 per cent) retailers that ship to China do not provide full duties calculations and pre-payment, which means that shoppers may be stung by unexpected charges or taxes.

Although more Chinese shoppers are open to shopping from international etail websites, many still have concerns. The biggest areas of concern are identity theft or fraud (54 per cent), currency exchange fluctuations (52 per cent), language issues (50 per cent) and shipping and delivery (47 per cent), according to research published by WorldPay. Merchants that will be able to address these concerns and give shoppers a seamless localised experience will be able to boost conversion rates.

Retailers must take a localised, customer-centric approach to tackle China's ecommerce market

As the world's biggest ecommerce market, and one of the fastest-growing markets worldwide for cross-border ecommerce, China offers UK retailers a great opportunity to grow sales internationally. However, the majority of retailers are failing to exploit this market fully.

Although more than half (55 per cent) of large online stores in the UK offer shipping to China, most retailers are falling short of Chinese shoppers' expectations by failing to offer pricing in Chinese yuan, adjusted content, Chinese local payment methods or import tax calculation, which can all help to improve the shopping experience and make shoppers feel more confident about making a purchase online.

To improve the experience and grow sales in China, retailers cannot afford to offer shoppers a second-rate experience. Unexpected delays to delivery or surprise fees for tax or shipping can quickly sour a great online experience, whilst failing to localise the online store can make shoppers nervous.

To make the most out of cross-border ecommerce opportunities in China, retailers should:

- *improve the experience of Chinese shoppers.* The first rule of international trade is that, in order to be successful, customers must enjoy the same experience, regardless of where they are in the world. Retailers should offer shoppers in China the same high-quality experience that shoppers in the UK and elsewhere expect to receive.
- *offer multiple shipping options at reasonable rates.* To give Chinese shoppers the confidence to buy, retailers must offer greater choice as well as competitive prices. This is especially critical in China where clearance processes can be very lengthy for non-experienced carriers. Moreover, it is important to have a simple and transparent returns process in place so, if something goes wrong, shoppers will be confident that it will be resolved quickly and easily.
- *display prices in Chinese yuan.* There are few things more off-putting than exchange rate uncertainty when buying from a retailer in another country, and this is particularly disconcerting at times of high currency fluctuation. Retailers should present shoppers in China with prices in the local currency, so that shoppers can feel confident about how much they are paying.
- *try to put the customer's mind at ease.* Most shoppers in China expect and prefer to pre-pay customs charges or handling fees when shopping online, so retailers should avoid any potential for nasty surprises by being upfront about these charges and offering pre-payment.

With ecommerce sales in China set to exceed $1 trillion next year, retailers must pay more attention to China in the years ahead. However, delivering a localised shopping experience does not have to require a dedicated Chinese website or months spent negotiating with the local supply chain. With a specialist partner, retailers can start tapping into China's ecommerce market in a relatively short timeframe and without a huge investment.

9.2 Case study: Vivobarefoot

Barefoot shoe manufacturer Vivobarefoot looks at replacing expensive distributor model in favour of direct-to-consumer sales strategy to support greater volumes.

By appointing three new specialist third-party providers in the areas of warehousing/logistics, payments and customer service, Vivobarefoot is able to support future growth of esales both in the UK and globally. By centrally locating everything in the UK, there is no need to duplicate facilities in individual countries and there is less time and expense in management and training. This approach allows the shoemaker to enter new markets easily, effortlessly and cost-effectively.

Key findings

- Ninety per cent increase in sales conversion due to the availability of multi-lingual speakers.
- Three hundred per cent increase in overall unit esales.
- The number of pairs of shoes sold on the company's own website and shops will increase from 70,000 this year to 311,000 in 2020.

Interviewee

Paul Walker is head of ecommerce at barefoot shoemaker Vivobarefoot, where he is responsible for the company's online global sales strategy. Previously, Walker worked at Carphone Warehouse creating website propositions and modelling and, prior to that, he was responsible for merchandising and esales of computing goods at Dixons.

About Vivobarefoot

Established in 2003, Vivobarefoot (www.vivobarefoot.com) makes what the company describes as the best barefoot shoes in the world. Created without compromise around its patented Pure Barefoot Technology, its products are the epitome of ancient wisdom with modern technology; designed in London, with a sole for every terrain, to live your life barefoot. The business was founded by two cousins Galahad and Asher Clark who are from seven generations of shoemakers.

The culmination of five years' research and development saw the release of the first Vivobarefoot shoe in 2004 – the first minimalist shoe with a patented, ultra-thin puncture-resistant sole. The shoe was designed to offer both maximum sensory feedback and maximum protection. Whilst growing its ecommerce business, the company also currently has 20 stores dedicated to the Vivobarefoot brand, with plans to double its global footprint in the next five years.

General online retail strategy

Over the last two years, Vivobarefoot has been on a journey to move away from a traditional, multi-tiered distribution model towards selling more directly to the consumer, combined with an underlying mission to become one of the most influential shoe brands in the world.

Previously, the shoemaker relied on an expensive and complex supply chain that included several suppliers and the transportation of goods between different third parties before finally reaching the end customer. The barefoot shoe specialist made the decision to simplify the way it sold its classic style of footwear that stands out anywhere in the world, by adopting a direct sales approach based via its ecommerce platform that serves a range of key markets, including the UK, Europe and USA.

The philosophy behind its direct sales strategy was to reduce the costs and to help them to 'sell the brand' of Vivobarefoot. The result of this 'personalised' brand experience would, in turn, sell the shoes themselves. To make this happen, the company completely redesigned its website so it was easy to navigate and also worked on simplifying its brand messages. Part of the branding was to appeal to what the company refers to as 'healthanistas' or people that are devoted to leading healthy lifestyles, such as yoga and running. This is also being achieved by targeting customers who engage with complementary brands through affinity marketing. In addition, Vivobarefoot recognised the importance of personalising the brand experience, which represented its next major challenge.

To help achieve this degree of personalised contact, all website visitors and prospects, whether new or existing customers, will be presented, with the aid of 'programmatics', tailored marketing messages and adverts that are unique to them and are based on buyer or search history. Similar to 're-marketing', programmatics goes one step further in that it replaces standard messaging with a customer's particular preferences unique to them.

With a growing community of 90,000 online followers, the company will also be exploring how it can optimise social media buying through the likes of Instagram, Facebook and Twitter.

Since 2014, the company has increased its online sales from 10,000 to 70,000 pairs of shoes per year. To fund its future global growth, in March 2016, Vivobarefoot launched its first crowd-funding initiative via Crowdcube to raise £750,000. Over the next four years, the company will focus on growing its ecommerce from 30 per cent to 60 per cent, by launching an updated brand experience website with enhanced functionality as well as 15 local language sites with multi-currency options. This identical experience will be backed up within its growing number of offline stores.

The Case

The problem

Faced with increasing online demand for its shoes across all its ecommerce sites in both the USA and Europe, Vivobarefoot decided that it needed to review its current fulfilment strategy so that it was better prepared to handle the growth potential that would be made possible through its direct-to-consumer sales model.

Head of ecommerce for Vivobarefoot, Paul Walker explains, 'Previously, we had a single supplier that handled customer service, payments and warehousing respectively. However, as online sales rocketed – 116 per cent growth from 2013–14 and 300 per cent growth from 2014–15 with further growth projected from 2015–16, we realised that we needed a greater number of external resources that were specialists in key areas that would be able to support the increase in volumes at a competitive price point.

▶

'We therefore wanted to find three UK-based partners that were specialists in customer service, payments and warehousing/distribution. In particular, the customer service partner would need to have experience of etailing already and, in particular, the shoe market. They also needed to have the resources to provide multi-channel (including social media) and multi-lingual native speakers for the USA and European countries, such as Portugal, Spain, Italy, France and the Netherlands.'

The background

According to Walker, the company addressed each supplier relationship in turn, but the overriding philosophy was to find partners that already had experience in their particular sectors as well as sufficient resources to scale in line with Vivobarefoot's own expansion. It was also essential that each partner would have the ability to operate on a cross-border basis, allowing the company to expand internationally, with minimal barriers.

The logistics/distribution partner was relatively simple, as they decided to go with an established ecommerce warehousing and logistics specialist PNC Global Logistics Ltd (PNC) in Birmingham, who already provided wholesale fulfilment and freight fowarding for Vivobarefoot. PNC already had facilities set up for other online brands, such as Rapha and Penfield, allowing Vivobarefoot to take advantage of their economies of scale and their understanding of a business model that mirrored its own. The online payments side of the business was also straightforward, with an agreement made with Sage to manage all etransactions globally, supported by PayPal.

For the customer services partner, this was slightly more complex as there were more providers to choose from, dependent on size, experience and location.

The company eventually selected outsourced customer contact centre Ventrica (www.ventrica.co.uk) for a number of reasons. 'Firstly,' says Walker, 'We felt that they had a genuine interest in our brand and product and we wouldn't just be another account to them. They already had experience of another shoe manufacturer and this was really important, as we require an exceptional level of knowledge across our extensive product range. We offer a range of barefoot shoes and, although they are fundamentally the same (barefoot!), there are, at any one time, between 50 and 60 different styles that differ based on the environment and terrain they are used in, in order that we can offer a shoe for all occasions – from mountains to oceans, with everything in-between, so there are subtle differences.' After visiting the supplier's team and their operation, Vivobarefoot was convinced they had the capability to support its growth and plans for the future.

According to Walker, Vivobarefoot has a policy of working with specialist third parties that share the same values and aspirations as themselves. 'What all the suppliers we picked had in common was that they genuinely showed that they wanted to work with us as a brand, and we could see that there would be mutual ongoing benefits for both parties as we grew. We believe this is critical as we wanted to be able to reward our partners and help them to share in our success over the long term.'

The fact that all suppliers were UK-based was also driven by the company's strategy of centralisation and simplification that would make all relationships easier and more cost-effective to manage, without also having the additional expense of setting up and duplicating supplier partnerships in every country.

The solution

The transition from a distribution to a direct sales channel was fairly seamless. There was a pure recognition within the business that, if it wanted to be able to reach more customers via ecommerce, then it would need to introduce new processes, infrastructure and services that would allow the company to grow rapidly. To achieve this goal it was clear that it had

▶

outgrown its current supplier who completely understood that the company needed to split the provision of its warehouse/ logistics, payments and service. Once they had made this decision, the migration to the new partners was very smooth.

The new warehousing and logistics facility was up and running within three months and the payment gateway was rolled out within weeks of initial contact. In parallel, after an intensive training course, the outsourced customer service provider began working for Vivobarefoot in 2014, in readiness for the seasonal peaks of Black Friday and Cyber Monday. Walker says, 'As with any ecommerce operation, our online business is subject to peaks and troughs through the year.

'When we first started the relationship, we expected there to be a lot of unknowns in terms of resource requirements and that it would be a learning experience. But, when we have experienced spikes in demand, as a result of an advertising campaign or promotion, our outsourced contact centre partner has always responded well and has up-scaled its resources accordingly.'

Walker continues, 'We are also seeing many benefits from centralising everything in the UK. Not only does it reduce our costs, it also saves time in training, as we only have to do this once rather than replicate in multiple countries for both the English and international language teams, plus it helps with the consistency of our overall customer communications.'

Vivobarefoot is also proud to be a London-based brand, so it made perfect sense for it to have everything in the UK. The USA is a significant market for the company and Americans like to speak with someone with an English accent, so it reflects its core brand values.

Most of its buyers are affluent and often speak English. However, since the company introduced native speakers, sales conversions have gone through the roof. In particular, in Spain and Italy, like-for-like sales grew by a massive 90 per cent in the first month of trade. This shows the impressive return on investing in multi-lingual speakers who they also use for translations for additional website updates, like a promotion.

The importance of 24/7 and multimedia communications

The fact that the service team is available 24/7 helps to meet and surpass customers' expectations, as they wish to be able to call or communicate over other channels, such as email or Facebook, at any time of the day. The team currently consists of four full-time equivalents (FTEs) as well as having access to the supplier's bureau facility that is a dedicated team that works across a range of different brands.

The outsourced contact centre operates three overlapping shifts with three separate dedicated teams that are all Vivobarefoot experts and manage emails, Facebook correspondence, Feefo responses and other customer care queries relating to the shoe manufacturer's Amazon merchant account.

Introduction of PayPal has seen conversion rates soar

As part of the brand's mission to simplify the buying experience for its customers, the company has also recently introduced support for PayPal that saw a 30 per cent transfer of payments from Sage, with a marked increase in conversion rates.

Results

Since making the changes to reach more customers via ecommerce and the appointment of specialist partners based in the UK with capacity to support additional volumes, Vivobarefoot has seen some impressive results in terms of increased sales and customer satisfaction ratings.

By using tools such as Google Analytics and its ecommerce platform Divendo, data has been collected to measure such stats, as the average website conversion rate that has risen from 1.9 to 2.5 per cent (25 per cent above what is considered 'good' for other comparative brands) with regional variations, including the UK site performing at 3.6 per cent, peaking at over 7 per cent, and a 90 per cent increase in sales conversion

▶

due to the availability of multi-lingual speakers, better delivery options and solutions, and a 300 per cent increase in overall unit sales due to better availability of sales thanks to a centralised stock pool.

With its revised model, Vivobarefoot is now entering the Swedish and Danish markets and will also focus on expanding its presence in the USA, which accounts for 40 per cent of overall sales. Overall, shoe sales are estimated to rise from 273,000 pairs this year to 664,000 in 2020. Crucially, though, the number of pairs of shoes sold on the company's own website and shops will increase from 70,000 this year to 311,000 in 2020.

Critical success factors

For VivoBarefoot, there have been a number of critical success factors. One of these has been the careful choice and selection of suitable third-party suppliers that are all experts at what they do. Without this access to knowledge in the areas of warehousing, logistics, payment processing and service, it would have been more difficult for Vivobarefoot to compete on a level playing field with rivals or larger competitors. In parallel with Apple, the ability to control and reinforce the brand experience through its own Vivobarefoot stores has also been invaluable in building a loyal fan base of online customers.

Lessons learned

Walker recommends:

- Do not be afraid to try out different marketing techniques across different channels. You need to be prepared to take a few risks, as this will help you to develop in the long term.
- Always work with third parties where there is mutual trust, respect and, of course, a two-way beneficial relationship, otherwise it will not work in the long run.
- There is a lot of noise out there in terms of what retailers should be doing, but the key is to really focus on what is

best for your particular business, your brand and your customers' expectations. Find the right tools, platforms and providers that fit your specific objectives rather than just follow the crowd.

Recommendations

- Centralise your operations in one country and draw on the help of third-party suppliers that are experts in their field.
- Personalise the brand experience and use native-language speakers for different countries.
- Keep control of the brand experience, e.g. via own-branded stores.

10. Inventory management

Increased demand is good, but creates a few new challenges for retailers:

1. How to build the perfect online assortment.
2. How to best leverage online data
3. What steps to take to be able to forecast returns.
4. How to balance stock between online and stores.
5. How to ensure the supply chain can manage all delivery methods.

This section examines how retailers can operate better inventory management online through optimising their ecommerce operations. As consumer expectations continue to rise, sustainable online operations have never been so pivotal in order to retain custom and remain ahead of competitors.

I met up with Tommi Ylinen, vice-president of product at RELEX Solutions, to understand the challenges facing an expanding retailer from a logistics point of view. RELEX Solutions is Europe's fastest growing provider of integrated retail and supply chain planning solutions. For more information about RELEX, visit their website: www.relexsolutions.com.

Whilst the rules around demand forecasting and inventory management are dependent upon the chosen channel, the approach is very different from traditional retail in a number of ways.

Key findings

- Retailers need to be able to build any new sales route into their offering so that the customer experience remains seamless. This level of flexibility requires a retailer to not just master its data but also make it work for them so they can remain ahead of trends rather than continuing to chase after them.
- When retailers are able to operate the best possible assortment and inventory management system, they are in a position to offer customers the choices they expect.
- Creating a supply chain planning system that is prepared for all of the channels that a customer may choose is vital, and there are advanced planning and forecasting systems that make it possible to handle several overlapping forecasts for different purposes.

The advice

Forecasting, analytics, assortment and inventory management are just some of the challenges that can cause retailers a headache. And these challenges can be even harder for those operating in an online environment. But that need not be the case and improving inventory management in ecommerce operations can result in numerous rewards for both retailers and customers.

Forecasting and ordering can, of course, be more straightforward for a retailer who just sells online and delivers orders from its warehouse against online sales, with only having inventory for one channel and the need to forecast for one channel to factor in. The interesting point in this case is the ability to capture more data, thanks to all shopping taking place digitally via computers and, more frequently, via mobile devices. Companies can complement forecasting and assortment management through the introduction of page-view information from its website within its processes. Additionally, pricing is more impactful when it comes to online, as a digital shopper can compare prices between different sites and could decide to go elsewhere easily. Therefore, integrating such data into a forecasting system can be invaluable.

Retailers who have a presence both online and on the high street have to contend with a slightly more complex scenario. For them to be able to manage supply chains more accurately, channel-level forecasting is vital, as different channels have different sales patterns. The Christmas peak, for example, usually starts earlier for online sales. Although some retailers have separate warehouses for digital and physical stores, this eventually increases the total stock holding, as products can become double-stocked.

There are a number of advantages to having a single pool of stock and a virtual stock ring-fencing, which can help manage availability between channels.

It also makes sense for retailers offering both home delivery and click & collect to forecast these separately, as home delivery orders, for instance, can be fulfilled from a separate ecommerce delivery channel (DC), when click & collect orders could be delivered from the store stock. In order to have a complete overview of the split between the delivery models, both at product and store level, having good analytics is required.

This chapter explores best practice for retailers offering supply chain operations online and discusses in detail the five main challenges they face and how these can be overcome.

1. Building the perfect assortment

Inventory management gives a retailer the ability to offer its customers a vast array of items without having to store everything in its own warehouse. And this is true for a pure ecommerce retailer, as well as those within an omni-channel strategy.

Often, the majority of items in an online assortment are being ordered from a supplier once an order has been placed by a customer; that means that the constraints that apply to traditional inventory management are removed. This enables a retailer to offer an extensive range and a high volume of products on its website. Although the decision of what to stock still has to be made.

In the world of ecommerce, things can happen and change at the drop of a hat and it is imperative that quick decisions are made. As a result, retailers need to monitor their stock continuously to ensure it does not become outdated. The answer to how to identify a few thousand products from the millions of options, not only once but also constantly, boils down to a fact- and cost-based model.

Retailers need to consider the cost of holding items that are in stock in their warehouse, the obsolescence-risk and capital for each of them. Purchasing larger batches means less time spent per product in all phases of the ordering process, and retailers can take advantage of freight-free limits and cheaper means of transportation. In contrast, ordering only against customer orders means the cost of warehousing moves towards zero, but ordering costs increase significantly when a retailer sources in small batches that are needed urgently.

The advice is to compare both models and proceed with the cheaper one. This is because it makes sense to stock cheaper items that sell reasonably well and keep the expensive goods that, perhaps, do not sell so well at the supplier's warehouse.

It sounds easy, but it is collecting and retaining cost data and then running an efficient process that become the hard part.

When we talk about cost data, the aim should always be how to maintain continuous improvement. Focusing on a subset of products would be a good starting point; perhaps the most challenging or those that are integral to the bottom line. It is actually not that hard to design such an approach into a well thought out and automated system. The results can be seen relatively fast to improve the decision-making process.

2. Capitalising on data within the supply chain

Because so much data can be captured automatically online, retailers need to work out how they can best leverage the data within their supply chain planning and analytics to improve both inventory management and demand forecasting.

Unlike when customers visit a store, where it is near on impossible for a retailer to track where a customer goes and what items they look at, online makes it easier to monitor and record the customer journey. Product views, for example, are an important data source for a supply chain manager as they can be used within the supply chain planning and analytics tool.

Bringing viewing rates and click data into your supply chain can help identify those items that need to always be in stock. By reviewing such data, delivery times can be reduced, customer experience improved and savings made by the retailer.

Pricing plays an important role in any retailer's business. The online environment not only makes it easy for customers to see a competitor's price for the same item, but retailers too, who can take advantage by reflecting a competitor's price within their own planning system.

Analysing sales volumes against retail pricing enables retailers to understand in detail the price elasticity of different products, which makes for more precise pricing decisions and improved demand forecasting.

It can be, however, difficult to tie forecasting directly to price changes because there are a variety of factors that influence sales. An example could be not enough data on a single product or the times between sales increases being too short to be useful. Results that are achieved semi-automatically through exception-based workflows are typically best as they highlight big price changes.

3. Forecasting sales with or without returns?

Product returns are a big consideration to every retailer with an online operation, and return rates rise significantly when customers are not able to see, touch or try products. Furthermore, when customers are unable to return the item back to store and have to mail them, the cost of returns becomes relatively higher.

Monitoring returns data as well as sales data undoubtedly helps to identify problematic brands, categories or items.

A question that is asked often is whether forecasting should be based on sales, including returns. We advise forecasting them separately, rather than trying to forecast sales including returns. With sales forecasts, the aim is to maximise availability – a retailer needs to know what will be shipped and, most importantly, when, irrespective of whether it will be returned or not. Forecasting returns separately also provides a clear overview of the associated costs and requirements, for example, logistics capacity, which therefore aids both the operational and financial planning.

In order to take returns forecasting to the next level, retailers can calculate it in two ways: first, as a separate independent time series, and then as a percentage of sales – tracking the differences between the two provides an early indication of whether the rate of returns is rising too much. If the independent forecast clearly starts to surpass the percentage-driven forecast, it means the trend is pointing to the wrong way. Action should therefore be taken. A budget for returns can also be used as an alert threshold and can help make decisions about what levels of returns are acceptable within the retailer's overall financial and business plans.

If a retailer wants to really take advantage of the return forecast, it could be used to test different what-if scenarios. For instance: 'So, if I have an increasing rate of sales of X and an increasing rate of Y of returns, what would that mean in terms of DC operations in total, end-of-season stock, markdown-costs or total margin?' – having a system that manages all this information, and keeps it available, enables operations to be managed more efficiently and helps support strategic decisions affecting the retail offering and returns policy.

4. Avoiding a stock imbalance between online and stores

Many will recall that it was only 10 years ago that senior retail executives were still looking at the world of ecommerce and saying, in a few words: 'It's not for us.' Oh, how the world has definitely changed since! With the rise of ecommerce, many traditional retailers have established an online presence to complement core business operations.

The whole ecommerce concept is still relatively new, and volumes often are quite small, but can grow at pace. The supply chain strategies in response can vary somewhat. Retailers can, however, optimise inventory levels whilst maximising sales across all channels.

A number of companies have decided to operate separate warehouses for online and for stores. Often, this is due to physical constraints: such as the DC currently responsible for delivering to stores cannot hold more stock, or the picking process (single items for online and cases for stores) differs too much. When this occurs, it is relatively straightforward simply to calculate forecasts separately for both warehouses and replenish them separately. This is, of course, far from ideal from a stock-holding perspective. As a retailer has to buffer against uncertainty in both warehouses, they are likely to end up having notably higher stock in the business than they would with a single-stock-pool scenario. Plus, there is still a risk – particularly if their forecasting process is not precise enough – that one channel sells better than predicted and the other not so well, with the result that the retailer creates a stock imbalance: no stock for online and too much for its stores, or the reverse. This may lead to lost sales, mark-downs or costly shipments between warehouses.

5. Planning delivery methods more accurately

Quite often, when discussing ecommerce, the view is somewhat simplified by the assumption that the online world is synonymous with home delivery. These days, though, we know that simply is not the case. The more options a retailer offers to its customers, the more complex the supply chain becomes, and that complexity understandably has implications when planning.

From delivery to the door, picking up items from a store, a special collection point or even sometimes the warehouse – the delivery options for customers have increased. Thankfully, in most cases, a business's basic operations are unaffected by the choice of delivery method. A retailer sells items on its website and then delivers them to the customer from its warehouse with only the delivery address being different.

When it comes to the model of click & collect from store, adding collection information to each store's sales figures supports the supply chain, as it provides a better idea of the stores that are proving to be the most popular collection points for customers. Moreover, such data can be linked to assortment management. If a product is ordered regularly for collection from a particular store, then it could be added automatically to the store's range, saving on future delivery costs and protecting margins.

However, a slightly different approach to click & collect is needed in the e-grocery sector, because goods typically are picked from the store rather than from a warehouse. In such a model, a retailer would need to operate in a different way; combining click & collect orders with the store forecast as well as integrating the order and inventory management process to include online sales so as to ensure there is enough stock instore.

For a retailer to have a clear view of the value of the different delivery options to the business, it is beneficial to use the relevant data in its supply chain system to analyse and report on which delivery method is being used more and when. A business might, in some cases, take a step further and forecast different methods separately. This would make it possible to plan delivery operations more accurately and enables them to spot patterns and changes in the market faster.

Recommendation

Retailers need to be able to build any new sales route into their offering so that the customer experience remains seamless. This level of flexibility requires a retailer to not just master its data but also make it work for them so they can remain ahead of trends rather than continuously chasing after them. Those that are willing to ride the next wave of change will triumph over competitors, and there is simply no longer the option to not invest in ecommerce.

By using a cost-based model, a retailer can build a solid basis from which it will be easy to automate. When they bring online data into their supply chain, they can leverage product insight, control stock levels of important products and link click data to forecasts. Using delivery data can also help to analyse and report which delivery method is proving to be most popular amongst customers. In addition, it can monitor differences between independent and percentage of sales to highlight problematic items and test what-if scenarios.

It is recommended that retailers use one pool of stock to serve all channels in order to minimise stock holding and make sure stock is distributed equally across and sold at the best price.

Forecasting different channels separately produces more accurate results and vertical ring-fencing ensures all channels get their fair share of stock, allowing retailers to use different strategies in different situations, meaning they can prioritise channels as needed.

Overall, it is wise to build a supply chain planning system that will be able to handle anything a customer may throw at it. Today's advanced forecasting systems make it possible to manage several overlapping forecasts for different purposes. This means it is critical that retailers can identify the key needs and understand what actually drives the operational actions and prioritise those first.

With the growing demand for retailers to provide customers with an online option, it is important that they continue to optimise and enhance their assortment planning process. When they are able to operate the best possible assortment and inventory management system, they will be in position to offer customers the choices they expect.

11. Delivery delight

I met up with Andrew Hill, commercial director at Electio, a delivery management platform (for more information, visit: www.electiodelivers.com).Before Electio, Hill worked for Yodel and CollectPlus, developing delivery services for large retailers. Hill's claim to fame is being instrumental in the development and launch of the first Pick-Up Drop-Off (PUDO) network in the UK, a service that has transformed the etail delivery industry. I wanted to learn from him what retailers must think about when it comes to getting the delivery right.

Ensuring an on-brand experience end to end

Consumers are not as patient as they used to be. Alongside the increase in ecommerce spend, shoppers are becoming much more demanding of when and how they want their products delivered.

To thrive in the ever-competitive world of ecommerce, retailers must delight their customers at every stage of the journey – including delivery and beyond. Loyalty is hard won but easily lost and consumers judge brands on their whole experience, not just up to the point when they press the 'buy' button.

Delivery innovation

Fundamental to delighting customers is delivery. One of the biggest contributors to basket abandonment, delivery is key to converting sales. There has been some incredible innovation here recently – from a meteoric rise in click & collect, to nominated and same-day delivery and peer-to-peer offerings, essentially tapping into the sharing economy zeitgeist.

But whilst these options have helped the industry take huge strides in meeting customer expectations, they have to work to keep customers coming back. A buyer who has paid more for nominated day delivery is less likely to buy from you again if that product does not arrive on time.

Having relationships with multiple carriers means retailers can select the best carrier, depending on the criteria of the delivery. Matching the right service to the right carrier improves first time delivery success rates. Retailers with a delivery management strategy also have an advantage when it comes to offering more ambitious delivery options.

Trusting others to deliver

Retailers have had reason for concern over carrier performance in the past. Pictures of parcels flung over hedges or on the roof are quick to do the rounds on social media. Inconsistency in reporting is also a frustration. Whilst some carriers will tell you where a parcel is every step of the way, others won't. It's incredibly hard to standardise communications with customers without an accurate data feed from each carrier.

Capacity has also been a huge factor – with numerous carriers unable to scale up for the peaks that occur across the retail calendar. Rolling out alternative delivery options can lighten some of those loads. Click & collect can help tackle capacity issues, for example, whilst also being extremely convenient for customers. Pick-up points popping up in local stores, petrol stations or even car boots are also innovative ways of relieving the pressure on carriers whilst ticking the convenience box.

Too much choice?

We all want options, but too much choice can be confusing. Research we conducted around Black Friday 2015 revealed that delivery preferences vary considerably between different types of customers. Younger shoppers, in the 18–25 age group, for example, are prepared to wait longer for a delivery, if the price is right. For other buyers, the convenience of the delivery is valued as highly as the speed.

With a wealth of data at their fingertips, ecommerce companies should analyse their customers' behavioural patterns to tailor their delivery options. It is not the quantity of options available, it is knowing they are the right ones and being confident that they work.

Delivery is not the end

The final piece of the jigsaw, when it comes to delighting customers, is to help them return what they do not want. Many retailers make the mistake of thinking that the journey is over when the product arrives with the customer. This attitude will not wash with modern consumers.

In reality, you cannot be sure you have reached the end until one month after shipping as, under the new Consumer Rights Act, consumers can return their items to you in that timeframe.

Retailers need as many returns options as they do choices around delivery to make it as easy as possible for people to buy. More enlightened retailers see returns as a vital part of the sales process. A lack of options can put customers off making a purchase, so an investment in it in the short term will pay dividends over time.

The customer knows best

Consumer demands will continue to grow, so retailers must keep innovating. But you need to understand what that choice means – the age-old adage of 'know your customer'. From same day, nominated day, peer to peer, click & collect and standard 3–5 day deliveries – spend time understanding which options will work best for your customers. Then make sure your processes are watertight and you have the capacity to scale up or down, whatever the demand. Getting these right = delivery delight.

This is also echoed by Niklas Hedin, CEO at Centiro logistics software company (www.centiro.com). He notes that online delivery has become an area of considerable innovation over the last few years, with retailers and carriers taking part in a race to deliver products more quickly than ever before. For example, Shutl (https://shutl.com/uk/) has pioneered deliveries to customers within an hour, whilst Amazon has expanded its Prime same-day delivery service to new parts of the UK.

Give them an all-in-one solution

No customer would ever say having multiple delivery options is a bad thing, but retailers would be much better off giving them a single option that could be adapted, according to their individual requirements.

Research conducted last year by YouGov revealed that customers are increasingly seeking delivery *convenience* over just choice: 20 per cent of UK adults said for them it was most important to be able to change the delivery date or timeslot for an order after it has already been shipped. A further 7 per cent stated it was important that they were able to change the delivery destination after an order was placed. Such flexibility can ensure a positive customer experience, encourage loyalty and give you a bigger share of the marketing in the long run.

How to give customers what they want now the power has shifted

YouGov's research also highlighted the fact that consumers are choosing retailers based on the delivery and returns experience they offer. Indeed, delivery flexibility could be a key differentiator for smaller retailers as they try to appeal to customers who want to make changes to their deliveries on the fly.

But why would this appeal to the modern shopper? Customers now prioritise convenience and expect items to be delivered at a time and place that works for them. There is no reason why delivery networks cannot work the other way around: if a customer waiting for an order needs to leave the house, they should also be able to collect from a store they are passing. Greater flexibility can create new efficiencies when it comes to reverse logistics. If customers are, for example, able to receive and return items at the same time, not only will it prove more convenient for the customer, but you can also halve the cost of transportation.

11.1 Deep dive: packaging

I met up with the team at Duo UK to learn how packaging and delivery is an intrinsic part of the online customer's journey. The company manufacture and supply branded packaging to retailers like Tesco, JD Williams, JD Sports, etc. For more information about Duo UK, visit: www.duo-uk.co.uk.

In essence, businesses spend time developing their product offering, making significant investments in customer acquisition and retention, refining marketing messages and analysing the customer journey – but, according to a 2013 *Retail Week* report, goods not for resale (GNFR) account for 12–15 per cent of net sales and, despite postal packaging being an integral part of the customer experience, businesses are quick to try and reduce spend on packaging.

The four key elements of retail packaging design used to be: it must be seen, it must be engaging, it must communicate a message, and it must sell. However, the online shopping environment, unlike its retail store counterparts, is an extremely fertile atmosphere for customer anxiety, due to its inherent risks and dangers (e.g. privacy infringement, credit card fraud)[1] particularly for a customer shopping with an online retailer for the first time and, through the browse-to-buy journey, the customer will develop pre-purchase expectations.

For online businesses to build brand equity and customer loyalty, packaging and delivery must not be viewed as just GNFR, but as an opportunity to improve business performance. The pre-purchase expectation compared to the post-purchase performance[2] will have a significant influence on the customer's intention to repurchase. That decision will be made based on the first moment of truth – the moment the parcel lands in the customer's hands.

Rather than the packaging selection falling solely to procurement buyers, a multi-functional collaborative approach, which also includes representatives from CSR, logistics and warehouse and marketing, will ensure the final range performs functionally, in-budget, on brand and ethically. These are the brands that come

---

[1]Hakan Celik, (2016) 'Customer online shopping anxiety within the Unified Theory of Acceptance and Use Technology (UTAUT) framework', *Asia Pacific Journal of Marketing and Logistics*, 28:2, 278–307.

[2]Hu, M., Huang, F., Hou, H., Chen, Y. and Bulysheva L. 'Customized logistics service and online shoppers' satisfaction: an empirical study', *Internet Research*, 26:2, 484–97.

full circle, from simply wanting the cheapest and most practical packaging products to understanding how considered packaging, whilst an initial investment, is cost-effective in the long term and will deliver a greater competitive advantage.

Overview

Packaging is a valuable marketing tool. Treating this particular GNFR spend as an investment can improve business performance and increase customer satisfaction, leading to loyalty and repeat sales. The packaging that protects a product in transit plays an important role in the customer's journey and may be their first tangible experience of the online brand. Considering the purpose, design and branding of the postal packaging used has a significant influence on the customer's first moment of truth.

Key findings

- Goods not for resale account for 12–15 per cent of net sales.
- In 2015, online weekly spending rose to £753.3 million, as ecommerce grew 12 per cent.

The advice

1. GNFR – The hidden secret to a maximising profitability and long-term customer loyalty

For an ecommerce business, packaging to protect a product in transit from the warehouse to the delivery destination is an unavoidable spend, although this goods not for resale (GNFR) item has vast potential to maximise sales success and influence customer loyalty.

Converting this necessary spend into a business asset requires some clever planning and collaborative thinking. This starts at the end of the packing line, understanding the customer's average basket size per order and trend of items purchased together. This data will help you to create a range of packaging products to optimise the performance of your outbound deliveries. Having the correct size packaging range will:

- improve presentation;
- reduce outbound delivery costs (if using volumetric weight delivery option);
- save time in the pick and pack operation.

Many start-ups order a large quantity of one size of postal packaging to achieve economies of scale and use this single packaging item to pack all outbound orders. As a result, some orders may have to be split into two packages – adding additional delivery costs – or the packaging item may need to be reduced in size by folding to fit around the product, creating excess packaging waste, additional wrapping costs, i.e. tape, and a drastically reduced aesthetic.

Although it is true that a business will achieve a cheaper price per postal packaging item by buying in vast quantities, the waste material when folding, the extra time packaging, the additional delivery charges and negative customer perception come at a much greater cost than the initial investment in a suitable packaging range for an online business.

According to a *Retail Gazette* report released in February 2015, online weekly spending rose to £753.3 million, as ecommerce grew 12 per cent ('ONS Retail Sales' report for January 2015), indicating that further growth can be expected. To manage growth and attract repeat sales, product ranges will, naturally, change and evolve and so may a packaging range. Audit the packing line at least every six months to review if the current packaging range is still performing at its optimum.

2. The moment of truth

In marketing circles, the first moment of truth is the exact moment at which a customer is confronted with a product in real life so, for an online sale, that is when the parcel is in their hands.

At this moment, everything about the parcel will affect the customer's first moment of truth: the packaging design, the touch of the packaging, its durability and condition, the time of delivery and the packaging material used.

If the first moment of truth fails to deliver, customer satisfaction will drop and this will significantly affect post-purchase behaviour. A consumer buying online will form an expectation about the shopping experience on offer. Based on a brand's ecommerce website and the purchase process, this creates a 'perceived performance level'.

When the purchase is received, the customer's satisfaction will arise from discrepancies between pre-purchase expectations and post-purchase performance and influence future engagement with the brand.

Making packaging design work harder

Brands devote hours and hours to developing their product offering, making significant investments in customer acquisition and retention, refining marketing messages and analysing the customer journey – but, according to a 2013 *Retail Week* report, GNFR account for 12–15 per cent of net sales and, despite postal packaging being an integral part of the customer experience, businesses are quick to try and reduce spend on packaging.

In many instances, packaging selection falls solely to procurement buyers. However, the role packaging plays and its catalytic properties to improve profitability and customer satisfaction are important, so deciding on the specification should not be decided in isolation. A multi-functional collaborative approach, which also includes representatives from CSR, logistics and warehouse and marketing, will ensure the final range performs functionally, in-budget, on brand and ethically.

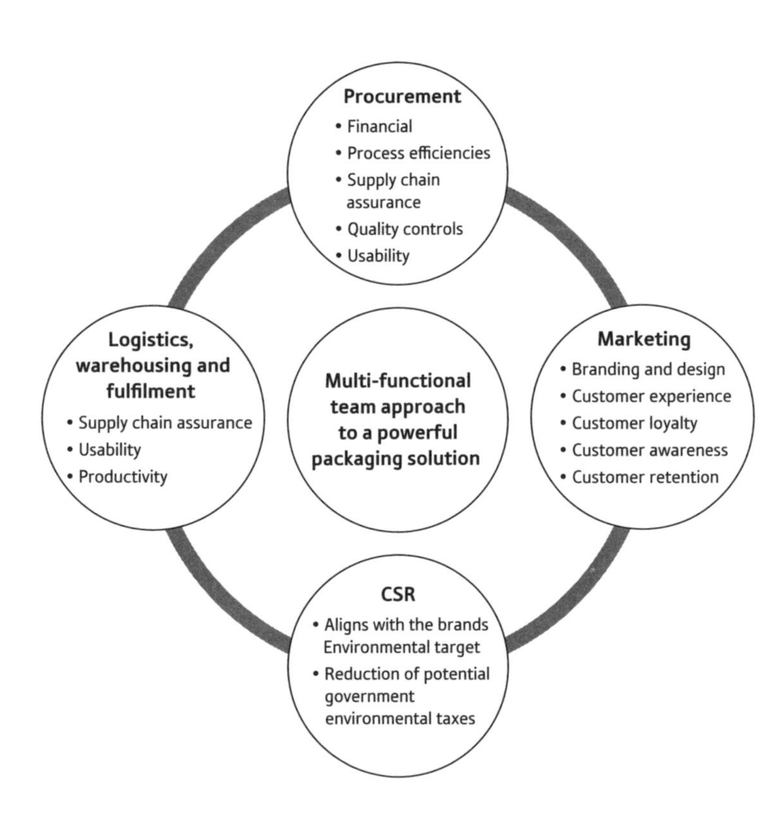

Customer convenience is driving demand for a wider range of delivery options and pick-up locations, resulting in an increased exposure of postal packaging outside the home; in retail stores with click & collect facilities, convenience stores and workplaces, for example.

Design enhancements, such as carry handles, twin glue lines and engaging branding that captures the attention of passers-by, as well as the shopper, has transformed postal packaging from practical protection to a powerful marketing tool that can increase brand awareness.

Including marketing messages in a packaging design is a cost-neutral option to achieve a good ROI from GNFR. Social media icons, calls-to-action, contact information and key messages are all regularly used by the likes of JD Williams and Amazon to engage with the customer before they have even touched their purchase, whether that is to encourage engagement with social media channels or inspire them to share a picture of their new purchase.

From new product launches to seasonal trends reflected in the colour of the postal packaging, gone are the days of the standard grey mailing bag or brown boxes; postal packaging designs have, and should, become more elaborate to capitalise on the increased visibility these bags now get.

The brands that come full circle, from simply wanting the cheapest and most practical packaging products to understanding how smart packaging, whilst an initial investment, is cost-effective in the long term, have a greater competitive advantage.

Recommendations

- Do not underestimate the importance of GNFR; it can build brand strength and profitability.
- Remember, the first moment of truth is in the customer's hands.
- Apply a multi-functional collaborative approach to your packaging design, to include representatives from procurement, CSR, logistics and warehouse and marketing, to ensure the final range performs functionally, in-budget, on brand and ethically.

An example

Claudio Lugli is a high-end Italian fashion brand that has gained a reputation for producing inspirational unique garments in strictly limited numbers. The brand is available in more than 250 physical stores across the UK and also sells online.

The company has been selling shirts in retail stores for more than 25 years and, in June 2014, it launched an online store. Selling online was new to the company and, in the first few months, it had less than 100 unique user visits per month. To emulate its success selling in stores, it knew it needed to a deliver the same luxury shopping experience online as customers receive instore.

Although new to selling online, it was imperative that the postal packaging Claudio Lugli chose reflected its core brand values. It realised very early on that, whilst you can buy cheaper mailing bags that do the same job in terms of practicalities (i.e. they get the product to the customer in a protective material), they do not deliver the same first impression.

The company believes that delivery presentation and packaging design has been a key component to the success of its online packaging sales – which now account for more than £30,000 of sales per month and more than 1,000 unique visits per month – but getting the right sized packaging range provided huge back-of-house benefits, such as increasing packing speeds and optimising delivery costs.

Even though Claudio Lugli has a low returns rate, it wanted to make this process as convenient as possible for the customer, should they need to return an item, so it added a second glue line to the mailing bag so that the same packaging can be used to return the item.

Any returns the company does receive always arrive in the outbound packaging, so it knows that its customers appreciate and use this additional feature as well as ensuring its goods are protected on the way back.

Enhancing customer satisfaction

For an online retailer, the customer journey does not stop when a product has been posted. It is the retailer's responsibility to ensure that the customer receives the product in perfect condition, the product meets pre-determined expectations and is delivered on time.

Packaging acts as a communication tool between the brand and the consumer and has the ability to influence satisfaction levels. Its function is to complete the practical 'protection' duty as well as act as an enabler to satisfy a customer's expectations of the brand.

Enhancements to the packaging specification to influence customer satisfaction levels could include:

- adding a twin glue line to double the uses of the packaging item and avoid the customer incurring additional costs to return their items; plus, it positions the brand as proactive at reducing waste;
- including a perforation on a mailing bag lip or between glue lines to make the package easy to open for the customer; it also preserves the packaging item so it can be re-used for returns;
- adding a handle to the postal packaging to enable the customer to carry their item with ease to their final destination;
- checking mailing bag opacity – remember, the package also includes your customer's invoice, so ensure opacity above 97 per cent to protect their data. This is achieved through darker coloured single-layer polythene films or, if you want to print on white, go for a co-extruded film white layer on the outside and a dark colour layer on the inside.

According to DUO UK, there has been a sharp rise in demand for postal packaging that features additional glue lines and carry handles, providing a multi-purpose ability for delivery, transport and re-use. This style of packaging can be more expensive than a standard mailing bag, as more raw material and additional processes are required. However, a satisfied customer carrying their product home easily together with the ability to use this for a return and being happy with their shopping experience, could result in a long-term loyal customer, optimising the return of investment in the GNFR item.

12. Beefing up security

The retailer is highly dependent on the security practices of the customer, leaving them over-exposed. But, it is possible to create a better balance, if the retailer takes proactive measures to secure customer data. We take a look at the changing data landscape and how the retailer can proactively manage this aspect of the customer relationship.

I sat down with the team at Pen Test Partners to find out how retailers should start thinking proactively about security threats. Pen Test Partners provides security testing, consultancy and training to businesses. To find out more about them, visit: www.pentestpartners.com.

Online retailing has seen a strange dichotomous relationship emerge between the seller and the customer. The retailer has more data at their disposal, can build a closer, longer-lasting relationship with the customer and can leverage this to create cross-sales opportunities. But the reverse side of this sees the retailer exposed and reliant upon the customer to protect that relationship by observing security best practice. Changes in customer buying habits, the emergence of the Internet of Things (IoT) and an imminent escalation in data generation means online retailers should act now to improve their data security practices. We will specifically look at:

- managing data over multiple touchpoints;
- the security impact of the IoT paradigm;
- responsible retailing and the need to provide security advice, channels to report issues and processes to update products and services to create a responsive retailing experience.

Key findings

- The omini-channel retail model and the ramifications for data security.
- The IoT and the problem posed by connected data.
- Customer care and the need to get security smart.

The advice

At first glance, data breach statistics suggest that the retail sector is performing well in mitigating data breaches. Globally, the Breach Level Index (BLI) states that the retail sector saw a decrease (down 93 per cent) in the number of stolen records compared to the previous year, with the total number of records affected standing at 40.1 million, or just under 6 per cent of all stolen records.[1] The 217 data breaches in the industry accounted for 13 per cent of the total number of breaches worldwide in 2015. Therefore, even though statistically there were more breaches in 2015, the number of records stolen was down dramatically in the same period.

In the UK, data breach incidents seem to have plateaued, with the retail sector coming in fifteenth place out of the 43 industries analysed by the Information Commissioner's Office (ICO) in the Data Breach Audit 2015.

Yet, the statistics tell a different story when the data breaches are analysed by type. The BLI survey found identity theft accounted for 53 per cent of all data breaches, followed by financial access (22 per cent) and account access (11 per cent). These three causes all relate to the online retail experience. In the future, identity theft or unauthorised account access could see information obtained that could then facilitate an attack against an online retailer.

---

[1]Gemalto (23 February, 2016) '2015: The Year Data Breaches Got Personal: Findings from the 2015 Breach Level Index', www.gemalto.com/brochures-site/download-site/Documents/ent-Breach_Level_Index_Annual_Report_2015.pdf.

Omni-channel access and social media data leakage

The omni-channel world has enabled the consumer to conduct purchases over any touchpoint (mobile, PC, laptop, tablet, wearables) and this is seeing an increase in the take-up of mobile purchasing. According to the PricewaterhouseCoopers (PwC) 'Global Total Retail Survey 2016', 34 per cent of those surveyed believed their mobile phone would become their main tool through which to purchase items going forward.[2] This raises the issue over whether the apps being developed for mobile purchasing are robust enough.

The Tinder premium app, for instance, was recently exposed as being easy to reverse-engineer and recompile, allowing fraudsters to use premium services for free.[3] Then there is the danger posed by mobile payment processing itself. The Starbucks mobile app can be used to pay for purchases instore and can top up the 'wallet' in the app by drawing funds direct from PayPal or bank accounts. This had profound implications when the app was hacked, with Starbucks' customers seeing funds siphoned from their bank accounts.[4]

The threat posed by mobile purchasing can be mitigated by better security design and testing. When developing a mobile app, the retailer should:

- decide on the security approach and use this to develop a scope of work or a specification which includes the correct controls;
- examine frameworks like OWASP, NIST, SANS and others that detail what good security is and how it should be approached. Ask to see the secure application development lifecycle;

---

[2]PricewaterhouseCoopers (PwC) (February 2016) 'They say they want a revolution – Total Retail 2016', www.pwc.com/us/en/retail-consumer/publications/assets/Total-Retail-Global-Report.pdf.

[3]Fox-Brewster, T., *Forbes* (9 February 2016), 'Tinder Not Bothered By Clone App That Dodges Premium Payment', www.forbes.com/sites/thomasbrewster/2016/02/09/tinder-bad-security-design/#69da0bf449ba.

[4]Pagliery, P., CNN (14 May 2015) 'Hackers are draining bank accounts via the Starbucks app', http://money.cnn.com/2015/05/13/technology/hackers-starbucks-app/.

- look to see if the developer uses source code control, practices peer code review and performs unit testing;
- if using a hosted managed solution, look at the security provisions. If there is IDS/IPS, look at how logs are monitored and reacted to;
- consider app security as an ongoing process, making regular security testing a must.

Other media sources are also increasingly influencing purchase decisions. Customers are no longer simply looking to compare prices but also want to use recommendations and user experiences to inform their choice. The same PwC survey found 45 per cent of respondents worldwide (33 per cent in the UK) use reviews, comments and feedback from social media sites to influence their online shopping.

The role of social media in the shopping experience can expose the retailer, however. Users often take to social media, such as Twitter or Facebook, to publicise their purchase, post an online query or vent their frustrations. They may use a common hashtag or even write a post directly on the manufacturer's social media company page. The savvy attacker who is aware of a product vulnerability can use this information to identify potential targets and then use directory sites and geolocation applications to physically locate the victim.

A recent investigation into the Smarter iKettle found the device could be used to steal WPA PSKs, enabling the attacker to compromise the router and DNS, before stealing other details, such as online emails, account logins, etc. Twitter users who tweeted about the kettle to @wifikettle could be identified, even down to determining Android versus Apple iOS users, and information used to determine where they lived. (The Android-configured kettle is much less secure than the iPhone-configured version and the time taken to crack the PIN should take, on average, four hours. So this information would be key to an attacker.)

Protect the password to protect the data

Customers often reuse passwords for multiple sites and presume that it is down to the site owner to ensure that password is kept secure. For the retailer, a reused password increases exposure to attack exponentially. In effect, the security measures adopted by the responsible retailer are only as effective as the security provisions made by the least secure site where that password is used.

There are numerous cases of stolen password hashes, obtained from less secure sites, being cracked and then reused against other sites. The retailer can take a proactive stance against this by using sites such as http://haveibeenpwned.com to collate breach data that has been dumped publicly (an API is available that can make the process easier). If the hashes have already been cracked and published, it is also possible to run the plaintext through the retailer's website's own hashing/salting process to verify if the password has, indeed, been reused.

These methods are far preferable to the blanket password resets that have been adopted by online retailers in the past and which can prove frustrating for the end user. But, if the compromise is so severe and there is no alternative but to issue a reset, some key considerations that should be observed include:

- Do not reset the user's password immediately on submitting the forgotten password form. Mail the customer a link and only reset it when the link is clicked and the reset page is landed on. If not, the hacker can, potentially, create a denial of service by scripting a wide-scale reset of valid customer account passwords.
- Do not allow enumeration in the forgotten password form. Return generic errors, not 'this account doesn't exist', otherwise the above attack becomes much easier. Also, if the username is the customer's email address, customer contact addresses can be leaked through mining the form.
- Before allowing a password reset, ask for another item of data. Ideally, a pre-shared secret question or, at the very least, an item of data that the customer is not going to forget. Bear in mind addresses, etc. are available online for anyone to look up.
- Make sure that reset link or token is one-time only.
- If a temporary password is used, the app must force it to be changed on first use.
- When storing passwords, one-way hash them. Even if the hashes are stolen, it is a slow process to crack complex passwords, even using Hashcat (hashcat.net).

- Enforce a good password policy. Consider password length, use of alphanumerics, case and special characters.
- Do not leave password reset requests live. Find a sensible duration, maybe a few hours, and set the reset to expire then.

Customers are for life, not just for Christmas

Customer relationships are changing because the retailer is becoming more involved in the data management process. The Internet of Things (IoT) has ushered in a new wave of invention that is seeing common household devices reinvented and connected to the internet. IoT devices typically connect using a mobile app or over WiFi and generate data that, in turn, can be used by the retailer to track usage behaviour and predict trends.

Yet, the rush to market has seen many of these devices shortcut the security process as a result of which they are hitting the shelves with startlingly obvious vulnerabilities. From broadcasting sensitive data in the clear, to default settings, to war walking, these devices are now providing a weak point over which to launch an attack on the home network or the mobile device to devastating effect, providing access to account logins, email, contacts, etc.

Typically, an Over The Air (OTA) update is seen as a cure-all for any security issues, but this is naïve. It fails to allow for the kind of serious network compromise already outlined. Plus, what manufacturers and their retail partners fail to appreciate is that IoT will redefine their relationship with the customer by making them responsible for securing that data for the lifetime of that product. From data collection, to how it is transmitted and stored, and the device updated and patched, the IoT retailer will need to demonstrate unprecedented levels of customer care.

IoT is a nascent industry, but there are already examples of manufacturers who are eager to reduce the odds of data leakage. FitBit was quick to rectify a firmware update vulnerability on its Aria bathroom scales, which saw the device surrender the WiFi PSK. Similar issues were found with the Crane Sports Connect bathroom scales and wrist fitness monitor, with the added complication that an online database of customer accounts was also susceptible to attack and could be brute-forced to obtain user login details or even delete all accounts. Again, Crane moved quickly to address the issues, but this case is interesting because it illustrates how data held remotely, in the Cloud, is also at risk.

The retailer as role model

Building a better relationship with the customer and their data is vital to the brand. The recent VTech debacle over the reissuing of terms and conditions that sought to absolve the manufacturer of any responsibility in the event of a data breach is both irresponsible and untenable as we move towards mandatory data protection legislation in the form of the EU General Data Protection Regulations (GDPR) due to come into force in the next two years.[5]

For online retailers, there is a real opportunity to steal a march on market developments by occupying the middle ground between customer and manufacturer and promoting data security. Security procedures that can be considered include:

- *promotion of password managers* – password managers or vaults can be used to create strong unique passwords for each site the user goes to, without the need to remember them, reducing the risk of password reuse. Retailers should offer a password app or link to a free password vault and incentivise its use.
- *use of 2FA/2SA* – this might seem like overkill for a retail site, but a breach could be far more devastating. Retailers typically capture customer mobile numbers anyway for delivery information, etc., so why not use this to SMS as a one-time code? This will also make authentication easier on subsequent visits to the website.
- *consideration of federated authentication or social login* – Facebook and others make it easy to integrate their login process. It is an attractive method to make authentication easy for customers. This does mean the retailer is reliant upon the provider and that is worth bearing in mind: if the provider has an outage, then this could impact the retail site. Plus, if the social media account is compromised, this exposes the retail site.

---

[5]Kelion, L., BBC Technology (10 February 2016) 'Parents urged to boycott VTech toys after hack', www.bbc.co.uk/news/technology-35532644.

Retailers also need to look at the procedures they have in place for incident reporting. Is the customer able to reach the retailer other than by social media? Is that the best place for customers to voice issues? Or are more formal disclosure processes needed that encourage and actively respond to data issues as and when they are flagged?

Recommendations

Online retail has predominantly focused on price comparison, speed of and ease of use but, in the future, security will become increasingly important not just as a differentiator but as a key staple of the customer service offering. Responsible retailing recognises the need to pre-empt attacks through secure app design, to protect access channels and secure data through the effective management of data generated by products and services in the future. But it should also encourage disclosure and engagement with the customer in an open way so that, when the inevitable happens, the retailer can react quickly to dispel fear and demonstrate customer commitment.

Index